King George County, Virginia

Court Orders

1728–1731

Abstracted and Edited by
Mary Marshall Brewer

HERITAGE BOOKS
2025

HERITAGE BOOKS

AN IMPRINT OF HERITAGE BOOKS, INC.

Books, CDs, and more—Worldwide

For our listing of thousands of titles see our website
at
www.HeritageBooks.com

Published 2025 by
HERITAGE BOOKS, INC.
Publishing Division
5810 Ruatan Street
Berwyn Heights, MD 20740

International Standard Book Number
Paperbound: 978-0-7884-3250-7

CONTENTS

Introduction v

Abbreviations and Terms vi

King George Order Book, original pages 409 - 550 (1728-1731) 1

Index 147

iii

INTRODUCTION

This book contains abstracts of court orders from 1728 to 1731. The original page number is given at the end of each entry. Punctuation has been added in numerous instances for clarity.

<u>Earlier works</u>

Brewer, Mary Marshall, King George County, Virginia Order Book 1721-1724, Lewes, DE: Colonial Roots (2007)

Brewer, Mary Marshall, King George County, Virginia Order Book 1724-1728, Lewes, DE: Colonial Roots (2007)

Brewer, Mary Marshall, Abstracts of Land Records of King George County, Virginia 1752-1783, Lewes, DE: Colonial Roots (2001)

King, George Harrison Sanford, *King George County, Virginia, Will Book A-1, 1721-1752, and Miscellaneous Notes*. Fredericksburg: King (1978)

Sparacio, Ruth and Sam, *King George County, Virginia Deed Abstracts, 1721-1793*, 7 vols. McLean, VA: Antient Press (1987, 1994, 2002)

Sparacio, Ruth and Sam, *King George County, Virginia Wills Abstracts 1752-1780*, McLean, VA: Antient Press, 1987

Sparacio, Ruth and Sam, *King George Inventory Book, 1745-1765*, McLean, VA: Antient Press

Sparacio, Ruth and Sam, *King George Order Books, 1721-1728*, 3 vols. McLean, VA: Antient Press

F. Edward Wright
Lewes, Delaware
2007

ABBREVIATIONS and TERMS

Some of the abbreviations are those made by the original clerk and others
are by the abstractor.

adj. - adjoining
afsd - aforesaid
agt - against
atty - attorney
co. - county
complt(s) - complainant(s)
dau. - daughter
decd - deceased
def - defendant
DShf. - Deputy Sheriff
entrd - entered
esqr - esquire
in account with - estate was administered by
gent. - gentleman
pd - pounds
pg - page
plt(s) - plaintiff(s)
pn - pennies
pt/o - part of
Quarter - usually a slave quarter at a different location than the home
    plantation
Returned - submitted to the authority (York Co. Court)
sl - shillings
wit - witness or witnesses

KING GEORGE COUNTY, VIRGINIA
ORDER BOOK
1728-1731

[Continuation of Court held 7 June 1728]

In the suit brought by Thomas Monteith agt Jeremiah Bronaugh & Rose his wife adminrs with the will annext of John Dinwiddie decd the defs being called & not appearing judgment is granted the plt agt the defs & Joseph Strother gent sheriff of this co for what of the sum sued for in the declaration shall appear to be justly due unless the defs appear at the next court & answer the sd accon. (Pg 409)

In the suit brought by Samuel Tuson & Mary his wife agt Wm Grant the def being called & not appearing judgment is granted the plts agt the def & Joseph Strother gent sheriff of this co for what of the sum sued for in the declaration shall appear to be justly due unless the def appear at the next court & answer the sd accon. (Pg 409)

In the suit brought by Angus Mackay agt William Fickling the def being called & not appearing judgment is granted the plt agt the def & Joseph Strother gent sheriff of this co for what of the sum sued for in the declaracon shall appear to be justly due unless the def appear at the next court & answer the sd action. (Pg 409)

In the suit brought by Angus Mackay agt Jeremiah Brown the def being called & not appearing judgment is granted the plt agt the def & Joseph Strother gent sheriff of this co for what of the sum sued for in the declaration shall appear to be justly due unless the def appear at the next court & answer the sd accon. (Pg 409)

In the suit brought by Jeremiah Brown agt John Stribling the def being called & not appearing judgment is granted the plt agt the def & Joseph Strother gent sheriff of this co for what of the sum sued for in the declaracon shall appear to be justly due unless the def appear at the next court & answer the sd accon. (Pg 409)

Ord'd the court be adjourn'd to court in course.

Court held 2 Aug 1728. Present: Wm Robinson, Nicho Smith, Wm Thornton, Saml Skinker, Rowld Thornton, gent justices. (Pg 409)

Daniel Robertson a servt boy belonging to William Robinson gent is adjudged by the court to be 15 years of age which was ord'd to be recorded. (Pg 409)

Edward Barradall produced a deputation from the Honble William Gooch esqr his Majesties Lt Govr of this Colony for the Kings attornies place for this co & took the oaths by law appointed & signed the test. (Pg 409)

Jeremiah Murdock gent took the oaths by law appointed as also the oath of a justice of the peace for this co at common law & chancery & signed the test. (Pg 410)

Ord'd that Robert Jones be surveyor of the Main Road from the Great Falls to the upper side of Deep Run. (Pg 410)

Present Wm Strother & Jereh Murdock gent.

On the petition of John Lomax gent setting forth that Jane Bowshott is not capable to make him satisfaction if any damages should be given in an accon depending in this court brought by the sd John agt the sd Jane the sd John is admitted to enter a retrazit & the suit is ord'd to be dismist in course. (Pg 410)

Jane Bowshott being before the court on the motion of John Lomax gent & by the evidence of Christopher Folicopher, Katherine Mumford & Caleb Hundley it appeared that the sd Jane had maliciously & falsely scandalized the sd John, it is ord'd that the sheriff take the sd Jane to the whipping post & give her 15 lashes on the bare back well laid on & it is further ord'd that the sheriff keep her in custody till she enter into bond with good & sufficient security herself in the sum of £10 & her security in £5 that she be of the good behaviour for 12 months & a day next coming. (Pg 410)

William Mcbee ackn his lease, release & receipt unto Thomas Barnes & Susannah w/o the sd William relinquished her right of dower thereto which on the motion of the sd Thomas is admitted to record. (Pg 410)

On the petition of Walter Anderson & he together with Aaron Thornley ackn their bond to our Sovereign Lord the King for 10,000 lbs of tobacco the sd Walter is admitted to keep ordinary on his now dwelling plantation for the ensuing year. (Pg 410)

In the ejectione firma between John Chilton gent next friend to Richard Wats plt & John Taylor def the jury & surveyor having returned their reports & the special verdict being found upon arguing the whole the court is of opinion that the law is with the def & the sd suit is ord'd to be dismist with cost & one atty fee. (Pg 410)

In the ejectione firma between John Chilton gent next friend to Richard Watts plt & Maxfield Rose def the jury & surveyor having returned their report & the special verdt being found upon arguing the whole the court is of opinion that the law is with the def & the sd suit is ord'd to be dismist with cost & one atty fee. (Pg 410)

In the ejectione firma between John Chilton gent next friend to Richd Watts plt & William Tippet def the jury & surveyor having returned their report & the special verdt being found upon arguing the whole the court is of opinion that the law is with the def & the sd suit is ord'd to be dismiss'd with cost & one atty fee. (Pg 411)

In the ejectione firma between John Chilton gent next friend to Richard Watts plt & Edward Fagan def the jury & surveyor having returned their report & the special verdt being found upon arguing the whole the court is of opinion that the law is with the def & the sd suit is ord'd to be dismiss'd with cost & one atty fee. (Pg 411)

Ord'd that the court be adjourned till tomorrow morning 8 o'clock.

Court held 3 Aug 1728. Present: Wm Robinson, Wm Thornton, Thos Vivion, Saml Skinker, Jereh Murdock, gent justices. (Pg 411)

Ord'd that John Hardy pay Mary Archard her legacy contained in the will of Patrick Maggee. (Pg 411)

The suit brought by John Lomax gent agt Jane Bowshott is ord'd to be dismiss'd with cost & one atty fee. (Pg 411)

The suit brought by Joseph Wing agt Jno Jennings is ord'd to be dismist. (Pg 411)

The suit brought by Mosely Battaley agt Jno Triplet is ord'd to be dismist. (Pg 411)

The suit brought by Jos Wing agt Chas Dean is ord'd to be dismist. (Pg 411)

The suit brought by Robt Wilson agt Jos Reade is ord'd to be dismist. (Pg 411)

The suit brought by Ralph Hughs agt Jno Duncan is ord'd to be dismist. (Pg 411)

Special imparlance is granted unto Thos Smith in the suit brought agt him by James Sparks. (Pg 411)

The suit brought by Edwd Philsher agt Jno Jones is ord'd to be dismist. (Pg 411)

The suit brought by Thomas Turner agt Thomas Vivion gent is ord'd to be dismiss'd with cost. (Pg 411)

The suit brought by Richard Longman agt William Hensly is dismist. (Pg 411)

In the accon of debt between Samuel Skinker gent plt & John Stribling def the def being called & not appearing judgment is granted the plt agt the def & Samuel Hoyle his security for what of the sum sued for in the declaration shall appear to be justly due unless the def appear at the next court & answer the sd accon. (Pg 412)

In the suit brought by John Branham agt Mary Brock the last courts order not being complied with is ord'd to be cont'd & that the def make oath to her discounts. (Pg 412)

In the suit brought by Giles Easter agt William Hensly the plt having replied to the defs plea the def joines the issue. (Pg 412)

The suit brought by John Coburn agt Jeremiah Bronaugh & Rose his wife adminrs of John Dinwiddie decd is cont'd. (Pg 412)

Ord'd that John Miller be sumoned to the next (court) to answer the petition of Margt Simmond. (Pg 412)

The suit brought by Benja Berryman agt Jeremiah Bronaugh is ord'd to be cont'd. (Pg 412)

In the suit in chancery depending between William Morrison complt & Jeremiah Bronaugh & Rose his wife respts the sd respts is ord'd to make oath to their answer before the next court. (Pg 412)

The suit brought by Thomas Chew agt John Hullock is ord'd to be dismiss'd with an atty fee. 3 Jun 1728 by virtue of this writ to me directed I have taken the within named Thos Chew whose body before the justices within named at the day & place within contained there ready to sattisfie John Hullock of the debt & damages within mentioned as to me is commanded, Larkin Chew sheriff. (Pg 412)

The accon of debt brought by Thomas Chew agt John Hullock is ord'd to be dismiss'd with cost & one atty fee. 3 Jun 1728 by virtue of this writ to me directed I have taken the within named Thos Chew whose body before the justices within named at the day & place within contained there ready to sattisfie John Hullock of the debt & damages within mentioned as to me is commanded, Larkin Chew sheriff. (Pg 412)

In the suit brought by George Davis agt George Parsons, Charles Seale enter'd himself special bail & the def pleads he owes nothing the plt joines the issue. (Pg 412)

The suit brought by Fras Triplet agt Jno Jones is dismist. (Pg 412)

In the suit brought by Robert English agt Charles Jones the def pleads he owes nothing & the plt joines the issue. (Pg 412)

The attachmt obtain'd by William Sebastian agt Higgason King is ord'd to be dismist. (Pg 412)

The suit brought by James Markham agt Robert Dudley the def pleads he owes nothing & the plt joines the issue. (Pg 412)

In the suit brought by Wm Skrine agt Ann Griffis the def pleads in writing & the plt has time till next court to consider the defs plea. (Pg 412)

The suit brought by Jereh Murdock gent agt John Long is dismist. (Pg 413)

In the suit brought by John Savage agt John Mooney the def being called & not appearing judgmt is granted the plt agt the def & Joseph Strother gent sheriff of this co for what of the sum sued for in the declaration shall appear to be justly due on a writ of enquiry for damages to be had at the next court. (Pg 413)

In the suit brought by Jeremiah Murdock gent agt Randolph Holebrooke the def being called & not appearing the last courts order is confirm'd agt him for the cost of this suit which is ord'd to be paid with one atty fee. (Pg 413)

In the accon upon the case between James Markham plt & John Mitchell def the def being called & not appearing the last courts order is confirm'd agt him & William Mumford & John Hardy his securities for 523 lbs of tobacco which is ord'd to be paid with cost. (Pg 413)

In the suit brought by William Strother gent agt Peter Cassedy the def being called & not appearing judgmt is granted the plt agt the def & Owen Greening his security for what of the sum sued for in the declaration shall appear to be justly due on a writ of enquiry for damages to be had at the next court. (Pg 413)

Judgment is granted unto Thomas Turner agt Thomas Riphley for 30 lbs of tobacco ballance of his note which is ord'd to be paid with cost. (Pg 413)

In the suit brought by Richard Brookes agt George Downing the def not appearing the order of last May court is confirm'd agt the def & Charles Lewis his security for the sum of £1:7:6 which is ord'd to be paid with cost. (Pg 413)

Walter Ross came into court & confess'd judgmt in custody unto Richard Todd for 600 lbs of tobacco which is ord'd to be paid with cost & one atty fee. (Pg 413)

In the suit brought by Daniel Hornby agt Charles Seale the def pleads he owes nothing & the plt joines the issue. (Pg 413)

The suit brought by Hugh Roberts agt Wm Strother gent is dismiss'd. (Pg 413)

In the suit by petition between Charles Bushnel plt & Wm Grant def the def pleads in writing & the plt has time till next court to consider the defs plea. (Pg 413)

The suit brought by John Champe agt Eliza Holdsworth is dismist. (Pg 413)

The suit brought by Thos Barnes agt Samuel Bromadge is ord'd to be cont'd to the next court. (Pg 413)

On the petition of Daniel French & Margaret his wife late widow & relict of John Pratt decd it is ord'd that Jeremiah Murdock, Thomas Vivion & Maximilian Robinson gent audit, state & settle the accts between the sd petitioners & Evan Price executor of the will of the sd Pratt decd in relation to the estate of the sd decd & report specially to the next court. (Pg 414)

In the suit brought by Thomas Monteith agt Jeremiah Bronaugh & Rose his wife adminrs of Jno Dinwiddie decd the defs have leave to plead divers matters, viz, that the sd decd owed him nothing & that they have fully administred. (Pg 414)

In the suit brought by Samuel Skinker gent agt John Trice the def not appearing judgmt is granted the plt agt the def & John Lomax his security for what of the sum sued for shall appear to be justly due unless the def appear at the next court & answer the sd accon. (Pg 414)

The suit brought by Saml Skinker gent agt Jno Mcnemara is ord'd to be dismist. (Pg 414)

Judgment is granted unto Angus Mackay agt William Fickling for the sum of £3:4:2 which is ord'd to be paid with cost & one atty fee. (Pg 414)

Jeremiah Brown came into court & confess'd judgmt unto Angus Mackay for 800 lbs of tobacco & cask which is ord'd to be paid with cost & one atty fee. (Pg 414)

John Stribing came into court & confess'd judgmt unto Jeremh Brown for 670 lbs of tobacco which is ord'd to be paid with cost. (Pg 414)

Ord'd that the sheriff take Eliz Elliot into custody till she enter into bond with good & sufficient security for her appearance at the next court to answer the presentment of the grand jury. (Pg 414)

Judgment is granted unto John Marr agt Thomas Davis for 312 lbs of tobacco which is ord'd to be paid with cost & one atty fee. (Pg 414)

Judgment is granted unto Andrew Leitch agt William Fewell for 266 lbs of tobacco which is ord'd to be paid with cost & one atty fee. 13 7r 1728 the within named not to be found in my bailiwick per B. Rush sub sheriff. (Pg 414)

The suit brought by Samuel Tuson & Mary his wife agt William Grant is dismist. (Pg 414)

Ordered that Robert Benson be surveyor of the Main Road from Markhams Run to the upper side of the Dogue Bridge. (Pg 415)

Ord'd that Thomas Turner be surveyor of the highways between Gingoteague & Markhams Run. (Pg 415)

Ord'd that the precinct from Thatchers Dam reach up to Pulleins Swamp.

In the information brought by George Eskridge for & on behalf of the Sovereign Lord the King agt Benjamin Rush, John Champe, George White, Saml Hoyle, Thomas Benson, Wm Grant, John Hardy, Joseph Wing, Jno Grant, Chas Seale, Jno Roy, Evan Price & Robt Smith was sworne a jury to try the issue joined who having heard the evidence & argmts withdrew & sometime after returned the following verdt (viz) we find the def guilty, Jno Champe foreman, which verdt is admitted to record & judgmt is granted our Sovereign Lord the King agt the def for 1200 lbs of tobo according to the information which is ord'd to be paid with cost. (Pg 415)

In the suit brought by Thos Dillen agt John Long, John Champe &c was sworne a jury to try the issue joined who having heard the arguments & evidence withdrew & in a short time returned the following verdt (viz) we find for the def, John Champe foreman, which verdt on the defs motion is adm'd to record & the sd suit is ord'd to be dismiss'd with cost & one atty fee. (Pg 415)

The suit brought by Hannah Sheilds agt Thomas Benson the jury having returned that they found for the def is ord'd to be dismist. (Pg 415)

In the suit brought by Owen Sullivan agt Francis Triplett, John Champe &c was sworne a jury to try the issue who having heard the evidence & argumts withdrew & sometime after return'd the following verdt (viz) we find for the plt 1 shilling damages, John Champe foreman, which verdt on the plt motion is admitted to record & judgmt is granted the plt agt the def for the sd sum which is ord'd to be paid with cost & one atty fee. (Pg 415)

In the suit brought by Robert Dudley agt James Markham, John Champe, George White, Saml Hoyle, Wm Grant, Jno Hardy, Jos Wing, Jno Grant, Evan Price, Walter Anderson, Wm Fewell, George Parsons & Jno Diskins was sworne a jury to try the issue who having heard the evidence & arguments of both parties withdrew & sometime after returned the following verdt (viz) we find for the plt £16 damages, John Champe foreman, which verdt on the plts motion is adm'd to record & judgment is granted the plt agt the def for the sd sum which is ord'd to be paid with cost & one atty fee. (Pg 415)

William Morrison being sumoned an evidence by Owen Sullevan agt Francis Triplett & making oath he attended five days on the sd suit it is ord'd that he pay him for the same according to law with cost. (Pg 416)

Mary Morrison being sumoned an evidence by Owen Sullevan agt Francis Triplett & making oath he attended five days on the sd suit it is ord'd that he pay her for the same with cost according to law. (Pg 416)

John Roy of Caroline Co being sumoned an evidence by James Markham agt Robert Dudley & making oath that he attended four days on the sd suit, it is ord'd that he pay him for the same & for four times two miles going & two miles coming according to law. (Pg 416)

James Gillison of Caroline Co being sumoned an evidence by James Markham agt Robert Dudley & making oath that he attended four days on the sd suit it is ord'd that he pay him for the same & for four times two miles coming & two miles going according to law. (Pg 416)

Roger Prosser of Caroline Co being sumoned an evidence by Robert Dudley agt James Markham & making oath that he attended four days on the sd suit it is ord'd that he pay him for the same & for four times coming & going two miles according to law. (Pg 416)

Thomas Stranghan of Caroline Co being sumoned an evidence by Robert Dudley agt James Markham & making oath that he attended four days on the sd suit it is ord'd that he pay him for the same & for four times coming & going one mile according to law. (Pg 416)

Thomas Blassingham of Essex Co being sumoned an evidence by Robert Dudley agt James Markham & making oath that he attended two days on the sd suit it is ord'd that he pay him for the same & for two times coming & two times going 10 miles & ferriages according to law. (Pg 416)

Robert Smith of Caroline Co being sumoned an evidence by Robert Dudley agt James Markham & making oath that he attended four days on the sd suit it is ord'd that he pay him for the same & for four times coming & four times going two miles according to law. (Pg 416)

In the accon upon the case between William Fewell plt & Francis Griffis def the def being called & not appearing the order of last May court is confirmed agt him & John Ellkin his security for 665 lbs of tobacco which is ordered to be paid with cost. (Pg 416)

Upon the scire facias between Nicholas Smith gent & Elizabeth his wife plts & George Mason gent def on a judgment which the plt obtain'd agt John Mercer at a court held for this co 8 Apr 1727 for the sum of £150 in which sd suit the afsd George Mason gent came into court & entered himself special bail & it appearing by the return of the sheriff that the sd George Mason gent has been sumoned by two several scire facias's but not appearing to shew any cause why the sd judgment & execution may not be awarded agt him, it is therefore ord'd that execution issue agt the def for the sd sum of £150 as afsd with all the former & present cost of this suit. (Pg 417)

Ord'd that the court be adjourn'd to court in course.

Court held by virtue of a Commission of Oyer & Terminer 12 Aug 1728 to try Negro Dick belonging to the Bristol Iron Mines. Present: Nicho Smith, Wm Thornton, Thos Vivion, Saml Skinker, Jereh Murdock, gent justices. (Pg 417)

Dick a Negro slave belonging to the Bristol Iron Mines being comitted by mittimus under the hand & seale of William Robinson gent for feloniously stealing a stuff gown from the dwelling house of Christopher Edrington also now being indicted for the same, the court upon hearing the evidence is of opinion that the sd Dick is guilty of petit larceny & thereupon order that the sheriff take him to the whipping post & give him 10 lashes on the bare back well laid on & that he be then discharg'd. Nicho Smith. (Pg 417)

Court held 6 Sep 1728. Present: Wm Thornton, Thos Vivion, Saml Skinker, Rowld Thornton, Jereh Murdock, gent justices. (Pg 417)

Samuel Moon returned an additional inventory of the estate of Francis Thornton decd which is admitted to record. (Pg 417)

William Saltash & Ester his wife ackn their Letter of Atty to Richard Fry & the same was proved by the oaths of Edward Barradall & John Hellier evidences thereto which is ord'd to be certified. (Pg 417)

Richard Fry presented into court the deposition of John Hellier who made oath thereto & the same was ord'd to be certified. (Pg 417)

Richard Buckner gent ackn his lease & release unto John Williams & Thomas Turner by virtue of a power of atty from Elizabeth w/o the sd Richard proved by the oath of Archbell Mcpherson relinqt her right of dower which is adm'd to record. (Pg 418)

Present Wm Strother gent.

Ord'd that Rowland Thornton gent be cont'd surveyor of the highways from Gingoteague to Crows Swamp. (Pg 418)

Ord'd that Richard Tutt be surveyor of the highway from Crows Swamp to the mines & that he keep the same in repair according to law. (Pg 418)

Ord'd that John Gilbert be surveyor of the highway from the mines to Thatchers Dam & that he keep ye same in repair according to law. (Pg 418)

Ralph Falkner ackn his lease & release unto John Williams & Thomas Turner by virtue of a power of atty from Elizabeth w/o the sd Ralph proved by the oaths of Ralp Falkner & Roger Prosser relinqt her right of dower which is adm'd to record. (Pg 418)

Benjamin Johnson ackn his lease & release unto John King esqr & Company & Thomas Turner by virtue of a power of atty from Margaret w/o the sd Benjamin proved by the oaths of John Harvie & Caleb Hundly relinqt her right of dower which is adm'd to record. (Pg 418)

Ord'd that William Strother gent be surveyor of the highway from the Great Falls to the upper side of the Deep Run. (Pg 418)

Ord'd that the sheriff sumon Adam Christie & Mary his wife to appear at the next court to answer the petition of Wm Strother gent, Briant OBannon & John Ambrose. (Pg 418)

George a Negro boy belonging to Benjamin Berryman Junr is adjudged to be 10 years of age & ord'd to be recorded. (Pg 418)

Abraham a Negro boy belonging to Benjamin Berryman Junr is adjudged to be 9 years of age & ord'd to be recorded. (Pg 418)

Bristol & Negro boy belonging to John Piper is adjudged to be 10 & Bassett to 8 years of age & ord'd to be recorded. (Pg 418)

On the petition of Thomas Monteith if is ord'd that the clerk bring the will of John Dinwiddie decd to the next court. (Pg 418)

Ord'd that the sheriff take Elizabeth Edwards to the whipping post & whipp her according to law for having a bastard child & it further ord'd that the sd Elizabeth serve her master Thomas Davis according to law for the trouble of his house. (Pg 418)

Francis Attwood came into court & agreed to serve Jeremiah Murdock gent six years which is ord'd to be recorded. (Pg 419)

Edward Elmes & Mary Stringer servants to John Popham came into court & agreed to serve their sd master nine months after their time by transportation is expired on condition their sd master give them leave to intermarry. (Pg 419)

Ord'd that the sheriff sumon a grand jury to the next Nov court.

The suit brought by John Branham agt Mary Brock the auditors having returned their report is cont'd to next court at the defs cost. (Pg 419)

The suit brought by Giles Ester agt Wm Hensley is cont'd at the defs cost. (Pg 419)

12

Ord'd that John Mcguire be put in the stocks for fighting at the court door. (Pg 419)

The suit brought by John Coburn agt Jereh Bronaugh is cont'd till next court for the plt to produce his acct. (Pg 419)

The suit brought by Benjamin Berryman agt Jereh Bronaugh is ord'd to be dismist with cost & one atty fee. (Pg 419)

Samuel Skinker gent produced an acct of 551 ½ lbs of tobo agt Peter Hedgman & made oath thereto which is ord'd to be certified. (Pg 419)

William Strother gent produced an acct of £5:19:3 agt Alexander Maver & made oath thereto which is ord'd to be certified. (Pg 419)

John Mcguire being drunk is ord'd to pay the church wardens of Hanover Parish 5 shillings or receive 10 lashes on the bare back according to law & remain in custody till he pay fees. (Pg 419)

Ord'd that Snodel Horton be put in the stocks for fighting & that he pay the church wardens of Hanover Parish 5 shillings for being drunk or receive 10 lashes on the bare back according to law & remain in custody till he pay fees. (Pg 419)

Then the court adjourned to court in course.

Court held 4 Oct 1728. Present: Wm Thornton, Thos Vivion, Jereh Murdock, Saml Skinker, Rowld Thornton, gent justices. (Pg 419)

Thomas Thatcher returned an additional inventory of the estate of Elizabeth Jett which is adm'd to record. (Pg 419)

John Warner ackn his assignment of a deed unto John Champe which is admitted to record. (Pg 420)

In the accon upon the case between John Branham plt & Mary Brock def the auditors having returned their report judgment is granted the plt agt the def for 300 lbs of tobacco which is ordered to be paid with cost & one atty fee. (Pg 420)

In the accon upon the case between Giles Ester plt & William Hensley def, John Gilbert, James Hackley, John Sharp, John Ambrose, Bryant OBannon, George White, Charles Dean, Rowland Thornton, William Harrison, Isaac Arnold, Roger Abbott & Daniel Marr was sworne a jury to try the issue joined who having heard the evidences & arguments of both parties withdrew & sometime after returned the following verdt (viz) we find for the plt £6, John Gilbert foreman, which verdt on the plts motion is admitted to record & judgment is granted the plt agt the def for the sd sum of £6 which is ord'd to be paid with cost & one atty fee. (Pg 420)

John Mcnemara being sumoned an evidence for Giles Ester agt William Hensley & making oath that he attended two days on the sd suit it is ord'd that he pay him for the same according to law with cost. (Pg 420)

William Whiteing of Westmoreland Co being sumoned an evidence by Giles Ester agt William Hensley & making oath that he attended two days on the sd suit & it appearing that he lives 12 miles from the sd court it is ord'd that he pay him for the same & for twice coming & twice going 12 miles according to law. (Pg 420)

Alexander Rigby of Stafford Co being sumoned an evidence by William Hensley agt Giles Ester & making oath that he attended one day on the sd suit it is ord'd that he pay him for the same & for coming & going 18 miles according to law. (Pg 420)

Richard Barret of Stafford Co being sumoned an evidence by William Hensley agt Giles Ester & having attended one day on the sd suit it is ord'd that he pay him for the same & for coming & going 12 miles according to law. (Pg 420)

On the petition of William Thatcher it is ord'd that John Gilbert be his guardian the sd Gilbert together with Richard Tutt ackn their bond for £100 to save ye court harmless. (Pg 420)

On the petition of George White & Francis James it is ordered that Samuel Tuson & Mary his wife extrix of the will of Humphrey Quisenbury decd deliver to the sd George White & Francis James so much of the estate of the sd Humphry decd as amounts unto £64:8:6 the same being appraised by Isaac Arnold, Joseph Minto & Richard Tutt on 11 Nov 1727 & it is further ord'd that the sd Samuel Tuson & Mary his wife pay unto the sd George White & Francis James the sum of £125:12:10 the sd sum being due to ballance the original inventory of the estate of the sd Quisenbury decd. (Pg 421)

In the accon upon the case between John Coburn plt & Jeremiah Bronaugh & Rose his wife adminrs with the will annexed of John Dinwiddie decd defs the auditors having made their report that they find due to the plt from the estate of the sd John decd £35:18:3 judgment is thereupon granted the plt agt the estate of the sd decd in the hands of the sd defs for the sd sum which is ord'd to be paid with cost when assets. (Pg 421)

On the petition of William Thatcher it is ord'd that John Gilbert be his guardian the sd John together with Richard Tutt ackn their bond for £100 to save the court harmless. (Pg 421)

Then the court adjourn'd till tomorrow morning 8 o'clock.

Court held 5 Oct 1728. Present: Wm Thornton, Thos Vivion, Saml Skinker, Jereh Murdock, gent justices. (Pg 421)

Order'd that the sheriff take the bodies of William Hensley, William Hensley Junr & Benjamin Hensley Junr till they enter into bond with security themselves in the sum of £10 their securities in the sum of £5 that they be of the good behaviour 12 months & a day next ensuing. (Pg 421)

Ord'd that Richard Griffith be constable in the room of John Steward. (Pg 421)

Jonathan Gibson gent took the oaths by law appointed together with the oath of a justice of the peace for this co both at common law & chancery & signed the test. (Pg 421)

In the accon of debt between George Davis plt & George Parsons def the def being called & not appearing judgment by default is granted the plt agt the def for the sum of £1:1:8 due on ballance of his bill for three pistols which is ord'd to be paid with cost & one atty fee. (Pg 422)

In the suit in chancery depending between William Morrison complt & Jeremiah Bronaugh & Rose his wife respts the respts having put in their answer time is given the complt till next court to consider it. (Pg 422)

In the accon of debt between Robert English plt & Charles Jones def, Charles Seale, John Jennings, John Hardy, Evan Price, Thos Boyles, Saml Hoyles, Jos Steward, John Williams, Thos Grimsly, Geo Head, John Stribling & Robt Richards was sworne a jury to try the issue who having heard the evidence & arguments withdrew & sometime after returned the following verdt, viz, we find for the plt 600 lbs of tobacco, Charles Seale foreman, & judgment is granted the plt agt the def for the sd tobacco which is ord'd to be paid with cost & one atty fee. (Pg 422)

William Owens being sumoned an evidence by Charles Jones agt Robert English & making oath that he attended three days on the sd suit it is ord'd that he pay him for the same according to law. (Pg 422)

In the suit brought by William Skrine agt Ann Griffis the plt having replyed the def joines the issue & the same lies till next court for trial. (Pg 422)

The petition brought by Charles Birchnel agt William Grant by consent is dismist. (Pg 422)

The suit by petition depending between Daniel French & Margaret his wife agt Evan Price exr of John Pratt decd is cont'd by consent till next court. (Pg 422)

In the suit brought by Thomas Monteith agt Jereh Bronaugh & Rose his wife the plt joines the issue & the same lies till next court for trial. (Pg 422)

The suit brought by James Sparks agt Thomas Smith is dismiss'd by consent. (Pg 422)

In the suit brought by Samuel Skinker gent agt John Trice the def being called & not appearing Edward Barradall atty for the def came into court & pleaded not guilty on behalf of he security. (Pg 422)

In the accon upon the case between James Markham plt & Robert Dudley def, Walter Anderson, John Jennings, John Hardy, Evan Price, Thos Grimsley, Geo Head, Saml Hoyle, Robt Richards, Jos Steward, John Williams, Jereh Bronaugh & James Jones was sworne a jury to try the issue joined who having heard the evidence & argumts withdrew & sometime after return'd the following verdt, viz, we find for the plt 828 lbs of tobacco, Walter Anderson foreman, which verdt on the plts motion is adm'd to record & judgmt is granted the plt agt the def for the sd tobacco which is ord'd to be paid with cost & one atty fee. (Pg 423)

The suit brought by Samuel Skinker agt John Stribling is cont'd. (Pg 423)

Ord'd that the sheriff take the body of Thomas Davis into his custody till he give security for his appearance at the next court to answer the indictmt of our Sovereign Lord the King. (Pg 423)

In the scire facias between our Sovereign Lord the King plt & Thomas Cressap, Rowland Cornelious & Thomas Yates defs the defs being called & not appearing it is order'd that the Kings atty prosecute the sd Cressap & Yates on their recognizances & that the sd Cornelous pay to our sd Lord the King £10 unless he appear at the next court & answer the sd scire facias. (Pg 423)

Roger Prosser being sumoned an evidence by Robert Dudley agt James Markham & it appearing he lived in Caroline Co two miles from the sd court & making oath that he attended two days on the sd suit it is ord'd that he pay him for the same & for coming two miles & going two miles twice according to law. (Pg 423)

The suit brought by William Strother gent agt Peter Cassedy is ord'd to be dismiss'd. (Pg 423)

The suit brought by Daniel Hornby agt Charles Seale is cont'd till next court. (Pg 423)

The suit brought by Thomas Barnes agt Samuel Bromadge is cont'd till next court at the plts cost. (Pg 423)

The suit brought by Joseph Delany agt Willm Barnes is dismiss'd. (Pg 423)

The suit brought by David Stern agt Geo & Thos Davis is dismist. (Pg 423)

The suit brought by John Long agt John Plant is dismist. (Pg 423)

The suit brought by Rowld Cornelious agt Jno Moony is dismist. (Pg 423)

The petition exhibited by William Strother, John Ambrose & Bryant OBannon agt Adam Christie & Mary his wife is dismist. (Pg 424)

The petition preferr'd by Thomas Monteith agt Jeremiah Bronaugh & Rose his wife is ord'd to be cont'd & that the def be sumoned to the next court. (Pg 424)

The attachmt obtain'd by Richard Longman agt William Tomlinson is cont'd for James Jones to finish the crop. (Pg 424)

The attachmt obtain'd by Samuel Crawley agt William Tomlinson is dismist. (Pg 424)

In the accon upon the case between John Savage plt & John Moony def, Walter Anderson &c was sworne a jury to enquire into the damages who having heard the argmts withdrew & sometime after return'd the following verdt, viz, we find for the plt 50 shillings damages, Walter Anderson foreman, which verdt on the plts motion is adm'd to record & judgment is granted the plt agt the def for the sd sum which is ord'd to be paid with cost & one atty fee. (Pg 424)

In the accon of Trover & Conversion between William Skrine plt & Richard Barnes def for £100 damages the def being called & not appearing judgment is granted the plt agt the def & Thomas Barnes his security for what of the sum sued for in the declaration shall appear to be justly due unless the def appear at the next court & answer the sd accon. (Pg 424)

Judgment is granted unto the Rev. Esdras Theodor Edzard agt Thomas Grimsley for 500 lbs of tobacco which is ord'd to be paid with cost. (Pg 424)

In the suit by petition between Margaret Simmond plt & John Miller def it is ord'd that the def keep the plt on his plantation in this co until the sd petition is determined & it is further ordered that William Doyle be sumoned by the sheriff of Essex Co to give his evidence for & on behalf of the sd Miller if able to come if not that his deposition be taken before two majistrates in Essex Co. (Pg 424)

Then the court adjourn'd to court in course.

Court held 1 Nov 1728. Present: Wm Robinson, Wm Thornton, Thos Vivion, Rowld Thornton, Jere Murdock, gent justices. (Pg 425)

Ordered that John Pritchet son of Thomas Pritchet serve Christopher Pritchet till he arrive to the age of 21 years he being 9 years of age the 1st day of July last he the sd Christopher assuming before the court to give him education & it is further ord'd & agreed to by the sd Christopher that the sd John is not to serve any other person as by his indenture may appear which is also ord'd to be recorded. (Pg 425)

Ordered that Henry Williams serve Christopher Pritchet till he come to the age of 21 years he being 14 years of age the 12th day of Jan next he the sd Christopher promising before the court to give him education & it is also agreed to by the sd Christopher that the sd Henry is not to serve any other person as by his indenture may appear which is also ord'd to be recorded. (Pg 425)

In the suit in chancery depending between William Morrison complt & Jeremiah Bronaugh respt the complt has time till next court to consider the respts answer. (Pg 425)

The suit brought by William Skrine agt Ann Griffis is cont'd till next court at the plts cost. (Pg 425)

In the suit by petition between Daniel French & Margaret his wife late widow & relict of John Pratt decd plts & Evan Price execr of the will of the sd John decd def it is ord'd that the sd Evan produce an account of all the crops of tobacco that has been made belonging to the estate since the decease of the sd John fairly stated to the next court held for this co. (Pg 425)

In the suit by petition between Daniel French & Margaret his wife plts & Evan Price execr of the will of John Pratt decd def it is ord'd that John Gilbert, Daniel White & Christopher Edrington divide the Negroes belonging to the estate of the sd John decd & set a part one third for the dower of the sd Margaret & that the sd Daniel & Margaret be possess'd thereof according to law. (Pg 425)

In the suit by petition between Daniel French & Margaret his wife plts & Evan Price execr of the will of John Pratt decd def it is ord'd that Robert Richards, Francis Lacom & William Rush divide the Negroes belonging to the estate of the sd John decd that are in Westmoreland Co & set a part one third for the dower of the sd Margaret & that the sd Daniel & Margaret be possess'd thereof according to law. (Pg 425)

Thomas Quisenbury ackn his lease, release & bond to John Finch which on the motion of the sd Finch is adm'd to record. (Pg 426)

Thomas Harrison & Margaret his wife made oath to their answer to a bill in chancery exhibited agt them by William Thornton gent guardian to Catherine Rymer. (Pg 426)

John Gilbert, John Wright, John Ambrose, Abraham Kenyan, William Rowley, John Owens, Robert Doniphan, Daniel Marr, James Robertson, William Harrison, Francis Woffendale, Samuel Hoyle, Enoch Berry, John Jennings, George White, Daniel White & Thomas Monroe was sworn a grand jury for the body of this co who having had their charge withdrew & sometime after returned their presentments whereupon it is ord'd that Ann Simpson & Thomas Harwood be sumoned to appear at the next court to answer the presentmt of the grand jury. (Pg 426)

King George Co. Sums of tobacco to: Joseph Strother gent sheriff, Saml Skinker gent assignee of Jno Mcguire for 7 wolves heads, Thomas Turner clerk by acct, Wm Strother gent assignee of Rowld Cornelious for 6 wolves heads, Samuel Skinker gent by acct, Major George Eskridge Kings atty for 6 months, Edwd Barradall for ditto the other 6 months, Joseph Strother gent by acct, Chas Seale by acct, Jereh Bronaugh Senr & Junr for counting tobo plants, Lazarus Dameron & Joseph Hudnall for ditto, Thomas Barlett & William Marshall for ditto, Linsfield & John Sharp for ditto, John Farguson & John Diskins for ditto,

Isaac Arnold & William Pullein for ditto, John Kenyan & John Ambrose for ditto, John Gilbert & Christopher Edrington for ditto, Danl Marr & Wm Hackney for ditto, Antho Seale & Enoch Berry for ditto, Wm Harrison & Wm Strother for ditto, Thomas Grimsley by acct, James Jones by acct, Walter Anderson by acct, Linsfield Sharp, John Glendening, Wm Strother gent assignee of Wm Russel for 1 wolfs head, ditto assignee of James Morgan for 1 ditto, ditto assignee of Thos Davis for 3 ditto, ditto assignee of John Payton & Snodel Horton for 7 ditto, Nicho Smith gent his burges acct, Wm Strother gent his burges acct, Peter Bashaw by acct, Danl Marr for 6 wolves heads, John Jenkins for 6 ditto. 46,965 lbs tobacco. (Pg 426-427)

It is ord'd that every tithable person in this co pay to the sheriff 31 ½ lbs of tobacco to discharge the co levy & that the sheriff pay the same to the respective creditors according to law.

Court held for proof of publick claims & certifying propositions & grievances 1 Nov 1728. Present: Wm Thornton, Saml Skinker, Wm Strother, Jere Murdock, gent justices. (Pg 427)

Daniel Marr produced a cert under the hand of William Thornton gent justice of the peace for this co for the taking up a runaway man servant named James Wilson belonging to Alexr Clark of Richmond Co & made oath that the sd service was real & bona fide made, done & performed & that he had rec'd no satisfaction for the same which was ordered to be certified to the next General Assembly for allowance. (Pg 427)

Daniel White produced a cert under the hand of Thomas Vivion gent for the taking up two runaway servants one named Charles Morgan the other John Beby one belonging to John Bagge the other to Peter Dudley both of Essex Co & made oath no satisfaction had been rec'd for the same which was ord'd to be certified to the next General Assembly for allowance. (Pg 427)

Thomas James produced a cert under the hand of William Thornton gent for taking up a runaway Negro man slave belonging to Major Robert Alexander of Stafford Co & made oath that no satisfaction had been rec'd for the same which was ord'd to be certified to the next Genl Assembly for allowance. (Pg 428)

John Jennings produced a cert under the hand of Thomas Vivion gent for taking up a runaway servant man named Richard Winter belonging to John Travis of Stafford Co & made oath that no satisfaction had been rec'd for the same which was ord'd to be certified to the next Genl Assembly for allowance. (Pg 428)

Elizabeth Beversham produced a cert under the hand of Thomas Vivion gent for taking up a runaway woman servt named Mary Gray belonging to Thos Bumberry of Stafford Co & made oath that no satisfaction had been rec'd for the same which is ord'd to be sent to the next Genl Assembly for allowance. (Pg 428)

Nathan Turner produced a cert under the hand of Jeremiah Murdock gent for taking up a runaway woman servt named Rose Hews belonging to William Baxter of Westmoreland Co & made oath that no satisfaction had been rec'd for the same which is ord'd to be certified to the next Genl Assembly for allowance. (Pg 428)

Court held 2 Nov 1728. Present: Nicho Smith, Wm Thornton, Jona Gibson, Saml Skinker, Rowld Thornton, Wm Strother, Jere Murdock, gent justices. (Pg 428)

The suit brought by Daniel Hornby agt Chas Seale is cont'd. (Pg 428)

The suit brought by Saml Skinker gent agt Jno Stribling is dismist. (Pg 428)

In the accon of Trover & Conversion between William Skrine plt & Richard Barnes def the def pleads not guilty & plt joines the issue & the same lies till next court for trial. (Pg 428)

The attachmt obtained by Richard Longman agt William Tomlinson is cont'd for James Jones to finish the crop. (Pg 428)

Special imparlance is granted unto Elias Yates in the suit brought agt him by Simon Hughs. (Pg 428)

In the suit brought by Isaac Norman agt Mary Brown the def being called & not appearing judgmt is granted the plt agt the def for what of the sum sued for in the declaration shall appear to be justly due unless the def appear at the next court & answer the sd accon. (Pg 428)

In the suit brought by Jacob Bartlett agt William Bowlware the def being called & not appearing judgmt is granted the plt agt the def & Joseph Strother gent sheriff of this co for what of the sum sued for shall appear to be justly due unless the def appear at the next court & answer the sd accon. (Pg 429)

In the suit brought by Fras Kirtley agt John Retterford the def being called & not appearing judgmt is granted the plt agt the def & John Miller his security for what of the sum sued for in the declaration shall appear to be justly due unless the def appear at the next court & answer the sd accon. (Pg 429)

In the suit brought by Davis Stern agt George & Thomas Davis the def pleads not guilty the (plt) joines the issue & the same is cont'd to next court for trial. (Pg 429)

John Mcnemara & Patrick Raines came into court & confess'd judgmt unto Samuel Skinker gent for 650 lbs of tobacco which is ord'd to be paid. (Pg 429)

Joseph Strother, Samuel Skinker & William Strother gent ackn their bond to our Sovereign Lord the King for 84,150 lbs of tobacco which is ord'd to be recorded. (Pg 429)

John Jennings being sumoned an evidence by Thomas Barnes agt Samuel Bromadge & making oath he attended five days on the sd suit it is ord'd that he pay him for the same according to law with cost. (Pg 429)

Richard Barnes of Richmond Co being sumoned an evidence by Thomas Barnes agt Samuel Bromadge & making oath that he attended five days on the sd suit & it appearing he lives 35 miles from the sd court it is ord'd that he pay him for the same & for four times coming & four times going according to law with cost. (Pg 429)

On the petition of Margaret Simmond agt John Miller setting forth the sd John detain'd her his servant upon hearing the evidence & arguments … [*illegible*] … it is ord'd that the sd Margaret be sett free & discharged from the sd Miller's service & that he pay the cost with one atty fee. (Pg 429)

In the accon upon the case between Thomas Barnes plt & Samuel Bromadge def, Walter Anderson, John Ambrose, Briant OBannon, Rowland Cornelious, James Greenian, Charles Lewis, Charles Seale, Jeremiah Bronaugh, Willm Strother, John Miller, Robert Taliaferro & Thomas Stribling was sworne a jury to try the issue who having heard the evidence & arguments of both parties withdrew & sometime after returned the following verdt, viz, we find a receipt dated 14 Jan 1726/7 under the hand of the def. We find by the evidence of Richard Barnes that after the sd receipt was passed the def promised to deliver to the plt a protested bill of exchange of one Joseph Hasells (or Hasetts?) for £18:3:1. We find a discharge in full of all demands under the hand of the plt dated 14 Mar 1727/8. We find by the evidence of the afsd Barnes that the def promised to send the plt some thread & a faggot of steel. If the law be for the plt we find for the plt £22, if not we find for the def, Walter Anderson foreman, which verdt is admitted to record & the sd suit is cont'd till next court to argue the matters of law. (Pg 429)

Then this court adjourn'd to court in course.

Court held 23 Dec 1728 for the examination of Jno Wilson. Present: William Thornton, Jona Gibson, Samll Skinner, Rowld Thornton, Jereh Murdock, gent justices. (Pg 430)

John Wilson being comitted under hand & seale of Thomas Vivion gent & accused of stealing large quantities of Indian corn, wheat, oates & Indian pease out of the house of Augt Washington gent of Westmoreland Co upon his examination the court is of opinion that he is a notorious thief & their upon order the sheriff take him to the whipping post & give him 39 lashes on the bare back well laid on & that he give security in the sum of £40, his security in the sum of £20 by the next court held for this co & that he be discharged paying the charge of his prosecution. (Pg 430)

Court held 3 Jan 1728. Present: Willm Thornton, Jona Gibson, Jereh Murdock, Samll Skinner, Willm Strother, gent justices. (Pg 430)

Willm Roof ackn his indenture to Richard Griffin which on the motion of the sd Griffin is admitted to record. (Pg 430)

Robert Doniphan ackn his deed together with the livery & seizing thereon to William Thornton gent which on the motion of the sd Thornton is admitted to record. (Pg 430)

Order'd that Robert Peck be constable in the room of Thomas Grimsley. (Pg 431)

Richard Gill ackn his lease, release & bond to Marmaduke Beckwith which at the instance of Edward Barradall atty for the sd Beckwith is admitted to record. (Pg 431)

On the petition of Mary Thornly administration of the estate of Aron Thornly decd is granted unto her she having with William Peck, Robert Strother & Robert Peck ackn their bond for £300 for her faithfull administration of the sd estate. (Pg 431)

Richard Tankersley, Samuel Wharton, Robert Elliston & James Robertson or any three of them are appointed to appraise in money the estate of Aron Thornly decd that shall be presented to their view & make report to the next court. (Pg 431)

Ordered that Dominic Newgen son & heir at law to Edwd Newgen decd be sumons by the sheriff to the next court to shew cause if any he hath why the will of the sd Edward may not be proved by the executors therein named. (Pg 431)

On the petition of George Franklin administration of the estate of Thomas Wells decd is granted him he having with John Jennings ackn their bond for £40 for the sd George's faithfull administration of the sd estate. (Pg 431)

John Tiller, Jos Minton, John Payne & Anthony Carnaby or any three of them are appointed to appraise in money the estate of Thomas Wells decd that shall be presented to their view & make report to the next court. (Pg 431)

Ordered that John Jett be summons agt next court to answer the petition of Samll Kindall. (Pg 431)

On the petition of Thomas Philips licence is granted him to keep an ordinary the ensuing year he having with Richard Gill & Thomas Harwood ackn their bond to our Sovereign Lord the King for 10,000 lbs of tobacco for his keeping the same according to law. (Pg 431)

In the suit in chancery depending between William Morrison complt & Jereh Bronaugh & Rose his wife respts the sd respts having return'd their answer the complt replies to the same & the respts has time till next court to consider it. (Pg 431)

The suit brought by William Skrine agt Ann Griffis cont'd till next (court) at the plts cost. (Pg 431)

The suit brought by Daniel Hornby agt Charles Senlvon the defs motion is cont'd till next court at his cost. (Pg 431)

In the suit by petition between Daniel French & Margaret his wife plts & Evan Price executor of the will of John Pratt decd def the last order not being comply'd with is cont'd till next court. (Pg 432)

The suit brought by Thomas Barnes agt Samuel Bromadge the plt being dead is order'd to be dismist. (Pg 432)

The suit in chancery depending between Catherine Rymer complt & Thomas Harrisson & Margaret his wife respondts is cont'd till next court. (Pg 432)

The suit brought by Samuel Skinker gent agt John Trice is cont'd till next court. (Pg 432)

The suit brought by William Skrine agt Richard Barnes is cont'd till next court. (Pg 432)

In the action upon the case between Thomas Montieth plt & Jeremiah Bronaugh & Rose his wife adminrs with the will annex'd of John Dinwiddie decd defs by consent of both parties it is order'd that William Thornton, Samuel Skinker gent & John Champe & Thomas Turner three or any two of them audit, state & settle all accounts in deferrance between the plt & the estate of the sd John decd & report their proceedings to the next court. (Pg 432)

In the action of trespass between Simon Hughs plt & Elias Yates def the def being called & not appearing judgt by nihil dicit is granted the plt agt the def for what of the sum sued for in the declaration shall appear to be justly due unless the def appear at the next court & answer the sd action. (Pg 432)

In the action upon the case between Isaac Norman plt & Mary Brown def judgmt is granted the plt agt the def for what of the sum sued for in the declaration shall appear to be justly due upon a writ of inquiry for damages to be had at the next court. (Pg 432)

The suit brought by Jacob Bartlett agt William Boldwire is cont'd till next court. (Pg 432)

In the action of debt between Francis Kirtly plt & John Ritterford def the def being called & not appearing the order of last Nov court is confirm'd agt the def & John Miller his security for 530 lbs of tobacco which is order'd to be paid with cost & one atty fee. (Pg 432)

In the suit brought by David Stern agt Thomas Davis is cont'd till next court. (Pg 432)

The attachmt obtained by George White & Francis James agt Samll Tuson is order'd to be dismist. (Pg 432)

The attachmt obtained by Richard Longman agt William Tomlinson cont'd till next court. (Pg 433)

In the action upon the case between Charles Burchnell plt & William Grant def the def being called & not appearing judgmt is granted the plt agt the def for what of the sum sued for in the declaration shall appear to be justly due unless the def shall appear at the next court & answer the sd action. (Pg 433)

In the suit brought by William Chamberlaine plt agt Thomas Smith def the def has oyer of the bill & the same is cont'd till next court. (Pg 433)

Special imparlance is granted unto Thomas Montieth in the suit brought agt him by Jeremiah Bronaugh & Rose his wife. (Pg 433)

In the suit brought by Jeremiah Bronaugh & Rose his wife plts agt Thomas Montieth the def has oyer of the acct & the same is cont'd till next court. (Pg 433)

The action upon the case between John Long plt & Francis Woffendale & Henry Bartlett defs the defs being called & not appearing judgmt is granted the plt agt the defs & William Harrison their security for what of the sum sued for in the declaration shall appear to be justly due unless the defs appear at the next court & answer the sd action. (Pg 433)

In the suit brought by William Dooling agt Geo Head the def appeared & pleaded not guilty & the plt joyned the issue & the same lyes till next court for triall. (Pg 433)

An alias capias is granted unto John Edwards agt John Triplett. (Pg 433)

The suit brought by our Sovereign Lord the King agt Thomas Harwood is cont'd. (Pg 433)

The scire facias brought by James Robirtson agt John Taliaferro & Mosely Battaley is ord'd to be dismist. (Pg 433)

In the action upon (the case) between William Strother plt & George Downing def the def being called & not appearing judgmt is granted the plt agt the def & Charles Lewis his security for what of the sum sued for in the declaration shall appear to be justly due unless the def appear at the next court & answer the sd action. (Pg 433)

The suit brought by Charles Seale agt James Greenian is order'd to be dismist. (Pg 433)

In the suit brought by Samuel Skinner agt Patrick Reins & John Mcmcmam is order'd to be dismist. (Pg 433)

In the suit brought by Catesby Cocke agt Richd Irish is ord'd to be dismist. (Pg 434)

In the suit brought by Antho Hainy agt John Elson is order'd to be dismist. (Pg 434)

In the suit brought by William Strother agt John Jones is ordered to be dismist. (Pg 434)

In the suit brought by Thomas Griffin &c jutices (justices?) of Richmond Co agt William Tharp & Francis Woffendale the def has oyer of the bond & the same is cont'd till next court. (Pg 434)

The attachmt obtained by Walter Anderson agt Jos Hensley is order'd to be cont'd till next court. (Pg 434)

The suit brought by William Harper agt Isaac Farguson is ordered to be dismist. (Pg 434)

The attachmt obtained by Samuel Skinker agt Jos Hensley is ordered to be cont'd till next court. (Pg 434)

Ordered that Mary Spicer be sumon'd to next court to answer the petition of Charles Dean. (Pg 434)

On the petition of Thomas Monteith setting forth that he was appointed one of the executors in the will of John Dinwiddie decd & praying he might prove the sd will & be admitted executor thereto the court upon hearing the evidence & arguments is of opinion that the sd Monteith is excluded from proving the sd will from which judgment the sd Monteith prayed an appeal to the 9th day of the next General Court which is granted him he having with John Taliaferro gent entered into bond to prosecute the sd appeal according to law. (Pg 434)

Thomas Catlett gent of Caroline Co being sumoned an evidence by Jeremiah Bronaugh agt Thomas Monteith & making oath that he attended one day it is ordered that he pay him for the same & for coming three miles & going three miles with ferriage according to law. (Pg 434)

Then the court adjourned to court in course.

Court held 7 Mar 1728. Present: William Robinson, William Thornton, Thomas Vivion, Samuel Skinker, William Strother, Jereh Murdock, gent justices. (Pg 434)

The will of Richard Tutt decd was presented into court by Mary Tutt his widow & extrix who made oath thereto & the same was proved by the oaths of Adam Chininghane, Joshua Farguson & Richard Tutt & admitted to record. (Pg 435)

Mary Tutt, Jeremiah Murdock & William Strother gent ackn their bond for £100 for the sd Mary's true & faithfull administration of Richard Tutt's estate. (Pg 435)

Joshua Farguson, John Fox, John Plunkett & Mosses Knighton or any three of them are appointed to appraise in mony the estate of Richard Tutt decd that shall be brought to their view & make report to the next court. (Pg 435)

George Franklin returned the inventory of Thomas Wells estate & made oath thereto which is admitted to record. (Pg 435)

Enoch Innis ackn his lease & release to the Honble Robert Carter esqr which on the motion of Thomas Turner atty for the sd Carter is admitted to record. (Pg 435)

John Quisenbury & William Quisenbury ackn their feeofment together with the livery & seizing thereon to Nicholas Smith gent which on the motion of Edward Barradall atty for the sd Nicholas Smith is admitted to record & Thomas Turner by virtue of a power of atty from Elizabeth Quisenbury w/o the sd John Quisenbury relinquished her right of dower & thirds at common law hereto which is admitted to record. (Pg 435)

Edward Barradall by virtue of a power of atty from Nicholas Smith gent prov'd in court by the oaths of George Fishpool & Charles Dean ackn a deed of feeofment together with the livery & seizing thereon from the sd Nicholas Smith to John Quisenbury & Thomas Turner by virtue of a power of atty from Elizabeth Smith w/o the sd Nicholas Smith relinquished her right of dower & thirds at common law to the sd land which on the motion of the sd John Quisenbury is admitted to record. (Pg 435)

The inventory of the estate of Aaron Thornly decd is returned & admitted to record. (Pg 435)

A deed of lease & release from William Skrine to Nicholas Smith gent was presented into court by Edward Barradall & the same was proved by the oaths of Samuel Skinker, Thomas Turner & Jeremiah Bronaugh & Thomas Turner by virtue of a power of atty from Margt Skrine w/o the sd William Skrine proved in court by the oaths of Samuel Skinker & Jeremiah Bronaugh relinquished her right of dower & thirds at common law to the sd land which on the motion of Edward Barradall atty for the sd Nicholas Smith is admitted to record. (Pg 435)

William Russell ackn his lease & release to John Bradford & Grace the w/o the sd William relinquished her right of dower to the land therein conveyed which on the motion of the sd John is admitted to record. (Pg 436)

Joseph Allen ackn his deed together with the livery & seizing thereon to John Morehead which on the motion of the sd John is admitted to record. (Pg 436)

Ordered that the sheriff take the body of John Wilson into his custody till he gives bond with good & sufficient security in the sum of £20 for his good behaviour for 12 months & a day next ensuing. (Pg 436)

Present Jonathan Gibson gent.

On the petition of John Willis it is ordered that Thomas Goff be admitted his guardian the sd Goff with Neal McCormack ackn their bond for £50 to save the court harmless. (Pg 436)

William Foster came into court & agreed to serve William Thornton gent to the 23rd of Jan next & the same admitted to record. (Pg 436)

Thomas Turner by virtue of a power of atty from under the hand & seal of Margrett Strother w/o William Strother gent proved in court by the oaths of Mosely Battaley & Thomas Smith relinquished her right of dower & thirds att the common law to a certain tr of land sold & conveyed by her sd husband unto Samuel Skinker gent which on the motion of the sd Samuel is admitted to record. (Pg 436)

The will together with a codicill of John Matthews decd was presented into court by Moseley Battaley & on the motion of the sd Battaley was proved by the oath of Lewis Morris one of the evidences thereto by reason the sd Lewis designs to leave this Colony the first oppertunity. (Pg 436)

Ordered that Baldwin Matthews heir at law of John Matthews decd be sumoned to the next court to shew cause if any he hath why the will of the sd John may not be proved according to law. (Pg 436)

Robert Jackson a servant boy belonging to John Standly being brought before the court to have his age adjudged when to be a tithable is adjudged to be 12 years of age which is ordered to be recorded. (Pg 436)

Councellor a Negro boy belonging to James Kenney is adjudged to be 10 years of age & Judy a Negro girl to be 11 which is ordered to be recorded. (Pg 437)

Ordered that Elizabeth Tippet be sumoned to next court to answer the petition of Josua Farguson. (Pg 437)

In the information of William Flowers agt John Clark, Peter Hedgman gent came into court & assumed to pay unto our Sovereign Lord the King the sum of £15 if the sd Peter fail to produce a certain horse belonging to the sd John Clark that is seized on by precept under the hand & seal of William Thornton gent to the next court whereupon the sd def has time till next court to plead to the sd information. (Pg 437)

John Sharp being brought before the court to answer the complaint of Bryant OBanon for scandalizing his dau Ann the sd Sharp ackn himself in fault that he is very sorry for what is past is discharged paying cost with one atty fee. (Pg 437)

Thomas Turner presented into court a deed for two lotts No. 19 & 13 from the trustees of Falmouth Town to John Williams together with the livery & seizing thereon the same being proved by the oaths of Catesby Cocke, Robert Jones & John Warner evidences thereto on the motion of the sd Turner is admitted to record. (Pg 437)

William Thornton gent presented into court a deed for two lotts No. 9 & 17 from the trustees of Falmouth Town to him the sd William Thornton together with the livery & seizing thereon the same being proved by the oaths of Catesby Cocke, Robert Jones & John Warner evidences thereto which on the motion of the sd Thornton is admitted to record. (Pg 437)

William Thornton presented into court a deed for a lott No. 8 from the trustees of Falmouth Town to Nicholas Smith gent together with the livery & seizing thereon the same being proved by the oaths of Catesby Cocke, Robert Jones & John Warner evidences thereto which on the motion of William Thornton on the behalf of the sd Nicholas Smith is admitted to record. (Pg 437)

William Thornton gent presented into court a deed for two lotts No. 5 & 15 from the trustees of Falmouth Town to Charles Carter gent together with the livery & seizing thereon the same being proved by the oaths of Catesby Cocke, Robert Jones & John Warner evidences thereto which on the motion of the sd William Thornton on the behalf of the sd Charles Carter is admitted to record. (Pg 437)

William Thornton gent presented into court a deed for two lotts No. 16 & 24 from the trustees of Falmouth Town to Robert Carter Junr esqr together with the livery & seizing thereon the same being proved by the oaths of Catesby Cocke, Robert Jones & John Warner evidences thereto on the motion of the sd William Thornton on the behalf of the sd Robt Carter is admitted to record. (Pg 437)

William Thornton gent presented into court a deed for two lotts No. 20 & 21 from the trustees of Falmouth Town to the Honble John Carter esqr together with the livery & seizing thereon the same being proved by the oaths of Catesby Cocke, Robert Jones & John Warner evidences thereto on the motion of William Thornton gent on the behalf of the sd John Carter esqr is admitted to record. (Pg 438)

William Thornton gent presented into court a deed for two lotts No. 6 & 26 from the trustees of Falmouth Town to the Honble Mann Page esqr together with the livery & seizing thereon the same being proved by the oaths of Catesby Cocke, Robert Jones & John Warner evidences thereto on the motion of William Thornton gent on the behalf of the sd John Carter (*sic*) esqr is admitted to record. (Pg 438)

William Thornton gent presented into court a deed for two lotts No. 2 & 25 from the trustees of Falmouth Town to the Honble Robert Carter esqr together with the livery & seizing thereon the same being proved by the oaths of Catesby Cocke, Robert Jones & John Warner evidences thereto which on the motion of William Thornton gent on the behalf of the sd Robert Carter esqr is admitted to record. (Pg 438)

John Warner presented into court a deed for two lotts No. 22 & 28 from the trustees of Falmouth Town to him the sd John Warner together with the livery & seizing thereon the same being proved by the oaths of Catesby Cocke, Robert Jones & Benjn Rush evidences thereto which on the motion of the sd Warner is admitted to record. (Pg 438)

Robert Jones presented into court a deed for two lotts No. 7 & 14 from the trustees of Falmouth Town to him the sd Robert Jones together with the livery & seizing thereon the same being proved by the oaths of Catesby Cocke, John Warner & Benjn Rush evidences thereto which on the motion of the sd Jones is admitted to record. (Pg 438)

Thomas Turner presented into court a deed for a lot No. 3 from the trustees of Falmouth Town to William Beverley gent together with the livery & seizing thereon the same being proved by the oaths of Robt Jones, John Warner & Benja

Rush evidences thereto on the motion of Thomas Turner on the behalf of William Beverly is admitted to record. (Pg 438)

The will of Edward Newgent decd was presented into court by Frances Newgent his widow & extrix who made (oath) thereto & the same was also proved by the oaths of Robert Jones & Thomas Harwood two of the evidences thereto, Domine Newgent being at law to the sd Edward being sumoned appeared & objected that he was not mentioned in the sd will. (Pg 438)

Adam Christe, Thomas Harwood, John & Linefield Sharp or any three of them being first sworne are appointed to appraise in mony the estate of Edward Newgent decd that shall be brought to their view & make report to the next court. (Pg 439)

Administration of the estate of David Caldwalls is granted unto James Jones he having with James Hackley ackn their bond for £20 for the sd Jones' true & faithfull administration of the sd Caldwalls estate. (Pg 439)

John Farguson, John Owen, John Diskins & William Procter or any three of them being first sworne are appointed to appraise in mony the estate of David Caldwalls decd that shall be brought to their view & make report to the next court. (Pg 439)

Ordered that Edward Barradall make application to Westmoreland Court in order to have the road that leads from the head of Popes Cr to Popeter Bridge laid open it being now stopt up by John Jarvis. (Pg 439)

In the suit in chancery depending between William Morrison compt & Jeremiah Bronaugh respt the complt having replyed the respt joins the sd replication & the sd suit lies till next court for triall. (Pg 439)

In the action upon the case between William Skrine plt & Ann Griffis def the def making oath that she had not received any goods of the plt within three years of the bringing the sd suit it is therefore ordered to be dismist with cost & one atty fee. (Pg 439)

In the action upon the case between Daniel Hornby plt & Charles Seale def, Charles Dean, Francis Woffendale, George Franklin, Richard Ellkins, Mark Hardin, John Farguson, John Diskins, Abraham Kenyan, William Hackley, Thomas Smith, John Sharp & Samll Wharton was sworne a jury to try the issue who having heard the evidence & arguments withdrew & not returning their verdt according to law the sd suit is cont'd till next court & a vinne facias denovo to be had the next court. (Pg 439)

The suit depending between Daniel French & Margrett his wife plt & Evan Price executor of the will of John Pratt decd def is cont'd till next court. (Pg 439)

The suit brought by Samuel Skinker gent agt John Trice is ordered to be dismist. (Pg 439)

The suit brought by Thomas Monteith agt Jeremiah Bronaugh & Rose his wife adminrs with the will annext of John Dinwiddie decd is ordered to be cont'd for the auditors to finish & make their report. (Pg 439)

In the suit in chancery between William Thornton gent for & on the behalf of Katherine Rymer complt & Thomas Harrison & Margrett his wife respondts the sd Thomas came into court & confest judgment for £110:11:3 which is ordered to be paid. (Pg 440)

In the suit brought by Simon Hughs agt Elias Yates the def pleads not guilty the plt joins the issue & the same lies till next court for triall. (Pg 440)

The suit brought by Jacob Bartlett agt Richard Bowlware is ordered to be dismist the def paying cost. (Pg 440)

In the attachment obtained by Richard Longman agt William Tomlinson judgment is granted the sd Richard agt the estate of the sd William for 200 lbs of tobacco in the hands of James Jones which is ordered to be paid. (Pg 440)

William Strother being sumoned an evidence by Samll Skinker gent agt John Trice & making oath that he attended 5 days on the sd suit it is order'd that he pay him for the same with cost according to law. (Pg 440)

Then the court adjourned till tomorrow morning 8 o'clock.

Court held 8 Mar 1728. Present: William Robinson, William Thornton, Jonathan Gibson, William Strother. (Pg 440)

In the suit brought by Charles Burchnell agt William Grant the def being called & not appearing judgment per nihil dicit is granted the plt agt the def for what of the sum sued for in the declaration shall appear to be justly due unless the def appear at the next court & answer the sd action. (Pg 440)

In the suit brought by Jeremiah Bronaugh agt Thomas Monteith the def pleads in writing & the plt has time till next court to consider the sd plea. (Pg 440)

In the suit brought by Jeremiah Bronaugh agt Thomas Monteith the def pleads he did not assume the plt joines the issue & the same lies till next court for triall. (Pg 440)

In the suit brought by John Long agt Francis Woffendale & Henry Bartlett the defs plead not guilty & the plt joins the issue & the same lyes till next court for triall. (Pg 441)

The suit brought by John Edwards agt John Triplett is dismist. (Pg 441)

In the action upon the case between William Strother gent plt & George Downing def the def being called & not appearing the order of last Jan court is confirmed agt the def & Charles Lewis his security for 10 shillings due on ballance of account which is ordered to be paid with cost & one atty fee. (Pg 441)

In the suit brought by Thomas Griffin & justices of the peace for Richmond Co agt William Tharp & Francis Woffendale the defs plead conditions perform'd the plt has time till next to reply. (Pg 441)

Present Jeremiah Murdock gent.

The suit brought by William Skrine agt Richard Barns is cont'd till next court at the plts cost. (Pg 441)

The suit brought by Isaac Norman agt Mary Brown is ord'd to be dismist. (Pg 441)

In the action of trespass & assault between David Stern plt & Thomas Davis def, Charles Dean, Francis Woffendale, George Franklin, Richard Ellkins, Mark Hardin, John Farguson, John Diskins, Abraham Kenyan, Willm Hackney, Thomas Smith, John Sharp & Samuel Wharton was sworne a jury to try the issue joined who having heard the evidence withdrew & sometime after returned the following verdt, to wit, we find for the def, Charles Deane foreman, & the sd suit is ordered to be dismist with cost. (Pg 441)

The attachment obtained by Walter Anderson agt Joseph Hensley is cont'd till next court for Joseph Strother gent to finish the crop. (Pg 441)

The attachment obtained by Samuel Skinker gent agt Joseph Hensley is cont'd till next court for Joseph Strother gent to finish the crop. (Pg 441)

The petition brought by Samuel Kendall agt John Jett is dismist. (Pg 441)

The suit brought by William Hutchinson agt Isaac Johnson is dismist. (Pg 441)

In the suit brought by William Chamberlaine agt Thomas Smith the def pleads payment the plt joins the issue & the same lies till next court for triall. (Pg 441)

The suit brought by William Hackney agt James Turner is dismist. (Pg 442)

The suit brought by William Hackney agt William Brooks is dismist. (Pg 442)

The suit brought by William Hackney agt Timothy Rading is dismist. (Pg 442)

The suit brought by Wm Beverly agt Robt Evans is dismist. (Pg 442)

In the suit between Jeremiah OBriant plt & John Standley def the def appearing pleaded that he owed nothing the plt joined the issue upon hearing the arguments judgment is granted the plt agt the def for 400 lbs of tobacco which is ordered to be paid with cost & one atty fee. (Pg 442)

Robert Dudley of Caroline Co being sumoned an evidence by David Stern agt Thomas Davis & making oath that he attended four days on the sd suit it is ordered that he pay him for the same according to law for three times coming & three times going 7 miles & ferriages with cost. (Pg 442)

In the action of slander between William Dooling plt & George Head def, Charles Deane, Francis Woffendale, George Franklin, Richard Ellkins, Mark Hardin, John Farguson, John Diskins, Abraham Kenyan, William Hackney, Thomas Smith, John Sharp & Samuel Wharton was sworne a jury to try the issue joined who having heard the evidences & arguments withdrew & sometime after returned the following verdt, viz, we find for the plt 17 shillings 6 pence which verdt on the plts motion is admitted to record & judgment is granted the plt agt the def for the sd sum which is ordered to be paid together with 17 shillings 6 pence for cost. (Pg 442)

In the suit brought by our Sovereign Lord the King agt Thomas Harwood the def pleads not guilty & issue is joined for the King. (Pg 442)

The attachment obtained by Roger Abbot agt James Taylor the sheriff having returned that the attached 900 lbs of tobacco in the hands of the sd Roger is cont'd for the sd Roger finishing his crop. (Pg 442)

Ordered that the sheriff take the body of Ann Simpson & her in his safe custody keep unless John Farguson her master will be her security for her appearance at the next court to answer the grand jurys presentment. (Pg 443)

Judgment is granted unto Hanover Parish agt Eliza Lee for bringing a bastard child & it is ordered that the sheriff take her into his custody till she pay the fine according to law. (Pg 443)

The suit brought by Francis Woffendale agt William Harrison & George Head is cont'd till next court. (Pg 443)

In the petition preferred by Charles Dean setting forth that Mary Spicer has stopd up the road that he can neither go to Church nor mill, it is ordered that Nicholas Smith gent, George White & William Carter or any two of them view the sd road & make report to the next court. (Pg 443)

On the motion of John Lee the will of Isaac Lee decd is presented into court & admitted to record. (Pg 443)

Thomas Williams, being sumoned an evidence by William Dooling agt George Head & having attended three days on the sd suit it is ordered that he pay him for the same with cost according to law. (Pg 443)

Joel Bucy being sumoned an evidence by William Dooling agt George Head & having attended three days on the sd suit it is ordered that he pay him for the same with cost according to law. (Pg 443)

Administration on the estate of James Robertson decd is granted unto Ann his widow the sd Ann with Rowland Thornton & Abraham Kenyan ackn their bond of £300 for the sd Ann's faithfull administration of the sd estate. (Pg 443)

Robert Elliston, Samll Wharton, Walter Anderson & Richard Tankersley or any three of them being first sworne are appointed to appraise in mony the estate of James Robertson decd that shall be brought to their view & make report to the next court. (Pg 443)

Jeremiah Murdock gent produced an account agt Jonas Jenkins for 465 lbs of tobacco & made oath thereto which is ord'd to be certifyed. (Pg 443)

36

Then the court adjourned till court in course.

Court held 4 Apr 1729. Present: Nicholas Smith, Thomas Vivion, Samuel Skinker, Rowland Thornton, Jere Murdock, gent justices. (Pg 444)

Francis Newgent returned the inventory of the estate of Edward Newgent decd which is admitted to record. (Pg 444)

Nicholas Smith gent made oath to his disposition which on the motion of Edward Barradall is ordered to be certified. (Pg 444)

James Jones returned the inventory of the estate of David Caldwalls decd which is admitted to record. (Pg 444)

On the petition of Henry Long licence is granted him to keep an ordinary the ensuing year he having with Benja Strother gent ackn their bond to our Sovereign Lord the King for 10,000 lbs of tobacco for his keep the same according to law. (Pg 444)

Ordered that the sheriff summons a grand jury to the next court.

In the action upon the case between Danll Hornby plt & Charles Seale def, Richard Bryant, Saml Hensley, Jereh Bronaugh, James Jones, William Grant, Xopher Rodgers, William Harrison, Henry Head, Robt Johnson, Joshua Farguson, John Plunkett & John Fox was sworn a jury to try the issue who having heard the evidence & arguments withdrew & sometime after returned the following verdt, viz, we find for the def, Richard Bryant foreman, which verdt on the defs motion is admitted to record & the sd suit is ordered to be dismist with cost & one atty fee. (Pg 444)

Ann Robertson returned the inventory of the estate of James Robertson decd which is admitted to record. (Pg 444)

Ordered that John Champe be surveyor of the highways from the Dogue Swamp to Skrine Mill. (Pg 444)

Ordered that Isaac Arnold be surveyor of the highways from Crows Swamp to the Mines Swamp. (Pg 445)

In the suit brought by Thomas Monteith agt Jeremiah Bronaugh & Rose his wife adminrs with the will annext of John Dinwiddie decd is ordered to be cont'd for the auditors to finish & make their report. (Pg 445)

The attachment obtained by Walter Anderson agt Joseph Hensley is cont'd till next court for Joseph Strother gent to finish the crop. (Pg 445)

The attachment obtained by Samll Skinker gent agt Joseph Hensley is cont'd till next court for Joseph Strother gent to finish the crop. (Pg 445)

The suit brought by Frances Woffendale agt William Harrison & George Head is cont'd till next court at the defs cost. (Pg 445)

In the attachment obtained by Rodger Abbot agt James Taylor is cont'd till next court for the sd Roger finishing his crop. (Pg 445)

The suit brought by John Champ agt Peter Newgent is dismist. (Pg 445)

The suit brought by Samuel Skinker agt Charles Jones is dismist. (Pg 445)

On the petition of Robert Spotswood agt Francis Newgent is cont'd. (Pg 445)

In the action upon the case between William Kennan plt & Charles Seale def the def has oyer of the account. (Pg 445)

In the suit brought by Charles Burchnell agt William Grant the def having pleaded in wrighting the plt has time till next court to consider the plea. (Pg 445)

In the suit brought by Jeremiah Bronaugh & Rose his wife plt agt Thomas Monteith def the def having put in his plea the plt joins the issue & the same lyes till next court for triall. (Pg 445)

On the petition of Charles Dean it is ordered that Mary Spicer open the road that leads from the sd Deans to church & mill & that she pay the costs. (Pg 445)

Thomas Smith came into court & confessed judgmt to William Chamberlayne for the sum of £27:18:10 due on a protested bill of exchange which is ordered to be paid with cost & one atty fee. (Pg 445)

John Bell being sumoned an evidence by Danl Hornby agt Charles Seale & making oath that he attended six days on the sd suit it is ordered that he pay him for the same with cost according to law. (Pg 445)

John Ambrose being sumoned an evidence by Danl Hornby agt Charles Seale & making oath that he attended six days on the sd suit it is ordered that the sd Hornby pay the sd Ambrose for the same with cost according to law. (Pg 446)

Rowld Cornelius being sumoned an evidence by Danl Hornby agt Charles Seale & making oath that he attended six days on the sd suit it is ordered that the sd Hornby pay the sd Cornelius for the same with cost according to law. (Pg 446)

In the action of Trover & Conversion between William Skrine plt & Richard Barns def, Richard Bryant, Samll Hensley, Jeremiah Bronaugh, James Jones, William Grant, Xopher Rogers, William Harrison, Henry Head, Robert Johnson, Joshua Farguson, John Plunkett & John Fox were sworne a jury to try the issue joined who having heard the evidence & arguments withdrew & some time after returned the following verdt, viz, we find for the plt £31:4:10, Richard Bryant foreman, which verdt on the plts motion is admitted to record & judgment is granted the plt agt the sd def for the sd sum which is ordered to be paid with cost & one atty fee & on the motion of the sd def injunction & subpoena in chancery is granted him to stay execution till the matter be further heard in equity, Thomas Turner entering himself security for the same. (Pg 446)

In the suit brought by Richard Longman agt Abraham Stanning the def being called & not appearing judgment is granted the plt agt the def for what of the sum sued for in the declaration shall appear to be justly due unless the def appear at the next court & answer the sd action. (Pg 446)

In the suit brought by William Hackney agt Abraham Stanning the def being called & not appearing judgment is granted the plt agt the def & John Griggsby his security for what of the sum sued for in the declaration shall appear to be justly due unless the sd def appear at the next court & answer the sd action. (Pg 446)

Ordered that Robert Abbot, William Corbin & Benja Griggsby be sumoned to next court to answer the attachmt of William Strother gent agt James Taylor. (Pg 446)

Court held 5 Apr 1729. Present: William Thornton, Samuel Skinker, William Strother, Jere Murdock, gent justices. (Pg 447)

Ordered that John Jett be sumoned to next court to answer the petition of Henry Lewis & Martha his wife. (Pg 447)

Christopher Rodgers & Margrett his wife ackn their deeds of lease & release to Jos Strother gent the sd Margt by solely examined confessed her free consent to the same which on the motion of the sd Joseph Strother is admitted to record. (Pg 447)

Administration of the estate of Robert Keirn decd is granted unto Thomas Turner he having with Joseph Strother gent ackn their bond for £30 for the sd Turner's true & faithfull administration of the sd Keirn's estate. (Pg 447)

On the motion of Baldwin Matthews, Thomas Turner is appointed guardian to the sd Baldwin. (Pg 447)

In the suit brought by Simon Hughs agt Elias Yates is cont'd till next court at the plts cost. (Pg 447)

Ordered that Thomas Harwood be surveyor of the highways from the Great Falls to the upper side of Deep Run. (Pg 447)

Administration of the estate of William Tippet is granted unto Joshua Farguson he having with Willm Grant ackn their bond for £50 for the sd Farguson's true & faithfull administration of the sd Tippet estate. (Pg 447)

In the suit brought by Jeremiah Bronaugh agt William Morrison is cont'd. (Pg 447)

The suit brought by Danll French agt Evan Price is cont'd till next court & for the sd Daniel to account for the profits in the hands of Margrett his wife. (Pg 447)

John Plunkett, Moses Knighton, Willm Pullen & Thomas Dickenson or any three of them being first sworn are appointed to appraise in mony the estate of Wm Tippet decd that shall be brought to their view & make report to the next court. (Pg 447)

The probate of the will of John Matthews decd is cont'd till next court this court being divided. (Pg 447)

Judgmt is granted unto Hanover Parish agt Ann Simpson for bringing a mollatto bastard child. (Pg 447)

William Skrine came into court & confess'd judgment unto Nicholas Smith gent for £50:8 1 penny & 8,448 lbs of tobacco which is order'd to be paid with cost. (Pg 448)

William Skrine came into court & confessed judgment unto Nicholas Smith gent for £76:16:3 which is ordered to be paid with cost. (Pg 448)

Robert Green of Spotsylvania Co being sumoned an evidence by Willm Skrine agt Richard Barns & making oath that he attended four days on the sd suit & it appearing he lived 50 miles from the sd court it is ordered that the sd Skrine pay him for the same & for two times coming & two times going with cost according to law. (Pg 448)

John Carder of Spotsylvania Co being sumoned an evidence by William Skrine agt Richard Barns & making oath that he attended four days on the sd suit & it appearing he lived 50 miles form the sd court it is order'd that the sd Skrine pay him for the same & for three times coming & going with cost according to law. (Pg 448)

Aaron Pinson of Spotsylvania Co being sumoned an evidence by William Skrine agt Richard Barns & having attended two days on the sd suit it appearing he lived 50 miles from the sd court it is ordered that the sd Skrine pay him for the same & for coming & going with cost according to law. (Pg 448)

Peter Newgent being sumoned an evidence by William Skrine agt Richard Barns & making oath that he attended six days on the sd suit it is ordered that the sd Skrine pay him for the same with cost according to law. (Pg 448)

In the information between William Flowers plt & John Clark def for importing three horses from New England contrary to Act of Assembly made in the year 1669, the sheriff having returned that he had taken two of the sd horse pursuant to a precept under the hand of William Thornton gent justice of the peace it was ordered in Mar court that the sd def should have time till this court to plead & now being called offered his plea in writing which the court would not admitt of & thereupon ordered the sd sheriff cause the sd horses to be disposed of according to the sd Act of Assembly from which judgmt the sd def prayed an appeal to the 9th day of the next Generall Court which is granted him he having with Peter Hedgman gent entered into bond to prosecute the sd appeal according to law. (Pg 448)

In the action of Trover & Conversion between John Long plt & Frances Woffendale & Henry Bartlet defs, Richard Bryant, Samll Hensley, James Jones, Wm Grant, Christopher Rogers, Robert Johnson, Joshua Farguson, John Plunkett, John Fox, Jeremiah Bronaugh, John Farguson & Daniel French was sworne a jury to try the issue joined who having heard the evidence & arguments withdrew & sometime after returned the following verdt, viz, we find for the def, Richard Bryant foreman, which verdt on the defs motion is admitted to record & the sd suit is ordered to be dismist with cost & atty fee to each of the defs. (Pg 449)

Henry Head being sumoned an evidence by John Long agt Frances Woffendale & Henry Bartlett & having attended two days on the sd suit it is ordered that the sd Long pay him for the same with cost according to law. (Pg 449)

John Suttle being sumoned an evidence by John Long agt Frances Woffendale & Henry Bartlett & having attended two days on the sd suit it is ordered that the sd Long pay him for the same with cost according to law. (Pg 449)

John Burton being sumoned an evidence by John Long agt Frances Woffendale & Henry Bartlett & having attended two days on the sd suit it is ordered that the sd Long pay him for the same with cost according to law. (Pg 449)

In the action upon the case brought by Jeremiah Bronaugh & Rose his wife plts & Thomas Monteith def judgment is granted the plts agt the def for £12:19:11 which is ord'd to be paid with cost & one atty fee. 10 Apr 1729 by vertue of this writ I have taken ye within named Thos Monteith before the justices to sattisfie Jere Bronaugh of the debt & damages within mentioned, John Foster dep sheriff. (Pg 449)

The indictment brought by our Sovereign Lord the King agt Thomas Harwood, Richard Bryant, Samll Hensley, James Jones, William Grant, Xopher Rogers, Robert Johnson, Joshua Farguson, John Plunkett, John Fox, Danll French, John Farguson & Jere Bronaugh was sworne a jury to try the issue joined who returned the following verdt, viz, we find the def not guilty, Richard Bryant foreman, which verdt on the plts motion is admitted to record. (Pg 449)

Then the court adjourned to court in course.

Court held 2 May 1729. Present: Wm Thornton, Saml Skinker, Rowld Thornton, Wm Strother, Jere Murdock, gent justices. (Pg 449)

Thomas Davis ackn his lease & release to William Remey & William Grant by virtue of a power of atty from Elizabeth w/o the sd Thomas relinquished her right of dower thereto which at the instance of the sd William is admitted to record. (Pg 449)

William Hackney presented into court the will of Henry Calfee decd & made oath thereto & the same was proved by the oaths of Joseph Hudnall & John Morehead & admitted to record. (Pg 450)

John Morehead, Joseph Hudnall, Thomas Duncomb & John Hopper or any three of them being first sworne are appointed to appraise in money the estate of

Henry Calfee decd that shall be brought to their view & make report to the next court. (Pg 450)

William Hackney by virtue of a power of atty from Elinor Calfee widow & relict of Henry Calfee decd relinquished the right of dower of the sd Elinor to a certain tr of land devised by the sd Henry to John Hudnall which at his motion is adm'd to record. (Pg 450)

William Hackney by virtue of a power of atty from Mary Allen w/o Joseph Allen relinquished her right of dower to a certain tr of land conveyed by her sd husband to John Morehead which on the motion of the sd Morehead is adm'd to record. (Pg 450)

Administration of the estate of Ralph Sise decd is granted unto Martha Sise his widow the sd Martha with Samuel Wharton & Robert Benson ackn their bond of £200 for the sd Martha's faithfull administration of the sd estate. (Pg 450)

John Farguson, John Diskins, Robert Strother & Benjamin Stribling or any three of them being first sworne are appointed to appraise in mony the estate of Ralph Sise decd that shall be brought to their view & make report to the next court. (Pg 450)

The inventory of the estate of George Jones is returned into court & adm'd to record. (Pg 450)

On the motion of John Hudnall, Joseph Hudnall is entered atty for the sd John in this court in all causes whatsoever. (Pg 450)

The inventory of the estate of Richard Tutt decd is returned & adm'd to record. (Pg 450)

Ordered that Robert Bourne an orphan be bound to Katherine Jones untill he arrive to the age of 21 years & that the sd Katherine find him a full suit of cloths with shirts, shooes, stockings & hat at ye expiration of the sd time as also to pay a hhd of tobacco of 530 next fall to some lawyer that the sd Robert shall employ to secure his land. (Pg 450)

Ordered that Thomas Harwood be surveyor of the highway from the Great Falls to the upper side of the next bridge above Roger Abbot's & that the sd Harwood alter the road above & below over the Deep Run & make bridge over the sd run where he shall think proper. (Pg 451)

Ord'd that Robert Duncomb be surveyor of the precinct above Roger Abbot's in the room of the sd Abbot. (Pg 451)

Joseph Hudnall is appointed constable in the room of Charles Morgan. (Pg 451)

On the motion of John Farguson & he having with John Diskin ackn their bond to our Sovereign Lord the King for 10,000 lbs of tobacco the sd Farguson is adm'd to keep an ordinary at his dwelling plantation the year ensuing. (Pg 451)

The action upon the case between Jeremiah Bronaugh & Rose his wife plts & Thomas Monteith def is cont'd till next court. (Pg 451)

The suit brought by Daniel French & Margaret his wife agt Evan Price is cont'd till next court. (Pg 451)

In the suit in chancery between Richard Barnes complt & William Skrine respt the respt has time till next court to answer the bill. (Pg 451)

In the accon upon the case between Thomas Monteith plt & Jeremiah Bronaugh & Rose his wife adminrs with the will annex'd of John Dinwiddie defs the auditors not having returned their report the defs moved to have the sd cause tried by a jury & the plt objected agt it by reason it was before agreed by all parties that it should be put to William Thornton, Samuel Skinker, John Champe & Thomas Turner gent to audit, state & settle the accts in difference & report to the court the court being divided is cont'd till next court. (Pg 451)

William Strother gent ackn his lease & release to John Williams & Thomas Turner by virtue of a power of atty from under the hand & seale of Margaret Strother w/o the sd William relinquished her right of dower thereto which at the instance of the sd John Williams is adm'd to record. (Pg 451)

The suit brought by Simon Hughs agt Elias Yates is cont'd. (Pg 451)

In the suit brought by Charles Birchnell agt William Grant the def has time till next court to plead several matters. (Pg 451)

The suit in chancery between William Morrison complt & Jeremiah Bronaugh respt is cont'd till next court. (Pg 451)

In the suit brought by Thomas Griffin &c justices of the peace for Richmond Co agt William Tharp & Francis Woffendale the defs has further time to reply. (Pg 451)

The attachment obtained by Walter Anderson agt Joseph Hensley is cont'd till next court. (Pg 451)

The attachment obtained by Samuel Skinker gent agt Joseph Hensley is cont'd till next court. (Pg 452)

The suit brought by Francis Woffendale agt William Harrison & George Head is cont'd till next court. (Pg 452)

The attachment obtained by Roger Abbot agt James Taylor is cont'd. (Pg 452)

The petition of Henry Lewis & Martha his wife agt John Jett is ord'd to be dismist. (Pg 452)

In the accon upon the case between Richard Longman plt & Abraham Stannings def the def being called & not appearing the order of last court is confirm'd agt the def & John Grigsby his security for the sum of 1861 lbs of tobacco due by account which is ord'd to be paid with cost & one atty fee. (Pg 452)

In the accon upon the case between William Hackney plt & Abraham Stannings def the def being called & not appearing the order of last court is confirm'd agt the def & John Grigsby his security for the sum of 235 lbs of tobacco due by account which is ord'd to be paid with cost & one atty fee. (Pg 452)

The suit brought by Robert Spotswood agt Frances Newgent is cont'd. (Pg 452)

In the action upon the case between William Kennan plt & Charles Seale def the def being called & not appearing judgmt per nihil dicit is granted the plt agt the def for what of the sum sued for in the declaration shall appear to be justly due unless the def appear at the next court & answer the sd accon. (Pg 452)

An alias capias is granted to John Snell agt Adam Christie. (Pg 452)

The suit brought by Richard Longman agt Francis Woffendale is cont'd. (Pg 452)

The suit brought by Richard Griffis agt Bartholomew Redman is dismist. (Pg 452)

The suit brought by John Tayloe gent agt Richard Griffis is dismist. (Pg 452)

The suit brought by Samuel Skinker gent agt Willm Burbridge is dismist. (Pg 452)

Daniel White, Samuel Hoyle, Isaac Arnold, Samuel Wharton, George White, John Triplet, Francis Suttle, Richard Tankersly, Richard Gill, Bryant OBannon, John Sharpe, Abraham Kenyan, Rowland Thornton, William Hackney, John Farguson, Jeremiah Bronaugh & John Ambrose was sworne a grand jury for the body of this co who having rec'd their charge withdrew & sometime after returned their several presentments, whereupon it is ord'd that Bryant Chadwell, Edward Grady, John Mcnemara, William Knighton, Thomas Monteith, Ann Leitch, Hannah Morriss, Elizabeth Johnson, Richard Griffis & John Hillier be sumoned to the next court to answer the presentments of the grand jury. (Pg 452)

Court held for proof of public claims & certifying propositions & grievances 2 May 1729. Present: Wm Thornton, Saml Skinker, Rowld Thornton, Wm Strother, Jere Murdock, gent justices. (Pg 453)

William Welch produced a cert under the hand of William Thornton gent justice of the peace for this co for the taking up Samuel Pickford a runaway servant man belonging to Major Willm Kennan of Henrico Co & made oath the sd service was real & bona fide made, done & performed & that no satisfaction had been rec'd for the same which was ord'd to be certified to the next Genl Assembly for allowance. (Pg 453)

Thomas Apperson produced a cert under the hand of Samuel Skinker gent for the taking of William Smith a runaway servant man belonging to Thomas Osbourne of Richmond Co & made oath that no satisfaction had been rec'd for the same which is ord'd to be certified to the next Genl Assembly for allowance. (Pg 453)

Jeremiah Bronaugh produced a cert under the hand of William Thornton gent for the taking up of John Dier a runaway servant belonging to the Biddeford Man of War & made oath that no satisfaction had been rec'd for the same which is ord'd to be certified to the next Genl Assembly for allowance. (Pg 453)

Court held 6 Jun 1729. Present: Wm Thornton, Thos Vivion, Saml Skinker, Jere Murdock, Wm Strother, gent justices. (Pg 453)

The Rev. Esdras Theodore Edzard brought John Ross a servant man before the court to be adjudged for runaway time & expences for taking him up & making oath that he had paid 350 lbs of tobacco, it is ord'd that he serve his sd master for the same & for 14 days absence from his sd masters service according to law with cost. (Pg 453)

Martha Saise returned the inventory of the estate of Ralph Saise decd which is admitted to record. (Pg 453)

Thomas Vivion gent sheriff of ye co ackn the receipt of William Skrine's his being in the goal of this co by execucon at the suit of Cornelious Sarjant & Company merchants in Bristol for the sum of £41:8:10 & 182 lbs of tobacco & 50 shillings or 500 lbs of tobacco which on the motion of Jos Strother gent late sheriff of this co is admitted to record. (Pg 453)

John Lomax gent ackn his deed of gift to Lunsford Lomax gent which on the motion of the sd John is admitted to record. (Pg 454)

David Oswald ackn his power of atty to Thomas Ramsay which sd power was also signed by Isabell Oswald, Walter Kay & Betty Oswald & was proved by the oaths of George Cuningham, Alexander Oswald & Alexander Angus that they rec'd a letter from under the hands of the sd Isabell, Walter & Betty certifying that they had executed the sd power & requesting them to prove the same which sd power on the motion of the sd Thomas Ramsay is admitted to record. (Pg 454)

Ordered that William Thornton gent take the list of tithables from the upper end of the co down to Kays Swamp & that Samuel Skinker gent take em from Kays Swamp down to the mines & William Robinson gent from the mines down to the lower end of the co. (Pg 454)

The suit brought by Simon Hughs agt Elias Yates if cont'd till next court at the plts cost. (Pg 454)

The suit brought by Jeremiah Bronaugh & Rose his wife agt Thomas Monteith is cont'd at the defs cost. (Pg 454)

The suit brought by Daniel French & Margaret his wife agt Evan Price exr of John Pratt decd is cont'd. (Pg 454)

In the suit in chancery depending between Richard Barnes complt & William Skrine respt the respt has further time to answer the sd bill. (Pg 454)

In the suit brought by Charles Birchnell agt William Grant the def pleads in writing & the plt has time till next (court to) consider the plea. (Pg 454)

Thomas Griffin &c agt William Tharp &c def has time to consider the plts replication. (Pg 454)

Present Jos Strother gent.

In the attachment obtained by Walter Anderson agt Joseph Hensley the coroner having attached his crop of corn & tobacco in the hands of Joseph Strother gent it is ord'd that the sd Joseph pay the sd Walter 436 lbs of tobacco if so much of the sd crop be in his hands with the cost of this suit & one atty fee. (Pg 454)

Judgment is granted unto Samuel Skinker gent agt Joseph Hensley for the sum of £9:8:5 in the hands of Joseph Strother gent if assets the sd Hensley's crop being attached by the sheriff in the hands of the sd Joseph which is ord'd to be paid with cost. (Pg 454)

Judgment is renewed by scire facias unto Francis Woffendale agt George Head & William Harrison for the sum of £20 & 117 lbs of tobacco which is ordered to be paid with cost & one atty fee. (Pg 455)

The attachment obtained by Roger Abbot agt James Taylor is cont'd. (Pg 455)

The attachment obtained by William Strother gent agt Jas Taylor is cont'd. (Pg 455)

Judgment is granted unto Robert Spotswood agt the estate of Edward Newgent decd in the hands of Francis Newgent exrix of the will of the sd Edward for the sum of £3:3 ½ penny due by account which is ord'd to be paid with cost. (Pg 455)

In the suit brought by William Kennan agt Charles Seale the def pleads non assumpsit the plt joines the issue & the same lies till next court for trial. (Pg 455)

A plures capias is granted unto John Snell in the suit brought by him agt Adam Christie. (Pg 455)

Imparlance is granted unto Francis Woffendale in the suit brought agt him by Richard Longman. (Pg 455)

The suit brought by Richard Taylor agt Jeremiah OBrian is cont'd till next court this court being divided. (Pg 455)

The suit brought by Patrick Caves agt Benja Hensley is dismist. (Pg 455)

In the suit brought by Henry Fitzhugh esqr agt Edward Watts the def being called & not appearing judgmt is granted the plt agt the def & Roger Abbot & Richard Gill his securities for what of the sum sued for in the declaration shall appear to be justly due unless the def appear at the next court & answer the sd action. (Pg 455)

In the attachment obtained by Thomas Bridgforth agt John Cox, John Champe came into court & ent'd himself security & special imparlance is granted the def in the sd suit. (Pg 455)

Joshua Farguson returned the inventory of the estate of William Typett which is admitted to record. (Pg 455)

Special imparlance is granted unto Mark Hardin in the suit brought agt him by James Warren. (Pg 455)

Judgment is granted unto Robert Spotswood agt Adam Christie for £2:1:4 which is ord'd to be paid with cost & one atty fee. (Pg 455)

The suit brought by James Markham agt Nathl Hilling is dismist. (Pg 455)

The suit brought by James Markham agt John Mcguffy is dismist. (Pg 455)

The suit brought by William Kennan agt Martha Sise is dismist. (Pg 456)

The suit brought by William Kennan agt Edward Waters is dismist. (Pg 456)

The suit brought by Jas Defoe agt John Miller is dismist. (Pg 456)

The suit brought by Charles Seale agt David Miller is dismist. (Pg 456)

In the suit brought by William Strother gent agt Edward Watts the def being called & not appearing judgmt is granted the plt agt the def & William Burbridge & Mathew Hubbard his securities for what of the sum sued for in the declaration shall appear to be justly due unless the def appear at the next court & answer the sd accon. (Pg 456)

The suit brought by Samuel Skinker agt Samuel Hoyle is dismist. (Pg 456)

The suit brought by Samuel Skinker agt Benjamin Hensley is dismist. (Pg 456)

The suit brought by Samuel Skinker agt John Ellkins is dismist. (Pg 456)

Richard Gill came into court & assumed to pay to the church wardens of Hanover Parish 500 lbs of tobacco & cask the same being a fine for Hannah Morris's bringing a bastard child. (Pg 456)

Hannah Morris made oath that John Arlet servant to Richard Gill is father of the sd child which Richard Gill pays her fine for. (Pg 456)

Richard Griffis being presented by the grand jury for setting up tobo hogsheads contrary to law being called came into court & confessed himself guilty whereupon it is ord'd that he pay to our Sovereign Lord the King 500 lbs of tobacco for the sd offence. (Pg 456)

John Hillier being presented by the grand jury for setting up tobacco hogsheads contrary to law being called came into court & confessed himself guilty whereupon it is ord'd that he pay to our Sovereign Lord the King 500 lbs of tobacco for the sd offence. (Pg 456)

The will of John Mathews decd was presented into court by Mosely Battaley with a codicil thereto annexed who made oath thereto & the same was proved by the oaths of Lewis Morris & Peter Nugent & admitted to record. (Pg 456)

John Farguson, James Jones, John Diskins & John Steward or any three of them being first sworne & appointed to appraise in mony the estate of John Mathews decd that shall come to their view & make report to the next court. (Pg 456)

Charles Skaggs a servant belonging to Richard Bryant was brought before the court to be adjudged for runaway time & expences in taking him up, it is ord'd that he serve his sd master for 50 shillings expended in taking him up, for 20 shillings for goods he stole from Thomas Jefferys & for three months absence from his sd master service according to law. (Pg 456)

Ordered that Adam Christie be sumoned to the next court to answer the petition of William Strother gent. (Pg 457)

Judgment is renewed by scire facias unto Samuel Skinker gent agt George Head, James Head, Alford Head & Anthony Head for 3,301 lbs of tobacco which is ord'd to be paid together with the former & present cost. (Pg 457)

Thomas Vivion gent produced a commission from the Honourable William Gooch his Majesties Lt Govern for the sheriffs place of this co & he having took the oath by law appointed & signed the test is admitted sheriff of this co. (Pg 457)

On the motion of Joseph Strother gent late sheriff of this co the sd Joseph took the oaths by law appointed together with the oath of a justice of the pace both at comon law & chancery & signed the test. (Pg 457)

On the motion of Thomas Vivion gent, Benjamin Rush & John Coburn took the oaths by law appointed & signed the test & was admitted under sheriffs of this co. (Pg 457)

Thomas Vivion, William Thornton & Thomas Turner gent ackn their bond to our Sovereign Lord the King for £1,000 for the sd Vivion's faithfull performing his office of sheriff for this co which is admitted to record. (Pg 457)

In the suit brought by Thomas Monteith agt Jeremiah Bronaug & Rose his wife adminrs with the will annexed of John Dinwiddie decd the auditors not having returned their report the defs moved that they might be tried by the country which motion the plt opposed & insisted that since it was referr'd to auditors that they should make their report which was overruled by the court from which judgment the plt prayed an appeal but the court would not admit one & whereupon the defs pleaded in writing & the plt has time till next court to consider the plea. (Pg 457)

Then the court adjourned to court in course.

Court held 4 Jul 1729. Present: Willm Robinson, Nicho Smith, Wm Thornton, Saml Skinker, Rowld Thornton, Wm Strother, gent justices. (Pg 457)

Edward Taylor ackn his deed of gift to John Taylor which on his motion is admitted to record. (Pg 457)

Ordered that Samuel Skinker gent be surveyor of the Back Road & that he clear a road from John Piper's along the ridge by William Duff's up to the Poplar Swamp the most convenient way the sd road to be cleared by the inhabitants of the forest in each precinct. (Pg 457)

The suit brought by Jeremiah Bronaugh agt William Morrison is cont'd. (Pg 458)

The suit brought by Daniel French agt Evan Price is cont'd at the plts cost. (Pg 458)

In the suit in chancery between Richard Barnes complt & William Skrine respt the respt put in his answer & the complt has time to consider it. (Pg 458)

In the suit between Thomas Monteith plt & Jeremiah Bronaugh & Rose his wife defs the defs having pleaded in writing the plt has further time to consider the plea. (Pg 458)

The suit brought by John Snell agt Adam Cristie is cont'd. (Pg 458)

In the suit brought by Charles Birchnell agt William Grant the plt replies to the defs plea & the def has time to consider it. (Pg 458)

In the suit brought by Thomas Griffin &c agt William Tharp &c the plt replies & the def has time to consider the replication. (Pg 458)

The attachmt obtained by Roger Abbot agt Jas Taylor is dismist. (Pg 458)

In the attachmt obtained by William Strother gent agt James Taylor judgmt is granted the plt agt the def for 570 lbs of tobacco due by acct which is ord'd to be paid with cost & one atty fee, & it appearing that Roger Abbot has 361 ½ lbs of tobacco of the estate of the sd James it is ord'd that the sd Roger pay the sd tobacco. (Pg 458)

The inventory of the estate of John Mathews is returned & admitted to record. (Pg 458)

Present Joseph Strother & Jeremiah Murdock, gent.

Administration of the estate of Darby [*Owen scratched out*] Sullivant is granted unto Elizabeth his widow she having with William Thornton gent ackn their bond for £100 for her faithfull administration of the sd estate. (Pg 458)

Rowland Thornton, Anthony Hainey, William Morrison & Humphrey Sawyer or any three of them being first sworne are appointed to appraise in money the estate of Owen Sullivan decd that shall come to their view & make report to the next court. (Pg 458)

Ord'd that John Goble 5 years of age the 20th of June last be bound to Mosely Battaley untill he come to the age of 21 the sd Battaley is to teach him to read & write & at the expiration of his servitude to provide for him as the law directs for servants imported. (Pg 458)

On the petition of John Williams it is ord'd that the overseers of the Main Road keep the main Back Road in repair according to law in their respective precincts. (Pg 459)

John Triplett is appointed surveyor of the highways from the mines to Thatchers Dam & it is ord'd that he keep the same in repair according to law. (Pg 459)

In the accon upon the case between Jeremiah Bronaugh & Rose his wife plts & Thomas Monteith def, John Ambrose, George Franklin, Isaac Arnold, Chas Seale, Francis Woffendale, Joseph Hudnall, Robert Harrison, Jos Berry, Jno Hudnall, Wm Proctor, Jno Gilbert & Jno Farguson was sworne a jury to try the issue joined who having heard the evidences & arguments withdrew & sometime after returned the following verdt, viz, we find for the plts £13 damage, Chas

Seale foreman, which verdt on the plts motion is adm'd to record & judgmt is granted the plts agt the def for the sd sum which is ord'd to be paid with cost & one atty fee. (Pg 459)

In the suit brought by Simon Hughs agt Elias Yates, Chas Seale &c was sworne a jury to try the issue who having heard the evidence & argumts withdrew & soon after returned the following verdt, viz, we find for the def, Chas Seale foreman, which verdt on the defs motion is adm'd to record & the sd suit ord'd to be dismist with cost & one atty fee. (Pg 459)

In the suit brought by Richard Longman agt Francis Woffendale the def being called & not appearing judgmt per nihil dicit is granted the plt agt the def for what of the sum sued for in the declaration shall appear to be justly due unless the def appear at the next court & answer the sd accon. (Pg 459)

The suit brought by William Kennan agt Charles Seale is cont'd. (Pg 459)

In the accon upon the case between Peter Hedgman adminr of Nathaniel Hedgman decd plt & John Hudnall def, Chas Seale &c was sworne a jury to try the issue who having heard the evidence & argumts withdrew & sometime after returned the following verdt, viz, we find for the plt 1,000 lbs of tobacco damage, Chas Seale foreman, which verdt on the plts motion is adm'd to record & judgmt is granted the plt agt the def for the sd tobacco which is ord'd to be paid with cost & one atty fee. (Pg 459)

In the suit brought by Henry Fitzhugh esqr agt Edwd Watts the def pleads he owes nothing the plt joines the issue & ye same lies till next court for trial. (Pg 459)

In the attachmt obtained by Thomas Bridgforth agt John Cox the def pleas the plt has time to consider the plea. (Pg 459)

John Yerby of Lancaster Co being sumoned an evidence by Peter Hedgman agt John Hudnall it is ord'd that he pay him for 80 miles going & coming one days attendance & 15 pence ferriages. (Pg 460)

In the accon upon the case between William Strother gent plt & Edward Watts def the def being called & not appearing the last courts order is confirmed agt him & William Burbridge & Mathew Hubberd his securities for 602 lbs of tobacco due by acct which is ord'd to be paid with cost. (Pg 460)

An alias capias is granted unto Samuel Timmons in the suit brought by him agt Adam Christie. (Pg 460)

An alias capias is granted unto John Finlason in the suit brought by him agt Adam Christie. (Pg 460)

In the suit by petition between William Hensley plt & Mosely Battaley def judgment is granted the plt agt the def for 700 lbs of tobacco with cost & one atty fee & on the defs motion injunction & subpa in chancery is granted him to stay exo till the matter be heard in equity. (Pg 460)

On the petition of William Strother gent setting forth that he became security for Adam Christie & Mary his wife's faithfull administration of the estate of William Pattishall decd & that the sd estate was much lessened it is ord'd that the sd Adam & Mary his wife deliver up the sd estate unto the sd William. (Pg 460)

George Pain being sumoned an evidence by Simon Hughs agt Elias Yates & making oath he attended five days on the sd suit it is ord'd he pay him for the same according to law with cost. (Pg 460)

Judgment is granted unto Richard Taylor agt Jeremiah OBrian for 200 lbs of tobacco which is ord'd to be paid with cost & one atty fee. (Pg 460)

On the petition of Samuel Skinker gent it is ord'd that he have liberty to keep a ferry from his landing over to Kays Landing in Caroline Co. (Pg 460)

On the motion of Charles Seal & he having with James Jones ackn their bond to our Sovereign Lord the King for 10,000 lbs of tobacco the sd Seale is adm'd to keep ordinary for the year ensuing. (Pg 460)

Then the court adjourned to court in course.

Court held 1 Aug 1729. Present: Wm Robinson, Jos Strother, Saml Skinker, Rowld Thornton, Wm Strother, gent justices. (Pg 461)

The suit brought by Jeremiah Bronaugh agt Wm Morrison is cont'd till next court. (Pg 461)

The suit by petition between Daniel French & Margaret his (wife) plts & Evan Price execr of the will of John Pratt decd def is cont'd & it is ord'd that the sd def give in a particular acct of the crops both corn & tobacco to the next court. (Pg 461)

In the suit in chancery between Richard Barnes complt & William Skrine respt the sd complt has time till next court to consider the answer. (Pg 461)

In the suit between Thomas Monteith plt & Jeremiah Bronaugh & Rose his wife adminrs with the will annexed of John Dinwiddie decd defs the plt having replied to the defs plea has time to consider the replication & upon the motion of Edward Barradall atty for the defs suggesting that Gilbert Hamilton a wit in this cause was going out of the country & could not be present at the trial, it is ord'd that the deposition of the sd Gilbert be taken before two of the justices of the peace for Richmond Co & that the same shall be evidence at the tryal giving the plt legal notice of the time & place of taking such deposition. (Pg 461)

In the suit brought by Charles Birchnell agt William Grant the def demurs to the plts replication. (Pg 461)

In the suit brought by Thomas Griffin &c justices of the peace for Richmond Co plts agt Wm Tharp &c defs the plts having replied the def joines the issue. (Pg 461)

In the accon upon the case between William Kennan plt & Charles Seale def, Richard Briant, Francis Woffendale, Robt Strother, Mark Hardin, Anthony Hainey, Rush Hudson, Bloomfield Long, John Grant, Jeremiah Bronaugh, Thos Smith, Neal Mccormack & Darby Calliham was sworne a jury to try the issue joined who having heard the evidence & arguments withdrew & sometime after brought in their verdict in these words, we find for the plt 1,716 lbs of tobacco, Richard Briant foreman, which verdt on the plts motion is admitted to record & judgmt is granted the plt agt the def for the sd tobacco with cost & one atty fee which is ord'd to be paid. (Pg 461)

John Travise of Stafford Co being sumoned an evidence by William Kennan agt Charles Seale & being called & not appearing, it is ord'd that he pay the sd William 350 lbs of tobacco it being his fine according to law unless the sd John appear at the next court & show good & sufficient reason why he did not appear & give his evidence pursuant to the sd sumons. (Pg 461)

A plures capias is granted unto John Snell in the suit brought by him agt Adam Christie. (Pg 462)

In the suit brought by Richard Longman agt Francis Woffendale the def pleads in writing & the plt has time to consider the plea. (Pg 462)

In the attachment obtained by Thomas Bridgforth agt John Cox the def having pleaded the plt replies to the sd plea & the def joines the replication & the same lies till next court for trial. (Pg 462)

A plures capias is granted unto Samuel Timmons agt Ralph Hewes. (Pg 462)

55

A plures capias is granted unto John Finlayson agt Adam Christie. (Pg 462)

In the suit in chancery between Mosely Battaley complt & George Downing & William Hensley respts the respts has time to plead to the answer & demurrer. (Pg 462)

In the suit brought by French Mason agt Thomas Johnson the def being called & not appearing judgmt is granted the plt agt the def for what of the sum sued for in the declaration that appear to be justly due unless the def appear at the next court & answer the sd accon. (Pg 462)

In the suit brought by Sarah Martin & John Martin exrs &c of Jacob Martin decd agt James Nicholls, Thomas Vivion gent entered himself special bail & the def pleads non assumpsit the plts joines the issue & the sd suit lies till next court for trial. (Pg 462)

In the suit brought by John Chadwell agt Charles Seale the def pleads he owes nothing the plt joines the issue & the same lies till next court for tryal. (Pg 462)

In the suit brought by Robert Kennan agt Charles Seale the def pleads not guilty the plt joines the issue & the same lies till next court for tryal. (Pg 462)

In the suit brought by John Cooke &c exrs of Andrew Russell decd, Thomas Grigsby enter'd himself special bail the def pleads non assumpsit the plt joines the issue & the same lies till next court for trial. (Pg 462)

In the suit brought by Robert Spotswood agt John Simpson the def being called & not appearing judgmt is granted the plt agt the def & Thomas Vivion gent sheriff of this co for what of the sum sued for in the declaration shall appear to be justly due unless the def appear at the next court & answer the sd accon. (Pg 462)

An alias capias is granted unto William Stevenson agt John Wilson. (Pg 462)

The scire facias brought by Jeremiah Bronaugh & Rose his wife adminrs of John Dinwiddie decd agt James Kay is ord'd to be dismist. (Pg 462)

The suit brought by Saml Skinker agt Wm Hensley is dismist. (Pg 462)

Ord'd that Thomas Welch & Ignatius Robinson be sumoned to the next court to answer the attachment obtained by Darby Calliham agt Dennis Morgan. (Pg 462)

56

John Dodd Senr ackn his deed to John Dodd Junr which on the motion of the sd John Dodd Junr is adm'd to record. (Pg 462)

John Dodd Junr ackn his deed to Simon Hughs which on the motion of the sd Simon is admitted to record. (Pg 463)

Francis Stone is appointed constable in the room of William Jett. (Pg 463)

Lazarus Dameron is appointed surveyor of the highways in the room of Robert Duncan. (Pg 463)

Jeremiah Bronaugh & Rose his wife presented into court the account of the administration of the estate of John Dinwiddie decd & made oath thereto & the same is ord'd to be recorded. (Pg 463)

In the accon upon the case between Henry Fitzhugh esqr plt & Edward Watts def, Richard Bryant, Francis Woffendale, Robt Strother, Mark Hardin, Antho Hainey, Rush Hudson, Bloomfield Long, Jno Grant, Jere Bronaugh, Thos Smith, Neal McCormack & Darby Calliham was sworne a jury to try the issue joined who having heard the evidence & argumts withdrew & sometime after returned the following verdt (viz) we find for the plt 1256 lbs of tobacco, Richd Bryant foreman, which verdt on the plts motion is admitted to record & judgmt is granted the plt agt the def for the sd tobacco which is ord'd to be paid with cost & one atty fee. (Pg 463)

Then the court adjourned to court in course.

Court held 5 Sep 1729. Present: Nicho Smith, Wm Thornton, Jona Gibson, Rowld Thornton, Wm Strother, gent justice. (Pg 463)

Administration of the goods, chattels & creditts of William Skrine decd is granted unto Nicholas Smith gent he being greatest creditor, Margaret Skrine widdow & relict of the sd William appearing in court & relinquishing her right of administration to the sd Nicholas. (Pg 463)

Nicholas Smith & William Thornton gent ackn their bond of £250 for the sd Nicholas' faithfull administration of William Skrine's estate. (Pg 463)

Walter Anderson, John Farguson, John Diskin & James Jones or any three of them are appointed to appraise in money the estate of William Skrine decd that shall come to their view & make report to the next court. (Pg 463)

Joseph Strother & Samuel Skinker gent present.

Tobias Ingram ackn his deed of lease & release to Samuel Skinker gent which on the motion of the sd Samuel is adm'd to record. (Pg 463)

Anthony Hainey brought John Ross a servt man before the court & produced an acct of 760 lbs of tobacco for expenses in taking up, it is ord'd that the sd John serve the sd Anthony for the same & for 48 days absence from his sd master. (Pg 463)

The suit in chancery depending between Richard Barnes complt & William Skrine respondt upon an injunction granted unto the sd Richard the sd William having recovered a judgmt at comon law for £31:4:10 with the cost of that suit & one atty fee is dismist the sd William being dead. (Pg 464)

In the suit brought by Thomas Monteith agt Jeremiah Bronaugh & Rose his wife adminrs of Jno Dinwiddie decd the def joines issue on the plts replication & the same lies till next court for trial. (Pg 464)

In the suit brought by Charles Birchnel agt William Grant the plt joines issue on the demurrer & the same lies till next court for trial. (Pg 464)

In the suit in chancery between William Morrison complt & Jeremiah Bronaugh & Rose his wife adminrs with the will annexed of John Dinwiddie decd respts upon an injunction granted unto the sd William the respts having obtained a judgmt at comon law for 1901 lbs of tobacco with cost due by bill the court upon arguing the sd injunction, answer & proceedings is of opinion the bill afsd was fraudulently obtained & ord'd that the sd injunction be perpetuall & the respts pay the cost of this suit. (Pg 464)

Ord'd that Henry Raredon a boy of 9 years of age last Apr be bound to Bryant Chadwell to learn the trade of a cooper untill he be 21 years of age. (Pg 464)

On the motion of Mary Christie, it is ord'd that Peter Percivall son of the sd Mary serve William Strother gent four years from this day the sd William promising before the court to learn the sd Peter to read & write & at the expiration of the sd term to give him a suit of drugget & a mare colt. (Pg 464)

Capt John Williams brought before the court William Cooke & Isaac Bendall two servants belonging to the Bristol Iron Mines to be adjudg'd for runaway time & expences in taking them up & produced an acct of 715 lbs of tobacco, it is ord'd that they serve for the same & for 19 days absence from their service according to law. (Pg 464)

58

Administration of the estate of Peter Dunbarr is granted unto George James Dunbarr he having with John Jennings ackn his bond of £20 for his faithfull administration of the sd estate. (Pg 464)

George White, Daniel White, William Jett & William Carter or any three of them being first sworne are appointed to appraise in money the estate of Peter Dunbar that shall come to their view & make report to the next court. (Pg 464)

In the suit by petition depending between Daniel French & Margaret his wife plts & Evan Price exr of the will of John Pratt decd def by consent of both parties, it is ord'd that Jeremiah Murdock, Thomas Vivion, Benjamin Strother & Daniel White gent or any three of them state & settle all accts relating to the estate of the sd John Pratt decd & make report to the next court. (Pg 464)

Then the court adjourned to court in course.

Court held 3 Oct 1729. Present: Wm Thornton, Jona Gibson, Jos Strother, Rowld Thornton, Wm Strother, gent justices. (Pg 465)

Thomas Goff is appointed constable in the room of George Parsons. (Pg 465)

Ord'd that the sheriff sumon a sufficient number of freeholders to serve as a grand jury at the next court for the body of this co.

On the motion of Walter Anderson & he having entered into bond with Thomas Stribling his security to our Sovereign Lord the King for 10,000 lbs of tobacco the sd Walter is licenced to keep ordinary on his now dwelling plantation the year ensuing. (Pg 465)

Walter Anderson produced an acct of 29 shillings agt Robert Evans & made oath thereto which is ord'd to be certified. (Pg 465)

Samuel Wharton ackn his lease & release unto Thomas Turner & Benjamin Rush by virtue of a power of atty from Ann Wharton w/o the sd Samuel relinquished the sd Ann's right of dower & thirds in & to the sd land the sd power being duely proved on the motion of the sd Turner is admitted to record. (Pg 465)

Thomas Turner ackn his lease & release unto Samuel Wharton & Benjamin Rush by virtue of a power of atty duely proved in court from Sarah Turner w/o the sd Thomas relinquished the sd Sarah's right of dower & thirds in & to the sd land which on the motion of the sd Samuel is adm'd to record. (Pg 465)

The additional inventory of the estate of Henry Gollop decd is returned & adm'd to record. (Pg 465)

Thomas Grigsby & Rose his wife ackn their lease & release unto Samuel Skinker gent the sd Rose being solely examined ackn her free consent thereto & on the motion of the sd Samuel is adm'd to record. (Pg 465)

On the motion of Richard Elkins, John Corbin, John Settle Senr, John Mcnemara & Robert Jones, it is ord'd that they be free from paying their co levy for the future. (Pg 465)

In the accon by petition between Daniel French & Margt his wife plts & Evan Price exr of the will of John Pratt decd def the last courts order in this cause not being complied with, it is ord'd to be cont'd to next court & it is ord'd that Nicholas Smith, Jeremiah Murdock & Maximilian Robinson gent audit, state & settle all accts in difference & make report to the next court. (Pg 465)

In the accon upon the case between Thomas Monteith plt & Jeremiah Bronaugh & Rose his wife adminrs with the will annexed of John Dinwiddie decd defs the sd suit is cont'd & it is ord'd that a dedimus potestatem issue to take the depositions of Gilbert Hamilton of Richmond Co & George Mason gent of Stafford Co. (Pg 465)

King George Co to the several claims hereafter mentioned: To Thomas Vivion gent sheriff, Thomas Turner clerk, Edward Barradall Kings atty, James Markham assignee of John Mcguffy for 8 wolfes heads, John Hopper Junr for 1 ditto, Daniel Marr for 11 ditto, Edward Abbot for 1 ditto, William Strother gent assignee of Thos Little for 1 ditto, ditto assignee of Richard Brooke for 4 ditto, ditto assignee of Ralph Hughs for 2 ditto, Isaac Arnold & Robert Johnson for counting tobacco plants, Christopher Edrington & William Jett for ditto, John Kenyan & John Ambrose for ditto, Joseph Hudnall & Lazarus Dameron for ditto, William Hackney & John Wright for ditto, Thomas Stribling & Antho Seale for ditto, John Diskin & John Farguson for ditto, Jeremiah Bronaugh & David Seale for ditto, Bartho Redman his acct, Jos Strother gent for 3 barrels of tarr for the courthouse & prison & laying it on, Antho Handy assignee of Patrick Grady for 7 wolves heads, James Jones his acct, Walter Anderson his acct. 21, 343 lbs tobacco. (Pg 466)

Pursuant to the Act of Assembly for encouraging adventurers in iron works, it is ord'd that the clerk of this co certify to the next General Assembly that in computation for the exemption of 60 tithable persons employed in the Bristol Iron Works in the sd co for the year 1728 the respective levies were increased on the remaining tithables in the sd co 1800 lbs of tobacco for the sd year & for the year 1729 for the afsd number they are increased 885 lbs of tobacco to the end the same quantities of tobacco may be reimbursed to the sd co in the next public levy. (Pg 466)

Then the court adjourned till tomorrow morning 8 o'clock.

Court held 4 Oct 1729. Present: Wm Thornton, Jona Gibson, Saml Skinker, Rowld Thornton, gent justices. (Pg 467)

In the suit brought by John Snell agt Adam Christie the def being called & not appearing judgmt is granted the plt agt the def & Benjamin Berryman, Thomas Smith, Thomas Benson & Anthony Hainey his securities for what of the sum sued for in the declaration shall appear to be justly due unless the def appear at the next court & answer the sd action. (Pg 467)

The attachment obtained by Thomas Bridgforth agt John Cox is cont'd till next court. (Pg 467)

The attachment obtained by Thomas Bridgforth agt John Cox is cont'd till next court. (Pg 467)

A plures capias is granted unto Samuel Timmons in the suit brought by him agt Ralph Hews. (Pg 467)

In the suit brought by John Finlayson agt Adam Christie the def being called & not appearing judgmt is granted the plt agt the def & Benjamin Berryman, Thomas Smith, Thomas Benson & Anthony Hainy his securities for what of the sum sued for shall appear to be justly due unless the def appear at the next court & answer the sd action. (Pg 467)

In the suit in chancery between Mosely Battaly complt & William Hensly respt the respt replies & joins the demurrer. (Pg 467)

In the suit brought by French Mason agt Thomas Johnson, Jeremiah Bronaugh enters himself special bail & the def pleads he owes nothing the plt joines the issue & the same lyes till next court for trial. (Pg 467)

In the suit brought by Robert Spotswood agt John Simpson the def has oyer of the plts acct. (Pg 467)

In the attachment obtained by Darby Calliham agt Dennis Morgan the sheriff having returned that he has attached a black horse & 10 shillings cash in the hands of Thomas Welch, it is ord'd that the same be sold by the sheriff according to law to satisfy the sd Darby the sum of 430 lbs of tobacco & the cost of this suit & that he return the overplus if any there be. (Pg 467)

In the suit brought by Sarah Martin widow & John Martin exrs of the will of Jacob Martin decd plts agt James Nicholls def, Richard Bryant, Thos Stribling, Anthony Seale, Xopher Edrington, Samuel Wharton, William Rowley, Wm Smith, Jno Triplett, Fras Settle, Robt Doniphan, Jno Grant & Wm Proctor was sworne a jury to try the issue who having heard the evidence & argumts withdrew & sometime after returned the following verdt, viz, we find for the def, Richd Bryant foreman, which verdt on the defs motion is admitted to record & the sd suit ord'd to be dismist. (Pg 467)

Judgment is granted unto John Chadwell agt Charles Seale for the sum of 47 shillings 7 pence which is ord'd to be paid with cost & one atty fee. (Pg 467)

An alias capias is granted unto Alexr Parker in the suit brought by him agt Robert Wilson. (Pg 467)

In the suit brought by Robert Kennan agt Charles Seale, Richard Bryant, Thomas Stribling, Antho Seale, Christr Edrington, Saml Wharton, Wm Rowley, Wm Smith, Jno Triplett, Fras Settle, Robt Doniphan, Jno Grant & Wm Proctor was sworne a jury to try the issue & having heard the evidence & argumts withdrew & sometime after returned the following verdt, viz, we find for the plt 20 shillings, Richd Bryant foreman, which verdt on the plts motion is admitted to record & judgmt is granted the plt for the sd sum which is ord'd to be paid with cost & one atty fee. (Pg 468)

In the suit brought by Henry Fitzhugh esqr agt Jereh Bronaugh & Rose his wife adminrs with the will annexed of John Dinwiddie decd the defs has leave to plead divers matters & pleads non assumpsit & pleny administravit. (Pg 468)

In the suit brought by Robert Kennan agt John Fox the def pleads not guilty the plt joins the issue & the same lies till next court for trial. (Pg 468)

In the suit brought by George Downing agt Thomas Blassingham the def pleads he owes nothing & the plt joins the issue. (Pg 468)

In the scire facias brought by Jeremiah Bronaugh & Rose his wife adminrs with the will annexed of John Dinwiddie decd agt William Thornton gent special bail for James Kay the sd Kay came into court & rendered his body in discharge of his bail & the sd suit is ord'd to be dismist. (Pg 468)

Robert Finch being sumoned an evidence by Robt Kennan agt Charles Seale & making oath that he attended three days on the sd suit, it is ord'd that he pay him for the same with cost. (Pg 468)

Elizabeth Finch being sumoned an evidence by Robt Kennan agt Charles Seale & making oath that she attended three days on the sd suit, it is ord'd that he pay her for the same according to law. (Pg 468)

Katherine Thatcher being sumoned an evidence by Robt Kennan agt Charles Seale & making (oath that) she attended two days on the sd suit, it is ord'd that he pay her for the same according to law. (Pg 468)

In the suit brought by John Cooke & others exr of Andrew Russell agt Edward Sweeting, Richd Bryant &c was sworne a jury to try the issue who having heard the evidence & argumts withdrew & sometime after returned the following verdt, viz, we find for the def, Richd Bryant foreman, which verdt on the defs motion is admitted to record & the sd suit ord'd to be dismist with cost. (Pg 468)

The suit brought by Daniel French & Margt his wife agt Evan Price is ord'd to be cont'd. (Pg 468)

Ord'd that Thomas Blasingham be sumon'd to the next court to answer the attachmt of Charles Seale agt George Downing. (Pg 468)

In the suit brought by Thomas Griffin &c justices of the peace for Richmond Co agt Francis Woffendale & William Tharpe, Richd Bryant &c was sworne a jury to try the issue who having heard the evidence & argumts withdrew & sometime after returned the following verdt, viz, we find for the defs, Richd Bryant foreman, which verdt on the defs motion is adm'd to record & the sd suit is ord'd to be dismissed with cost & one atty fee. (Pg 469)

In the suit brought by Charles Birchnell agt William Grant the def having demurred to the plts replication upon arguing the demurer the sd demurer is overruled & a writ of enquiry for damages is ord'd to be executed the next court. (Pg 469)

The suit brought by Richd Griffis agt Bartho Redman is ord'd to be cont'd. (Pg 469)

In the suit brought by Thomas Riphley agt John Bolling the def being called & not appearing judgmt is granted the plt agt the def & Charles Seal his security for what of the sum sued for in the declaration shall appear to be justly due unless the def appear at the next court & answer the sd action. (Pg 469)

In the suit brought by Charles Seale agt Thomas Davis the def pleads he owes nothing & the plt joins the issue. (Pg 469)

Judgmt is granted unto Alexr Mcfarlane agt Richd Griffis for 647 lbs of tobo which is ord'd to be paid with cost & one atty fee. (Pg 469)

Special imparlance is granted unto John Wilson & Mary his wife in the suit brought agt them by Mary Durham. (Pg 469)

Special imparlance is granted unto Mark Jones in the suit brought agt him by Richard Bryant. (Pg 469)

In the suit brought by William Kennan agt Mosely Battaley exr of the will of John Mathews decd the def pleads the testator was not indebted as is declared & the plt joins the issue. (Pg 469)

In the suit brought by Thomas Davis agt Edward Merret the def has oyer of the bill. (Pg 469)

Imparlance is granted unto Robert Raddish in the suit brought agt him by John Wilson. (Pg 469)

John Wilson came into court & confessed judgment unto Charles Seale for 25 shillings 5 pence which is ord'd to be paid with cost. (Pg 469)

In the suit in chancery between Saml Reeds &c agt John Jett & Fras Jett the respondts has time till next court to answer the sd bill. (Pg 469)

In the suit brought by Richd Longman agt Fras Woffendale the plt replys & the def has time till next court to consider the replication. (Pg 469)

In the suit brought by Thomas Riphley agt Richard Green the def being called & not appearing judgmt is granted agt him & Charles Seale his security for what of the sum sued for in the declaration shall appear to be justly due unless the def appear at the next court & answer the sd accon. (Pg 470)

In the suit brought by Thomas Riphley agt Thomas Blassingham the def being called & not appearing judgmt is granted the plt agt the def & Francis Woffendale his security for what of the sum sued for shall appear to be justly due unless the def appear at the next court & answer the action. (Pg 470)

Lazarus Dameron is appointed oversee of the highways in the room of Robert Duncomb & it is ord'd that he keep the same in repair according to law. (Pg 470)

Thomas Duncomb is appointed overseer of the highways in the room of John Marr & it is ord'd that he keep the same in repair according to law. (Pg 470)

The suit brought by William Stevenson agt Jno Wilson is dismist. (Pg 470)

The suit brought by William Grant agt Jno Yewbank is dismist. (Pg 470)

The suit brought by Samuel Hearn agt Jno Peatross is dismist. (Pg 470)

The suit brought by Willm Hackney agt Ignatious Robisson is dismist. (Pg 470)

The suit brought by Richd Gill agt Jno Peyton is dismist. (Pg 470)

The suit brought by Richd Gill agt Jas Warren is dismist. (Pg 470)

The suit brought by Thomas Royston agt Saml Newbald is dismist. (Pg 470)

The suit brought by Robt Stuard agt Geo Parsons is dismist. (Pg 470)

The suit brought by Thos Benson &c agt Adam Christie is dismist. (Pg 470)

Then the court adjourned to court in course.

Court held 7 Nov 1729. Present: Wm Thornton, Jos Strother, Saml Skinker, Wm Strother, Jere Murdock, gent justices. (Pg 470)

John Conner ackn his indenture unto William Stringfellow which on the motion of the sd William is adm'd to record. (Pg 470)

William Stringfellow ackn his indenture unto John Conner which on the motion of the sd William is adm'd to record. (Pg 470)

Benjamin Rush came into court & confessed judgment unto the church wardens of Hanover Parish for 500 lbs of tobacco & cask it being for a fine for Dorothy Thompson's bringing a bastard child which is ord'd to be paid. (Pg 470)

Ord'd that Dorothy Thompson serve William Duff 12 months for the trouble of his house for the sd Dorothy's bringing a bastard child after her time is expired by indenture custom or hire. (Pg 471)

John Travis ackn his lease unto Joseph Crouch which on the motion of the sd Joseph is admitted to record. (Pg 471)

Joseph Crouch ackn his lease unto John Travis which on the motion of the sd Joseph is admitted to record. (Pg 471)

The will of Thomas Boyles decd was presented into court by Margaret his widdow the same was proved by the oaths of Samuel Hoyle & William Alsup & admitted to record. (Pg 471)

Samuel Hoyle, William Alsup, Robert Benson & William Mumford or any three of them being first sworn & appointed to appraise in money the estate of Thomas Boyles decd & make report to the next court. (Pg 471)

The additional inventory of the estate of James Robertson decd is returned & admitted to record. (Pg 471)

Judgment is granted unto John Hartshorne & Bersheba his wife for the sum of £18:14:11 ½ penny agt the estate of Katherine Waters decd in the hands of John Ambrose exr of the will of the sd Katherine it being the sd Bersheba's pt/o the sd estate which is ord'd to be paid. (Pg 471)

Adam Christie came into court & confessed judgmt unto William Strother gent for 4,285 lbs of tobacco & £1:5 which is ord'd to be paid with cost. (Pg 471)

On the petition of Adam Christie & Mary his wife it is ord'd that Robert Jones, Benjamin Berryman, Thomas Smith & Thomas Harwood or any three of them set a part one third of the personal estate of William Pattishall decd for the sd Mary's dower & make report to the next court. (Pg 471)

In the suit by petition between Daniel French & Margaret his wife plts & Evan Price execr of the will of John Pratt decd def the sd suit is ord'd to be cont'd & that William Robinson & Nicholas Smith gent & Thomas Turner or any two of them audit, state & settle all accounts relating to the sd estate & make report to the next court. (Pg 471)

Special imparlance is granted unto Rowland Cornelious in the suit brought agt him by Francis Thornton. (Pg 471)

Special imparlance is granted unto Thomas Smith in the suit brought agt him by Francis Thornton. (Pg 471)

Special imparlance is granted unto Anthony Head in the suit brought agt him by Miles Potter. (Pg 471)

In the suit brought by Philemon Cavenaugh agt Bartholomew Redman judgmt is granted the plt agt the def & [*blank*] his security for what of the sum sued for in the declaration shall appear to be justly due unless the def appear at the next court & answer the sd accon. (Pg 472)

The suit brought by Alexr Carson agt Charles Seale appearing to the court to be agreed is ord'd to be dismist. (Pg 472)

Thomas Vivion, John Champe & Christopher Edrington ackn their bond to our Sovereign Lord the King for 42,686 lbs of tobacco which is ord'd to be recorded. (Pg 472)

It is ord'd that the several & respective tithable persons in this co pay to the sheriff 15 ½ lbs of tobacco to discharge the co levy & that the sheriff pay the respective creditors according to law.

In the attachment obtained by William McBee agt Thomas Beach the sheriff having returned that he had attached ½ skirted saddle, 1 fustan vest, 1 pr of shoes & worstead stockings, 1 pr of garters & 5 old shirts & ½ lb of white thread, ¼ yard of druget, 1 gun, an old pr of linen breeches & 2 raw doe skins, it is ord'd that the sd goods be sold to satisfy the sd McBee for 575 lbs of tobacco & costs & one atty fee & that the sheriff return the overplus if any there be. (Pg 472)

The suit brought by John Elkin agt Esdras Theodor Edzard is dismist. (Pg 472)

The suit brought by Miles Potter agt John Williams is dismist. (Pg 472)

The suit brought by Miles Potter agt James Gillison is dismist. (Pg 472)

The suit brought by William Beverley agt Robert Jones is dismist. (Pg 472)

The suit brought by Thomas Blassingham agt Thomas Riphley is dismist. (Pg 472)

The suit brought by James Boddington agt Richard Griffis is dismist. (Pg 472)

The suit brought by Bloomfield Long agt Wm Mumford is dismist. (Pg 472)

The suit brought agt George Franklin by James Holland is dismist. (Pg 472)

The suit brought by Wm Clark agt George McDonald is dismist. (Pg 472)

The suit brought by Israel Illingsworth agt Thos Birk is dismist. (Pg 472)

Then the court adjourned till tomorrow morning 8 o'clock.

Court held 8 Nov 1729. Present: Wm Thornton, Jos Strother, Saml Skinker, Jere Murdock, gent justices. (Pg 473)

A power of atty from Robert Kennan to William Kennan was presented into court & the same was proved by the oath of Benjamin Hawkins & Thomas Thatcher which is ord'd to be certified. (Pg 473)

In the suit brought by John Snell agt Adam Christie, William Strother & Hugh French came into court & entered themselves special bail the def pleads payment & the plt joins the issue. (Pg 473)

In the suit brought by Richard Longman agt Francis Woffendale the plt have replyed the def demurs to the replication & the plt joins the demurrer. (Pg 473)

In the suit brought by John Finlason agt Adam Christie the def has oyer of the plts account. (Pg 473)

The suit brought by Robert Spotswood agt John Simpson is ord'd to be dismist with cost & one atty fee. (Pg 473)

In the suit brought by Alexander Parker agt Robert Wilson the def being called & not appearing judgment is granted the plt agt the def & Alexander Carson his security for what of the sum sued for in the declaration shall appear to be justly due unless the def appear at the next court & answer the sd action. (Pg 473)

In the suit brought by Richard Griffis agt Bartholomew Redman the def being called & not appearing judgment is granted the plt agt the def & Richard Ellkins his security for what of the sum sued for in the declaration shall appear to be justly due unless the def appear at the next court & answer the sd action. (Pg 473)

In the action of trespass & assault brought by Thomas Riphley agt John Bolling the def being called & not appearing the last courts order is confirm'd & a writ of enquiry for damages is ord'd to be executed the next court. (Pg 473)

In the action of trespass & assault brought by Thomas Riphley agt George Downing the def being called & not appearing the last courts order is confirm'd & a writ of enquiry for damages ord'd to be executed the next court. (Pg 473)

In the suit in chancery between Samuel Reeds, Mary Reeds, Thomas & Elizabeth Reeds complts & Francis Jett & John Jett respts by consent of all parties it is ord'd that William Robinson, Nicholas Smith, Rowland Thornton & Jeremiah Murdock three or any two of them audit, state & settle the accts in difference & make report to the next court & the same to be definitive. (Pg 473)

Judgment is granted unto Charles Seale agt Thomas Davis in custody for 463 lbs of tobacco which is ord'd to be paid with cot & one atty fee. (Pg 474)

In the suit brought by Mary Durham agt John Wilson & Mary his wife the defs plead not guilty & the plt joins the issue. (Pg 474)

In the suit brought by Richard Bryant agt Mark Jones the def pleads not guilty & the plt joins the issue. (Pg 474)

Judgment is granted unto William Kennan agt the estate of John Mathews decd in the hands of Mosely Battaley for the sum of £5 which is ord'd to be paid with cost. (Pg 474)

In the suit brought by Thomas Davis agt Edward Merret the def pleads he owes nothing & the plt joins the issue. (Pg 474)

In the suit brought by Charles Birchnel agt William Grant, John Champe, Jeremiah Strother, Anthony Seale, Saml Reed, Thos Thatcher, Thomas Stribling, Richd Bryant, Henry Berry, Saml Moon, John Jett, Richard Rosser & James Kay was sworne a jury to execute a writ of enquiry who having heard the evidence & arguments withdrew & sometime after returned the following verdt, to wit, we find for the plt £5, Jno Champe foreman, which verdt on the plts motion is adm'd to record & judgment is granted the plt agt the def for the sd sum which is ord'd to be paid with cost & one atty fee upon which the def assigned errors in arrest of the sd judgmt & the same is cont'd till next court to be argued. (Pg 474)

John Gilbert, Wm Reemy, John Quisenbury, Wm Jett, John Jennings, Isaac Arnold, Francis Woffendale, John Owens, Wm Proctor, Wm Flowers, Jere Bronaugh Junr, Robert Doniphan, Wm Marshall, Robert Strother, Thos Duncomb, Bryant OBannon & Thos Harwood was sworne a grand jury for the body of this co who after they had recd their charge withdrew & sometime after returned their presentments whereupon it is ord'd that the several persons presented by the grand jury be sumoned to the next court to answer the same. (Pg 474)

Ord'd that what depositions shall be taken of any of the wits in the suit between Thomas Monteith plt & Jeremiah Bronaugh & Rose his wife defs before a justice of the peace of any co both parties being present shall be allowed to be evidence on the trial. (Pg 474)

The suit brought by Thomas Monteith agt Jere Bronaugh & Rose his wife is ord'd to be cont'd. (Pg 474)

The attachment obtained by Thomas Bridgforth agt John Cox is ord'd to be dismist by consent. (Pg 474)

The suit brought by Samuel Timmons agt Ralph Hews is dismist. (Pg 475)

The suit in chancery between Mosely Battaley complt & Wm Hensley & George Downing respts is cont'd till next court. (Pg 475)

The suit brought by French Mason agt Thomas Johnson is cont'd. (Pg 475)

The suit brought by Henry Fitzhugh esqr agt Jere Bronaugh is cont'd. (Pg 475)

The suit in chancery brought by Daniel French & Margaret his wife agt Evan Price exr of the will of John Pratt decd is dismist. (Pg 475)

The attachmt obtained by Charles Seale agt George Downing is dismist. (Pg 475)

Then the court adjourned to court in course.

Court held 5 Dec 1729. Present: Nicho Smith, Wm Thornton, Jos Strother, Rowld Thornton, Jere Murdock, gent justices. (Pg 475)

Frances Sharp w/o John Sharp came into court & relinquished her right of dower to a certain tr of land sold by her sd husband John Sharp unto Bryant OBannon which on the motion of the sd Bryant is admitted to record. (Pg 475)

Judith Sharp w/o Linsfield Sharp came into court & relinquished her right of dower to a certain tr of land sold by her sd husband Linsfield Sharp unto Bryant OBannon which on the motion of the sd Bryant is admitted to record. (Pg 475)

Margaret Boyle returned the inventory of the estate of Thomas Boyle decd & the same is admitted to record. (Pg 475)

On the motion of Jane Humphrey it is ord'd that her sons William Humphrey being 9 years of age the 2nd day of Sep next & John Humphrey being 6 years old the 15th of Oct next be bound to John Bourne untill they respectively come to the age of 21 the sd John Bourne in consideration thereof is to learn them to read distinctly which on the motion of the sd Jane is admitted to record. (Pg 475)

Administration on the estate of Samuel Nicholls decd is granted unto Mary his widow the sd Mary with William Grant & Thomas Thatcher ackn their bond of £100 for the sd Mary's faithfull administration on the sd estate. (Pg 475)

William Thornton gent ackn his deed to Thomas Akers Ayres which on the motion of the sd Thomas is admitted to record. (Pg 475)

The suit in chancery depending between Richard Barnes complt & William Skrine decd respondt is by consent of the complt & Nicholas Smith gent adminr of the goods, chattels & creditts of the sd Skrine ord'd to be revived & the same stands cont'd over to the next court. (Pg 476)

Nicholas Smith gent returned the inventory of the estate of William Skrine decd which is adm'd to record. (Pg 476)

Ord'd that a dedimus potestatem issue to take the depositions of Robert Green, John Carder & Aaron Pinson of Spotsilvania Co between Richard Barnes complt & Nicholas Smith adminr &c of William Skrine decd before any two justices of the sd co. (Pg 476)

The will of Jonathan Gibson gent decd was presented into court by Elizabeth his widdow & extrix who made oath thereto & the same was proved by the oath of Thomas Turner & Anthony Strother two of the wits thereto & was adm'd to record. (Pg 476)

Joseph Strother, Samuel Skinker, Thomas Turner & Walter Anderson or any three of them are appointed being first sworne to appraise in money the estate of Jonathan Gibson gent decd & make report thereof. (Pg 476)

Alice Cale ackn her lease & release unto William Strother gent which on his motion is adm'd to record. (Pg 476)

Judgment is granted unto Nicholas Smith gent agt the estate of Samuel Nicholls decd in the hands of Mary Nicholls adminr &c of the sd estate for the sum of £2:13:9 which is ord'd to be paid with cost. (Pg 476)

Capt John Williams ackn his lease & release unto John Tayloe & Company which on the motion of the sd Tayloe is admitted to record. (Pg 476)

Richard Griffis ackn his lease & bond unto William Rowley which is adm'd to record. (Pg 476)

Wm Rowley ackn his lease unto Richard Griffis which is adm'd to record. (Pg 476)

William Strother gent produced three accts one agt Abraham Maxfield & Lazarus Tilly, one agt William Russell & the other agt John Garner & made oath to them which on his motion is ord'd to be certified. (Pg 476)

Present Wm Strother.

In the suit in chancery between Samuel Reeds, Mary Reeds, Thomas Reeds & Elizabeth Reeds complts & Francis Jett & John Jett respondts upon the return of the auditors report the court doth decree that the sd Francis & John pay to the sd complts £45:13:11 it being their pt/o the estate of William Reeds their late father decd & also that they deliver unto the sd complts four Negroes (to wit) Scipio, Mingo, Dingey & Dick now in the possession of the afsd John Jett & it is further ord'd that Rowland Thornton & Jeremiah Murdock gent divide the sd four Negroes between the sd Samuel, Mary, Thomas & Elizabeth & make their report to the next court. (Pg 477)

Samuel Reeds, John Gilbert & Thomas Harper came into court & assumed themselves securitys for that pt/o the estate of William Reeds decd in the hands of the sd Samuel Reeds that belongs to Thomas Reed & Elizabeth Reed infants under the age of 21. (Pg 477)

The suit brought by Thomas Monteith agt Jeremiah Bronaugh & Rose his wife adminrs with the will annexed of John Dinwiddie decd is cont'd. (Pg 477)

The division of the estate of William Pattishall decd is returned by Adam Christie & Mary his wife & the same is admitted to record. (Pg 477)

Robert Jones, Benjamin Berryman, Thomas Smith & Thomas Harwood or any three of them by consent of Adam Christie & Mary his wife are appointed to make partition of the land belonging to William Pattishall decd & lay off 1/3 thereof for the sd Mary's dower & it is further ord'd that they divide this present crop of corn & tobacco & set apart 1/3 thereof for the sd Mary's & make report to the next court. (Pg 477)

The suit brought by John Snell agt Adam Christie is cont'd. (Pg 477)

The suit brought by Richard Longman agt Francis Woffendale is cont'd. (Pg 477)

The suit brought by John Finlason agt Adam Christie is cont'd. (Pg 477)

The suit in chancery between Mosely Battaley complt & Wm Hensley respt is cont'd. (Pg 477)

The suit by petition between Daniel French & Margaret his wife plts & Evan Price exr of the will of John Pratt decd def the last courts order not being complied with is cont'd till next court for the auditors to make their report. (Pg 477)

Judgment is granted unto French Mason agt Thomas Johnson for the sum of 665 lbs of tobacco, Jeremiah Bronaugh Junr entered himself special bail in the sd suit & the sd tobacco is ord'd to be paid with cost & one atty fee. (Pg 477)

In the suit brought by Charles Birchnell agt William Grant the jury having found £5 damages for the plt upon executing a writ of enquiry & the def having assigned errors in arrest of judgment upon arguing the sd errors the court is of opinion the declaration is incertain & that no judgment can be founded thereon & do therefore order that the sd suit be dismist with cost & one atty fee. (Pg 478)

In the suit brought by Robert Kennan agt John Fox, Richard Bryant, Rowland Thornton, Anthony Hainy, John Steward, Rush Hudson, Francis Woffendall, Samuel Moon, Jno Farguson, Jereh Strother, Neal McCormack, John Triplett & William Gording was sworne a jury to try the issue joined who having heard the evidence & arguments withdrew & sometime after returned the following verdt, viz, we find for the def, Richd Bryant foreman, which verdt on the defs motion is adm'd to record & the sd suit is ord'd to be dismist with cost & one atty fee. (Pg 478)

Thomas Thatcher being sumoned an evidence by Robert Kennan agt John Fox & making oath he attended three days on the sd suit it is ord'd that the sd Kennan pay the sd Thatcher for the same 30 lbs of tobacco per day with cost. (Pg 478)

Benjamin Hawkings being sumoned an evidence by Robert Kennan agt John Fox & making oath he attend'd three days on the sd suit it is ord'd that the sd Kennan pay the sd Hawkings for the same 30 lbs of tobacco per day with cost. (Pg 478)

John Gilbert being sumoned an evidence by John Fox agt Robert Kennan & making oath he attend'd three days on the sd suit it is ord'd that the sd Fox pay the sd Gilbert for the same 30 lbs of tobacco per day with cost. (Pg 478)

Thomas Vivion gent being sumoned an evidence by John Fox agt Robert Kennan & having attend'd three days on the sd suit it is ord'd that the sd Fox pay the sd Vivion for the same 30 lbs of tobacco per day with cost. (Pg 478)

Then the court adjourned to court in course.

Court held 6 Feb 1729 for the examination of Thomas Turner. Present: Wm Robinson, Wm Thornton, Jos Strother, Saml Skinker, Rowld Thornton, Wm Strother, Jere Murdock, gent justices. (Pg 478)

Thomas Turner being comitted by mittimus under the hand & seale of William Robinson gent for feloniously stealing a bay horse gelding belonging to Nicholas Smith gent upon examination the sd Turner confessed he took the sd horse but without intent to steal him whereupon it is ord'd that the sheriff take him to the comon whipping post & give him 39 lashes on the bare back well laid. (Pg 478)

Court held 6 Feb 1729. Present: Wm Robinson, Wm Thornton, Jos Strother, Saml Skinker, Rowld Thornton, Wm Strother, Jere Murdock, gent justices. (Pg 479)

Anthony Hainey brought before the court a servt man named Thomas Harbut to be adjudged for runaway time & expences in taking him up & produced an acct of £2:15:2 & made oath thereto, it is ord'd that he serve him for the same according to law & for 12 days absence from his sd masters service. (Pg 479)

Ord'd that John Popham be sumoned by the sheriff of this co to appear at the next court to answer the information of our Sovereign Lord the King. (Pg 479)

Mary Nicholls returned the inventory of the estate of Samuel Nicholls decd & the same is adm'd to record. (Pg 479)

Robert Elliston & Elliner his wife ackn their lease & release unto Thomas Turner the sd Elliner being solely examined ackn her free & voluntary consent thereto which on the motion of the sd Turner is admitted to record. (Pg 479)

John Grayson gent of Spotsilvania Co ackn his lease & release unto Thomas Turner & Benjamin Rush by virtue of a power of atty from Susanah Grayson w/o the sd John relinquished the sd Susanah's right of dower & thirds in & to the same which on the motion of the sd Turner is admitted to record. (Pg 479)

Thomas Turner ackn his lease & release unto Elliner Elliston which on the motion of the sd Elliner is admitted to record. (Pg 479)

The petition of Jonas Williams for the administration of the estate of George McDonald is cont'd till next court. (Pg 479)

Edward Barradall produced a note for 1,050 lbs of tobacco under the hand of Isaac Bennet & made oath that 600 thereof was justly due which is ord'd to be certified. (Pg 479)

Ord'd that Thomas Riphley & Grace his wife be sumoned to the next court to answer the petition of Thomas Welch. (Pg 479)

The suit brought by Daniel French & Margt his wife agt Evan Price exr of the will of John Pratt decd is cont'd for the auditors to return their report. (Pg 479)

On the petition of Adam Christie & Mary his wife praying that the land belonging to William Pattishall decd might be divided & 1/3 laid off for the petitioners the division being returned, viz, we the subscribers in obedience to the within order have mett at the plantation of Adam Christie & by consent of Mary his wife have divided the land in manner following, from a spool house built on the Rolling Road through the plantation to the lower side the wheat patch from thence to the head of a br & down the sd br to Thomas Harwood's tobacco house within Christie's bounds we allot William Strother, 4 Jan 1729, Benjamin Berryman, Thomas Smith, Thos Harwood, which sd division is admitted to record. (Pg 479)

In the suit in chancery between Samuel Reeds, Mary Reeds, Thomas Reeds & Elizabeth Reeds complts & Francis Jett & John Jett exrs of the will of William Reeds decd respts the auditors having returned their report, viz, pursuant to an order of King George Co Court dated 5 Dec 1729, we the subscribers met at the house of Saml Reeds & did there value & set apart the following four Negroes (to wit) Dick to Mary valued at £16, Scipio to Samuel at £30, Mingo to Thomas at £27 & Dingey to Elizabeth at £15 & do award that Samuel Reeds pay to Mary £17:8:6, to Thomas £6:8:6 & to Elizabeth £18:8:6 being each pt/o their fathers estate now in the possession of the sd Samuel Reeds, given under our hands this 13th day of Dec 1729, Rowld Thornton, Jere Murdock, which sd report is admitted to record & it is ord'd that the sd Mary, Thomas & Elizabeth Jett [sic] pay unto the sd Samuel Reeds their proportional pt/o the expence that shall appear the sd Samuel hath been at in recovering the sd estate. (Pg 480)

In the action upon the case between Thomas Monteith plt & Jeremiah Bronaugh & Rose his wife adminrs with the will annexed of John Dinwiddie decd defs,

John Diskin, Thomas Stribling, Richard Ellkin, John Fox, Isaac Arnold, Rowland Thornton, Francis Woffendale, Anthony Hainey, Samuel Moon, Jonas Williams & Jeremiah Bronaugh was sworn a jury to try the issues joined who having heard the evidences & arguments withdrew. (Pg 480)

Then the court adjourned till tomorrow morning 9 o'clock.

Court held 7 Feb 1729. Present: Wm Robinson, Wm Thornton, Jos Strother, Saml Skinker, Rowld Thornton, Jere Murdock, gent justices. (Pg 480)

John Travis & Margaret his wife ackn their lease & release unto Catesby Cocke the sd Margaret being solely examined ackn her voluntary consent thereto which on the motion of the sd Catesby is admitted to record. (Pg 480)

The inventory of the estate of Peter Dunbar is return'd & admitted to record. (Pg 480)

Jeremiah Murdock gent produced an acct agt John Hasty for 550 lbs of tobacco & made oath thereto which is ord'd to be certified. (Pg 480)

John Chadwell of Stafford Co being sumoned an evidence by Thomas Monteith agt Jeremiah Bronaugh & Rose his wife adminrs with the will annexed of John Dinwiddie decd & making oath that he attended seven days on the sd suit, it appearing that he lived 8 miles from the sd court & that he came five times, it is ord'd that the sd Monteith pay him for the same according to law. (Pg 480)

Augustin Smith of Caroline Co gent being sumoned an evidence by Thomas Monteith agt Jeremiah Bronaugh & Rose his wife adminrs with the will annexed of John Dinwiddie decd & making oath that he had come four times & attended four days on the sd suit, it appearing that he lived 5 ½ miles from the sd court it is ord'd that the sd Monteith pay the sd Smith for the same & ferriages according to law. (Pg 481)

Benjamin Strother of Stafford Co being summoned an evidence by Thomas Monteith agt Jeremiah Bronaugh & Rose his wife adminrs with the will annex'd of John Dinwiddie decd & making oath he had come five times & attended seven days on the sd suit, it appearing that he lives 30 miles from the sd court it is ord'd that the sd Monteith pay the sd Strother for the same according to law. (Pg 481)

Elizabeth Parker of Spotsilvania Co being sumoned an evidence by Thomas Monteith agt Jeremiah Bronaugh & Rose his wife adminrs with the will annexed of John Dinwiddie decd & making oath that she had come four times & attended six days on the sd suit, it appearing that she lives 20 miles from the sd court it is ord'd that the sd Monteith pay the sd Parker for the same & two ferriages according to law. (Pg 481)

Benjamin Grayson of Stafford Co being sumoned an evidence by Thomas Monteith agt Jeremiah Bronaugh & Rose his wife adminrs with the will annexed of John Dinwiddie decd & making oath that he had come five times & attended seven days, it appearing that he came twice 80 miles & three times 50 miles it is ord'd that the sd Monteith pay the sd Grayson for the same according to law. (Pg 481)

John Mercer of Stafford Co being sumoned an evidence by Thomas Monteith agt Jeremiah Bronaugh & Rose his wife adminrs with the will annex'd of John Dinwiddie decd & making oath that he had come three times & attended four days on the sd suit, it appearing that he lived 15 miles from the sd court it is ord'd that the sd Monteith pay the sd Mercer for the same & ferriages according to law. (Pg 481)

Then the court adjourned till Monday morning 9 o'clock.

Court con't & held 9 Feb 1729. Present: Wm Robinson, Wm Thornton, Jos Strother, Saml Skinker, Rowld Thornton, Wm Strother, Jere Murdock, gent justices. (Pg 481)

Thomas Turner being comitted into the goal of this co for attempting to steal a horse belonging to Nicholas Smith gent the sd Turner upon his examination appearing to be a vagabond & confessing that he resided last with Capt John King of Hampton, it is considered by the court & ord'd that the sd Thomas be conveyed from constable to constable the nearest way to the sd Capt King's at Hampton pursuant to the late Act of Assembly in that [?] made & provided. (Pg 481)

The motion of Wm Thatcher to choose his guardian is cont'd till next court. (Pg 482)

Mathew Mcmahone being drunk before the court, it is ord'd that he pay the church wardens of Hanover Parish 5 shillings for the sd offence, John Fox assumed in court to pay the 5 shillings. (Pg 481)

Mathew McMahone being convicted of swearing one oath, it is ord'd that he pay the church wardens of Hanover Parish 5 shillings for the sd offence the sd Mcmahone refusing to pay the 5 shillings or to give security for the same, it is ord'd that the sheriff take him to the comon whiping post of this co & give him 10 lashes on the bare back well laid on. (Pg 482)

Mathew McMahone being of very ill behaviour before the court it is ord'd that the sheriff take him into his custody & him safely keep till he enter into bond with good & sufficient security in the sum of £20 for his good behaviour for 12 months & a day next coming. (Pg 482)

Imparlance is granted unto Thomas Harper in the suit brought agt him by our Sovereign Lord the King. (Pg 482)

Imparlance is granted unto Thomas Monteith in the suit brought agt him by our Sovereign Lord the King. (Pg 482)

An alias scire facias is granted to our Sovereign Lord the King agt William Hensley Junr. (Pg 482)

An alias scire facias is granted to our Sovereign Lord the King agt Jonathan Williams. (Pg 482)

Judgment is renewed by scire facias to our Sovereign Lord the King agt Benjamin Hensley for 20 shillings which is ord'd to be paid with cost & one atty fee. (Pg 482)

Judgment is renewed by scire facias to our Sovereign Lord the King agt Joseph Minton for 20 shillings which is ord'd to be paid with cost & one atty fee. (Pg 482)

The suit brought by Samuel Skinker gent agt James Kay is dismist. (Pg 482)

The suit brought by John Ambrose agt Thomas Harwood is dismist. (Pg 482)

The suit brought by John Cameron agt John Hilling is dismist. (Pg 482)

The suit brought by Charles Seale agt Thos Blassingham is dismist. (Pg 482)

The suit brought by John Champe agt John Ellkins is dismist. (Pg 482)

In the suit brought by Edward Barradall agt Charles Seale the def has oyer of the acct. (Pg 482)

Then the court adjourned till tomorrow morning 9 o'clock.

Court cont'd & held 10 Feb 1729. Present: Wm Robinson, Wm Thornton, Jos Strother, Saml Skinker, Rowld Thornton, Wm Strother, Jere Murdock, gent justices. (Pg 482)

The suit brought by Jas Hinson agt Wm Grant is dismist. (Pg 483)

An als capias is granted unto John Savage in the suit brought by him agt Thomas Riphley. (Pg 483)

The suit brought by John Farguson agt Miles Potter is dismist. (Pg 483)

In the suit brought by William Strother gent agt Thomas Phillips the def being called & not appearing judgment is granted the plt agt the def & Richard Gill his security for what of the sum sued for in the declaration shall appear to be justly due unless the def appear at the next court & answer the sd accon. (Pg 483)

The suit brought by John Champe agt Thomas Davis is dismist. (Pg 483)

The suit brought by Saml Skinker agt John Cameron is dismist. (Pg 483)

The suit brought by Thomas Duncan agt Robert Shelton is dismist. (Pg 483)

The suit brought by William Grant agt George James Dunbar is dismist. (Pg 483)

The suit brought by George Fishpool agt John Fleming is dismist. (Pg 483)

The suit brought by George Jas Dunbar agt John Yewbank is dismist. (Pg 483)

The suit brought by John Champe agt Christopher Rodgers is dismist. (Pg 483)

The suits brought by John Champe agt Robert Jones, Charles Jones, Wm Flowers, Richard Griffith, Thos Stribling, Thos Duncom, Jereh Bronaugh, Rosser Spicer, Thos Johnson & Thos Davis are dismist. (Pg 483)

In the suit brought by John Champe agt Richard Griffis the def being called & not appearing judgmt is granted the plt agt the def & [*blank*] his security for what of the sum sued for in the declaration shall appear to be justly due unless the sd def appear at the next court & answer the sd action. (Pg 483)

The attachment obtained by John Higdon agt Howell Jones is cont'd to next court. (Pg 483)

The suit brought by Chas Gamon agt Saml Oxshaw is dismist. (Pg 483)

The suit brought by Thomas Sinclair agt Benja Grigsby is dismist. (Pg 484)

The suit brought by Richard Ellkins agt Robert English is dismist. (Pg 484)

The suit in chancery between Richard Barnes & Wm Skrine is cont'd. (Pg 484)

The grand jurys presentmt agt Richard Ellkins is cont'd. (Pg 484)

Judgmt is granted unto Hanover Parish agt William Brown for 10 shillings for being drunk & swearing one oath which is ord'd to be paid. (Pg 484)

The suit brought by John Snell agt Adam Christie is cont'd. (Pg 484)

In the suit brought by Richard Longman agt Francis Woffendale the def having demurr'd to the plts replication upon arguing the demurrer the court is of opinion the demurrer is good & the sd suit is ord'd to be dismist with cost & one atty fee. (Pg 484)

The suit in chancery between Moseley Battaley & Wm Hensley is cont'd. (Pg 484)

In the suit brought by Alexr Parker agt Robert Wilson the def pleads he owes nothing the plt joines the issue & the same lies till next court for trial. (Pg 484)

Ord'd that Anthony Thornton & James Markham be sum'd to the next court to answer the courts objections. (Pg 484)

On the motion of Edward Barradall atty for Jeremiah Bronaugh & Rose his wife adminrs with the will annexed of John Dinwiddie decd that the jury might distinguish in their verdt when the assetts come to the hands of the sd adminrs the court did not think fit to give the sd jury any such directions. (Pg 484)

John Travis of Stafford Co being sumoned an evidence by Thomas Monteith agt Jeremiah Bronaugh & Rose his wife adminrs with the will annexed of John Dinwiddie decd & making oath that he had come six times & attended eight days on the sd suit & it appearing that he lived 10 miles from the sd court it is ord'd that the sd Monteith pay the sd Traviss for the same according to law. (Pg 484)

Richd Long of Caroline Co being sumoned an evidence by Thomas Monteith agt Jeremiah Bronaugh & Rose his wife adminrs with the will annexed of John

Dinwiddie decd & making oath that he had come four times & attended six days on the sd suit & it appearing that he lived 10 miles from the sd court it is ord'd that the sd Monteith pay the sd Long for the same & his ferriages according to law. (Pg 484)

Mott Doniphan of Stafford Co being sumoned an evidence by Thomas Monteith agt Jeremiah Bronaugh & Rose his wife adminrs with the will annexed of John Dinwiddie decd & making oath that he had come four times & attended eight days on the sd suit & it appearing that he lived 10 miles from the sd court it is ord'd that the sd Monteith pay the sd Doniphan for the same according to law. (Pg 485)

John Wheeler of Stafford Co being sumoned an evidence by Thomas Monteith agt Jeremiah Bronaugh & Rose his wife adminrs with the will annexed of John Dinwiddie decd & making oath that he had come five times & attended eight days on the sd suit & it appearing that he lived 20 miles from the sd court it is ord'd that the sd Monteith pay the sd Wheeler for the same according to law. (Pg 485)

James Seaton of Stafford Co being sumoned an evidence by Thomas Monteith agt Jeremiah Bronaugh & Rose his wife adminrs with the will annexed of John Dinwiddie decd & making oath that he had come six times & attended eight days on the sd suit & it appearing that he lived 12 miles from the sd court it is ord'd that the sd Monteith pay the sd Seaton for the same according to law. (Pg 485)

Thomas Sinclair of Stafford Co being sumoned an evidence by Thomas Monteith agt Jeremiah Bronaugh & Rose his wife adminrs with the will annexed of John Dinwiddie decd & making oath that he had come five times & attended eight days on the sd suit & it appearing that he lived 20 miles from the sd court it is ord'd that the sd Monteith pay the sd Sinclair for the same according to law. (Pg 485)

George Proctor of Spotsilvania Co being sumoned an evidence by Thomas Monteith agt Jeremiah Bronaugh & Rose his wife adminrs with the will annexed of John Dinwiddie decd & making oath that he had come four times & attended eight days on the sd suit & it appearing that he lived 20 miles from the sd court it is ord'd that the sd Monteith pay the sd Proctor for the same & his ferriages according to law. (Pg 485)

John Fox of Caroline Co being sumoned an evidence by Thomas Monteith agt Jeremiah Bronaugh & Rose his wife adminrs with the will annexed of John Dinwiddie decd & making oath that he had come three times & attended six days on the sd suit & it appearing that he lived 5 miles from the sd court it is ord'd that the sd Monteith pay the sd Fox for the same & his ferriages according to law. (Pg 485)

Robert Taliaferro of Caroline Co being sumoned an evidence by Thomas Monteith agt Jeremiah Bronaugh & Rose his wife adminrs with the will annexed of John Dinwiddie decd & making oath that he came four times & attended seven days on the sd suit & it appearing that he lived 12 miles from the sd court it is ord'd that the sd Monteith pay the sd Taliaferro for the same & his ferriages according to law. (Pg 486)

Thomas Jefferies of Stafford Co being sumoned an evidence by Thomas Monteith agt Jeremiah Bronaugh & Rose his wife adminrs with the will annexed of John Dinwiddie decd & making oath that he had come four times & attended eight days on the sd suit & it appearing that he lived 8 miles from the sd court it is ord'd that the sd Monteith pay the sd Jefferies for the same according to law. (Pg 486)

Darby Callihan being sumoned an evidence by Thomas Monteith agt Jeremiah Bronaugh & Rose his wife adminrs with the will annexed of John Dinwiddie decd & making oath that he attended seven days on the sd suit it is ord'd that the sd Monteith pay the sd Callihan for the same at 30 lbs of tobacco per day & cost. (Pg 486)

John Gilbert being sumoned an evidence by Thomas Monteith agt Jeremiah Bronaugh & Rose his wife adminrs with the will annexed of John Dinwiddie decd & making oath that he attended ten days on the sd suit it is ordered that the sd Monteith pay the sd Gilbert for the same at 30 lbs of tobo per day & cost. (pg 486)

John Bourne being sumoned an evidence by Thomas Monteith agt Jeremiah Bronaugh & Rose his wife adminrs with the will annexed of John Dinwiddie decd & making oath that he attended nine days on the sd suit it is ord'd that the sd Monteith pay the sd Bourne for the same at 30 lbs of tobo per day & cost. (Pg 486)

Richard Rosser being sumoned an evidence by Thomas Monteith agt Jeremiah Bronaugh & Rose his wife adminrs with the will annexed of John Dinwiddie decd & making oath that he attended seven days on the sd suit it is ord'd that the sd Monteith pay the sd Rosser for the same at 30 lbs of tobo per day & cost. (Pg 486)

Henry Berry being sumoned an evidence by Thomas Monteith agt Jeremiah Bronaugh & Rose his wife adminrs with the will annexed of John Dinwiddie decd & making oath that he attended eight days on the sd suit it is ord'd that the sd Monteith pay the sd Berry for the same at 30 lbs of tobo per day with cost. (Pg 487)

Frances Sawyer being sumoned an evidence by Thomas Monteith agt Jeremiah Bronaugh & Rose his wife adminrs with the will annexed of John Dinwiddie decd & making oath that he attended seven days on the sd suit it is ord'd that the sd Monteith pay the sd Sawyer for the same at 30 lbs of tobo per day & cost. (Pg 487)

Jeremiah Bronaugh being sumoned an evidence by Thomas Monteith agt Jeremiah Bronaugh & Rose his wife adminrs with the will annexed of John Dinwiddie decd & making oath that he attended eight days on the sd suit it is ord'd that the sd Monteith pay the sd Bronaugh for the same 30 lbs of tobo per day & cost. (Pg 487)

Henry Mckie being sumoned an evidence by Thomas Monteith agt Jeremiah Bronaugh & Rose his wife adminrs with the will annexed of John Dinwiddie decd & making oath that he attended eight days on the sd suit it is ord'd that the sd Monteith pay the sd McKie for the same at 30 lbs of tobo per day & cost. (Pg 487)

Jeas Mckie being sumoned an evidence by Thomas Monteith agt Jeremiah Bronaugh & Rose his wife adminrs with the will annexed of John Dinwiddie decd & making oath that he attended eight days on the sd suit it is ord'd that the sd Monteith pay the sd McKie for the same at 30 lbs of tobo per day & cost. (Pg 487)

Charles Seale being sumoned an evidence by Thomas Monteith agt Jeremiah Bronaugh & Rose his wife adminrs with the will annexed of John Dinwiddie decd & making oath that he attended four days on the sd suit it is ord'd that the sd Monteith pay the sd Seale for the same at 30 lbs of tobo per day & cost. (Pg 487)

John Coburn being sumoned an evidence by Thomas Monteith agt Jeremiah Bronaugh & Rose his wife adminrs with the will annexed of John Dinwiddie decd & making oath that he attended seven days on the sd suit it is ord'd that the sd Monteith pay the sd Coburn for the same at 30 lbs of tobo per day & cost. (Pg 487)

William Strother gent being sumoned an evidence by Richard Longman agt Francis Woffendale & making oath he attended five days on the sd suit it is ord'd that he pay him for the same at 30 lbs of tobacco per day with cost. (Pg 487)

Jeremiah Strother being sumoned an evidence by Richard Longman agt Francis Woffendale & making oath he attended 10 days on the sd suit it is ordered the sd Longman pay him for the same at 30 lbs of tobacco per day with cost. (Pg 487)

In the action upon the case between Thomas Monteith plt & Jeremiah Bronaugh & Rose his wife adminrs with the will annexed of John Dinwiddie decd defs, John Diskin &c was sworne a jury to try the issue joined who having heard the evidence & arguments of both parties withdrew & sometime after returned the following verdt (viz) we of the jury upon the two first issues joined we find for the plt damage £181:11:1, John Diskin foreman, we the jury find assetts to the value of £116:10:7 in the hands of the adminrs of John Dinwiddie decd, John Diskin foreman, which verdt on the plts motion is admitted to record & on the defs motion time is granted the defs till next court to consider the sd verdict. (Pg 488)

On the motion of William Robinson gent it is ord'd that Thos Clator be sumoned to the next court to shew cause why he stops up the road leading from his house to the church & it is ord'd that the old road be laid open in the mean time. (Pg 488)

Then the court adjourned to court in course.

Court held 6 Mar 1729. Present: Nicho Smith, Willm Thornton, Jos Strother, Saml Skinker, Jereh Murdock, gent justices. (Pg 488)

Martin Gollathan ackn his lease, release & bond to John Berkley & Mary the w/o the sd Gollathan relinquished her right of dower & thirds at the comon law she being solely examined confessed her free consent thereto which on the motion of the sd Berkley is admitted to record. (Pg 488)

John Quisenbury ackn his deed of feofment to John Dodd & William Remey by virtue of a power from Elizabeth Quisenbury w/o the sd John relinquished her right of dower in & to the same which on the motion of the sd Dodd is admitted to record. (Pg 488)

On the petition of Peter Hedgman it is ord'd that the sd Hedgman have liberty to clear a road from his quarter into the Cart Road now used by Col Robert Carter

& if any person thinks themselves aqrieved thereat the sd Hedgman is to desist till it is further heard before the court. (Pg 488)

On the motion of John [?] it is ordered that he be levy free for the future. (Pg 489)

The suit brought by Daniel French & Margt his wife agt Evan Price exr of the will of John Pratt decd is cont'd. (Pg 489)

The suit brought by Richd Griffis agt Bartho Redman is dismist. (Pg 489)

The suits brought by Thomas Riphley agt George Downing, John Bolling, Richd Green, Thos Blassingham are ord'd to be dismist. (Pg 489)

The suit brought by Thos Turner agt Thos Blassingham is ord'd to be dismist. (Pg 489)

The suit brought by Miles Potter agt Antho Head is ord'd to be dismist. (Pg 489)

On the motion of John Willis, Rush Hudson is appointed his guardian. (Pg 489)

The suit brought by Phil Cavenaugh agt Bartho Redman is dismist. (Pg 489)

The suit in chancery between Richard Barns & William Skrine is cont'd. (Pg 489)

Administration of the goods, chattels & credits of William Hudson decd is granted unto Sarah Hudson his widow the sd Sarah with Rush Hudson ackn their bond of £100 for the sd Sarah's faithfull administration of the sd estate. (Pg 489)

The suit brought by John Coburn agt Thomas James is dismist. (Pg 489)

The suit brought by John Gilbert agt Jos Burges is dismist. (Pg 489)

The suit brought by Henry Fitzhugh esqr agt Jeremiah Bronaugh & Rose his wife adminrs of the estate of John Dinwiddie decd is cont'd. (Pg 489)

The suit brought by John Willis agt Thos Golf is dismist. (Pg 489)

The suit brought by William Thatcher agt John Gilbert is cont'd. (Pg 489)

Ordered that Matthew McMahone be discharged from his bond to our Sovereign Lord the King paying fees. (Pg 489)

The suit brought by Richard Griffis agt William Duling is dismist. (Pg 489)

The suit brought by Lazarus Tilly agt Isaac Johnson is dismist. (Pg 489)

Samuel Wharton, Henry Long, Richard Tankersley & Henry Head or any three of them being first sworne are appointed to appraise in mony the estate of William Hudson decd that shall be brought to their view & make report to the next court. (Pg 490)

The suit brought by Josiah Farguson agt John Diskin the def being called & not appearing judgmt is granted the plt agt the def & Thomas Vivion gent sheriff of this co for what of the sum sued for in the declaration shall appear to be justly due unless the def appear at the next court & answer the sd action. (Pg 490)

In the suit brought by Jeremiah Murdock gent agt Charles Seale the def being called & not appearing judgmt is granted the plt agt the def & David Seale & John Fox for what of the sum sued for in the declaration shall appear to be justly due unless the def appear at the next court & answer the sd action. (Pg 490)

The suit brought by William Robinson gent agt Thos Clayter is cont'd. (Pg 490)

Ordered that the main Back Road by John Piper's be laid open as formerly. (Pg 490)

Ordered that the main Back Road by Fras Drake's be laid open as formerly. (Pg 490)

Administration of the goods, chattels & credits of George McDaniel decd is granted unto Jonas Williams the sd Jonas with John Mercer assumed in court in the sum of £30 for the sd Jonas his faithfull administration of the sd estate. (Pg 490)

Benja Berryman, John Ambrose, Abraham Kenyan & John Kenyan or any three of them being first sworne are appointed to appraise in mony the estate of George McDaniel decd that shall be brought to their view & make report to the next court. (Pg 490)

In the suit brought by John Wilson agt Robert Raddish the def pleads not guilty the plt joines the issue & the same lyes till next court for tryall. (Pg 490)

In the suit brought by Francis Thornton agt Rowland Cornelius the def pleads in writing the plt replies the def joins the replication the same lyes till next court for tryall. (Pg 491)

In the suit brought by Francis Thornton agt Thomas Smith the def pleads in writing the plt replies the def joins the replication & the same lyes till next court for tryal. (Pg 491)

A plures capias is granted unto John Savage in the suit brought by him agt Thomas Riphley. (Pg 491)

In the action upon the case brought by William Strother agt Thomas Phillips the def being called & not appearing judgment is granted the plt agt the def for what of the sum sued for shall appear to be due upon a writ of inquiry to be executed next court. (Pg 491)

In the scire facias brought by our Sovereign Lord the King agt Thomas Harper the def pleads in writing & Edward Barradall atty for our King has time till next court to consider the sd plea. (Pg 491)

In the scire facias brought by our Sovereign Lord the King agt Thomas Monteith the def pleads in writing & Edward Barradall atty for our King has time till next court to consider the sd plea. (Pg 491)

In the action upon the case between Edward Barradall plt & Charles Seale def the def being called & not appearing judgment per nihil dicit is granted the plt agt the def for what of the sum sued for in the declaration shall appear to be justly due unless the sd def appear at the next court & answer the sd action. (Pg 491)

Richard Griffis came into court & confessed judgment to John Champ for 500 lbs of tobacco which is ordered to be paid with cost. (Pg 491)

In the attachment obtained by John Higdon agt Howell Jones judgment is granted the sd John agt the sd Howell for 634 ½ lbs of tobacco which is ordered to be paid with cost. (Pg 491)

Special imparlance is granted unto Esdras Theodor Edzard clerk in the suit brought agt him by Saml Skinker gent. (Pg 491)

In the information brought by our Sovereign Lord the King agt John Popham the sheriff having returned the sd John not to be found in his bailiwick it is ordered that an alias sumons issue returnable to the next court. (Pg 491)

Mathew McMahone confessed judgment in custody unto Thomas Harper for £6:14:7 due by bill which is ordered to be paid with cost. (Pg 492)

Mathew McMahone confessed judgment in custody unto Mary Tutt for £5:6:9 due by account which is ordered to be paid with cost. (Pg 492)

In the petition brought by Thomas Welch agt Thomas Riphley is cont'd. (Pg 492)

In the suit brought by Edmund Dunahoe agt Thomas Thatcher the plt not prosecuting is nonsuit which is ordered to be paid with cost & one atty fee. (Pg 492)

William Strother being sumon'd by the sheriff to attend the court this day for a juryman being called & not appearing it is ordered that he be fined 5 shillings to our Sovereign Lord the King for the sd contempt which is ordered to be paid with cost. (Pg 492)

John Jennings being sumoned by the sheriff to attend the court this day for a juryman being called & not appearing it is ordered that he be fined 5 shillings to our Sovereign Lord the King for the sd contempt which is ordered to be paid with cost. (Pg 492)

Samuel Hoyle being sumoned by the sheriff to attend the court this day for a juryman being called & not appearing it is ordered that he be fined 5 shillings to our Sovereign Lord the King for the sd contempt which is ordered to be paid with cost. (Pg 492)

John Fox being sumoned by the sheriff to attend the court this day for a juryman being called & not appearing it is ordered that he be fined 5 shillings to our Sovereign Lord the King for the sd contempt which is ordered to be paid with cost. (Pg 492)

In the action upon the case between Thomas Monteith plt & Jeremiah Bronaugh & Rose his wife adminrs with the will annext of John Dinwiddie decd defs by Edward Barradall their atty having filed errors to stay judgment in the verdt found by the jury the last court the plt by Z. Lewis his atty has time till next court to consider them. (Pg 492)

An alias capias is granted unto John Savage in the suit brought by him agt Thomas Riphley. (Pg 492)

In the scire facias brought by our Sovereign Lord the King agt Thomas Harper the def pleads in writing & Edward Barradall atty for our King has time till next court to consider the sd plea. (Pg 493)

In the scire facias brought by our Sovereign Lord the King agt Thomas Monteith the def pleads in writing & Edward Barradall atty for our King has time till next court to consider the sd plea. (Pg 493)

In the scire facias brought by our Sovereign Lord the King agt Jonathan Williams the sheriff having returned the sd Jonathan not to be found in his bailiwick it is ordered that an alias scire facias issue returnable to the next court. (Pg 493)

In the scire facias brought by our Sovereign Lord the King agt William Hensley Junr the sheriff having returned the sd William not to be found in his bailiwick it is ordered that an alias scire facias issue returnable to the next court. (Pg 493)

In the suit brought by George Downing agt Thomas Blassingham the plt not prosecuting is nonsuit which is ordered to be paid with cost & one atty fee. (Pg 493)

Ordered that Rowland Cornelius be sumoned to next court to answer the attachment of Thomas Philips agt Richard Cornelius. (Pg 493)

In the suit brought by Francis Thornton agt Rowland Cornelius the def pleads in writing the plt replies & the def joins the replication & the same lies till next court for tryal. (Pg 493)

In the suit brought by Francis Thornton agt Thos Smith the def pleads in writing the plt replies & the def joins the replication & the same lies till next court for tryal. (Pg 493)

Ordered that the rates of liquors be as formerly.

In the gectiona firma between Thomas Thrustout plt & Willm Holdfast def for lands & appurtenances in Hanover Parish as is set forth in the declaration & it appearing by the return of the sheriff that Ann Marsh tenant in possession of the premises has been served with a copy of the sd declaration & of the indorsement thereon Ann Marsh by Z. Lewis her atty appeared & prayed that she might be admitted def which is granted & the sd Z. Lewis confessed lease, entery & ouster & pleaded not guilty & Edwd Barradall atty for the plt joined the issue & the same is referred till next court for tryall. (Pg 493)

Then the court adjourned to court in course.

Court held 30 Mar 1730 for the examination of James Scott, Mary Marshall, James Dickinson & Hugh Strahan. Present: William Robinson, William Thornton, Joseph Strother, Samuel Skinker, gent justices. (Pg 494)

James Scott being committed by mittimus under the hand & seale of William Strother gent for feloniously taking sundry goods out of the store of James Nicholls on the plantation of William Strother gent the sd Scott having made his confession & signed to the same it is the opinion of the court that the sd Scott ought to be tried for the sd fact before the General Court & it is ordered that the sd Scott be carried again to the goal of the sd co in order thereto. (Pg 494)

Mary Marshall being comitted by mittimus under the hands & seales of Joseph Strother & Saml Skinker gent for receiving several goods feloniously stolen out of the store of James Nicholls on the plantation of William Strother gent the court on consideration of the evidences being divided appoint to next Friday for her further examination. (Pg 494)

James Dickinson being commited by mittimus under the hands & seals of Joseph Strother & Saml Skinker gent for breaking open the store of James Nicholls on the plantation of William Strother gent & for the feloniously taking several goods out of the sd store (viz) four pair of shoes, three pair of stockings, a parcel of [?] gloves, one remnant of linen, one pair of yarn [?], 3 ½ yards of ticken & 9 ½ yards of plains which sd goods were produced & the sd Dickinson confessed to be the same he had stole out of the sd store about 6 weeks ago by getting into the store house loft with one James Scott through a scuttle hole in the sd loft where was a loose board & said he put himself on the mercy of God & the worshipfull court but being required by the court to sign the sd confession he refused saying he never had signed any papers whereupon the court is of opinion the sd Dickinson might to be tried for the sd fact before the General Court & it is ordered that the sd Dickinson be carried back again to the goal of the co in order thereto. (Pg 494)

Hugh Strahan being commited by mittimus under the hand & seale of Joseph Strother gent for receiving several goods supposed to be stole out of the store house of James Nicholls the court being divided on consideracon of the evidence appoints next Friday for his further examination. (Pg 495)

John Toward came into court & ackn himself to stand justly indebted to our Sovereign Lord the King in the sum of £40 to be levied on his lands & tenements, goods & chattels if he performe not the condition hereafter required. The condition of this recognizance is such that if the sd John Toward personally appear at Wmsburgh at the trial of James Scott & James Dickinson to give his evidence for & on the behalf of our King agt the sd Scott & Dickinson then this obligation to be void. (Pg 495)

Rebecca Quidley came into court & ackn herself to stand justly indebted to our Sovereign Lord the King in the sum of £40 to be levied on her lands & tenements, goods & chattels if she performe not the condition hereafter required. The condition of this recognizance is such that if the sd Rebecca Quidley appear at Wmsburgh at the trial of James Scott to give her evidence for & on the behalf of our King agt James Scott then this obligation to be void. (Pg 495)

James Nicholls came into court & ackn to be justly indebted to our Sovereign Lord the King in the sum of £40 to be levied on his lands & tenements, goods & chattels if he performs not the condition hereafter required. The condition of this recognizance is such that if Robert Taylor security to the sd Nicholls appear at Williamsburgh at the trial of James Scott & James Dickinson to give his evidence for the behalf of our King agt the sd Scott & Dickinson then this obligation to be void. (Pg 496)

Court held 3 Apr 1730. Present: Nicholas Smith, Wm Thornton, Jos Strother, Saml Skinker, Rowld Thornton, gent justices. (Pg 496)

Ordered that the sheriff sumons a grand jury to the next court.

Ordered that Thomas Benson be constable in the room of John Smith. (Pg 496)

On the petition of Joseph Berry it is ordered that he have licence to keep a ferry at his dwelling plantation the sd Berry entering into bond for the same according to law. (Pg 496)

Ordered that Richard Ellkins Senr be sumoned to the next court to answer the information of our Sovereign Lord the King. (pg 496)

Order'd that Richard Butler be sumoned to the next court to answer the petition of William Wood. (Pg 496)

Present William Robinson gent.

In the suit brought by John Finlason agt Adam Christie the def demures generally & plt joins the demurer & the same lyes till next court for tryall. (Pg 496)

Jonas Williams returned the inventory of George McDaniel. (Pg 496)

Ordered that Robert Washington be sumoned to answer the petition of Thomas Vivion. (Pg 497)

The inventory of the estate of William Hudson is returned & admitted to record. (Pg 497)

Robert Doniphan & Mott Doniphan ackn their lease, release & bond to Stephen Hansford which on the motion of the sd Hansford is admitted to record. (Pg 497)

The suit in Chancery between Moseley Battaley complt & William Hansley respt is ordered to be dismist with cost. (Pg 497)

In the action of debt between John Snell agt Adam Christie, Joseph Berry, Enoch Berry, Robert Strother, Saml Hensley, Rowland Thornton, John Jennings, Jeremiah Bronaugh Junr, John Diskin, Thomas Smith, John Ambrose, John Conner & John Grant was sworne a jury to try the issue joined who having heard the argumts & evidences of both parties withdrew & sometime after returned the following verdt (viz) we find for the plt £6, Joseph Berry foreman, which verdt on the plts motion is admitted to record & judgment is granted the plt agt the def for the sd £6 which is ord'd to be paid with cost & one atty fee. (Pg 497)

In the action upon the case between Alexr Parker plt & Robert Wilson def by consent of both parties it is ordered that Nicholas Smith gent state & settle the accounts in difference & make report to the next court & the same report to be definitive. (Pg 497)

The suit brought by Henry Fitzhugh esqr agt Jeremiah Bronaugh adminr with the will annext of John Dinwiddie decd is cont'd till next court. (Pg 497)

In the action of trespass & assault between Mary Durham by Samuel Durham her next friend plt & John Wilson & Margaret his wife defs, Joseph Berry, Enoch Berry, Robert Strother, Saml Hensley, Rowland Thornton, John Jennings, Jeremiah Bronaugh Junr, John Diskin, Thomas Smith, John Ambrose, John Conner & John Grant was sworne a jury to try the issue joined who having heard the arguments & evidences of both parties withdrew & sometime after returned the following verdt (viz) we find for the plt £2:10, Joseph Berry foreman, which verdt on the plts motion is admitted to record & judgment is granted the plt agt the sd def for the sd £2:10 which is ord'd to be paid with cost & one atty fee. (Pg 497)

Robert English of Stafford Co being sumoned an evidence by Mary Durham agt John Wilson & Margaret his wife & making oath that he had come five times & attended seven days on the sd suit & it appearing he lived 6 miles from the sd court it is ordered that the sd Durham pay the sd English for the same according to law. (Pg 498)

Jane English of Stafford Co being sumoned an evidence by Mary Durham agt John Wilson & Margaret his wife & making oath that she had come five times & attended seven days on the sd suit & it appearing she lived 6 miles from the sd court it is ordered that the sd Durham pay the sd English for the same according to law. (Pg 498)

Robert Raddish of Stafford Co being sumoned an evidence by Mary Durham agt John Wilson & Margaret his wife & making oath that he had come three times & attended five days on the sd suit & it appearing he lived 8 miles from the sd court it is ordered that the sd Durham pay the sd Raddish for the same according to law. (Pg 498)

Elinor Raddish of Stafford Co being sumoned an evidence by Mary Durham agt John Wilson & Margaret his wife & making oath that she had attended one day on the sd suit & it appearing she lived 8 miles from the sd court it is ordered that the sd Durham pay the sd Raddish for the same & coming & going according to law. (Pg 498)

In the suit brought by Thomas Davis agt Edward Merret judgmt is granted the plt agt the def for the sum of 30 shillings which is ord'd to be paid with cost & one atty fee & injunction & supena in chancery is granted the def to stay execution till the matter be further heard in equity. (Pg 498)

The suit brought by John Wilson agt Robert Raddish is cont'd. (Pg 498)

In the suit brought by Frans Thornton agt Rowland Cornelius, Joseph Berry &c was sworne a jury to try the issue joined who having heard the evidences & arguments of both parties withdrew & sometime after returned the following verdt (viz) we find that the def did catch or take fish in waters within the bounds of the plts land, Joseph Berry foreman, which verdt on the plts motion is admitted to record & judgment is granted the plt agt the def for 500 lbs of tobacco according to Act of Assembly in that case made & provided which is order'd to be paid with cost & one atty fee. (Pg 498)

Then the court adjourned till tomorrow morning 8 o'clock.

Court held 4 Apr 1730. Present: William Robinson, William Thornton, Joseph Strother, Samuel Skinker, Rowland Thornton, gent justices. (Pg 499)

Thomas Turner gent presented into court a deed from the Proprietors Office to Thomas Lee gent which on the motion of the sd Turner is admitted to record. (Pg 499)

The attachment obtained by Thomas Phillips agt Richard Cornelious is cont'd for Rowland Cornelious to finish the crop. (Pg 499)

In the suit in chancery between Richard Rasins complt & William Skrine respdt the complt not having taking the depositions of his evidences pursuant to the last courts order the sd suit is cont'd till next court for tryall & it is ord'd that the evidences be examined before the court. (Pg 499)

James Horsnail of Spotsilvania Co being sumoned an evidence by Frans Thornton agt Rowland Cornelious it appearing he lived 18 miles from the sd court & making oath he attended two days on the sd suit it is ord'd that the sd Thornton pay the sd Horsnail for the same & his ferriages according to law. (Pg 499)

George Hume of Spotsilvania Co being sumoned an evidence by Frans Thornton agt Rowland Cornelious & making oath that he attended two days on the sd suit & it appearing he lived 18 miles from the sd court it is ordered that the sd Thornton pay the sd Hume for the same & his ferriages according to law. (Pg 499)

A plures capias is granted unto John Savage in the suit brought by him agt Thomas Riphley. (Pg 499)

In the suit brought by our Sovereign Lord the King agt Thomas Harper the def having pleaded in writing, Edward Barradall atty for our King demurs to the sd plea the plt joines the demurer & same is cont'd till next court. (Pg 499)

In the suit brought by our Sovereign Lord the King agt Thomas Monteith the def having pleaded in writing, Edward Barradall atty for our King demurs to the sd plea the plt joins the demurer & the same is cont'd till next court. (Pg 499)

Judgment is renewed by scire facias to our Sovereign Lord the King agt Jonathan Williams for 50 shillings which is ord'd to be paid with cost & one atty fee. (Pg 500)

Judgment is renewed by scire facias to our Sovereign Lord the King agt William Hensley for 50 shillings which is ord'd to be paid with cost & one atty fee. (Pg 500)

In the suit brought by Edward Barradall agt Charles Seale the def pleads he owes nothing the plt joins the issue & the same lyes till next court for tryal. (Pg 500)

In the suit brought by Saml Skinker agt Esdras Theodor Edzard the def pleads & demurs the plt has time till next court to consider it. (Pg 500)

The petition exhibited by Thomas Welch agt Thomas Riphley is dismist. (Pg 500)

Special imparlance is granted to John Popham in the information brought agt him by our Sovereign Lord the King. (Pg 500)

In the suit brought by Josiah Farguson agt John Diskin the plt has liberty to mend his declaration paying the def 15 pence special imparlance is granted the def in the sd suit. (Pg 500)

Charles Seale came into court & confessed judgment unto Jere Murdock gent for 7,005 lbs of tobacco which is ordered to be paid with cost & one atty fee. (Pg 500)

The ejectione firma between Thomas Thrustout plt & John Brown def is cont'd. (Pg 500)

Judgment is granted unto John Coburn agt Thomas James for 468 ¾ lbs of tobacco which is ord'd to be paid with cost & one atty fee. (Pg 500)

Special imparlance is granted agt William Loney in the suit brought agt him by Thos Stribling. (Pg 500)

In the suit brought by Frans Thornton agt Thos Smith judgment is granted the plt agt the def for 500 lbs of tobacco with cost & one atty fee. (Pg 500)

In the suit brought by Richard Bryant agt Mark Jones, Joseph Berry, John Bourne, Richard Gill, David Seale, Darby Callihan, Thomas Thatcher, John Brown, John Jennings, Jno Diskin, Thomas Stribling, Enoch Berry & Robert Strother was sworne a jury to try the issue joined who having heard the evidences & arguments withdrew & sometime after returned the following verdt (viz) we find that about two years ago the def then being under the wardship of the plt that the def did kill four hogs, shoats or pigs belonging to the plt at several times, Joseph Berry foreman, which verdt is admitted to record & the def has time till next court to consider the sd verdt. (Pg 501)

In the suit brought by William Strother Junr agt Thomas Phillips, Joseph Berry &c was sworne a jury to try the issue joined who having heard the evidences & arguments withdrew & sometime after returned the following verdt (viz) we find for the plt 4,179 lbs of tobacco damage, Joseph Berry foreman, which verdt on the plts motion is admitted to record & judgment is granted the plt agt the def for the sd sum of tobacco which is ordered to be paid with cost & one atty fee. (Pg 501)

The suit brought by Samuel Nubald agt Thomas Williams is dismist. (Pg 501)

Special imparlance is granted agt Richd Gill & Joseph Seamons in the suit brought agt them by Marm Beckwith. (Pg 501)

An alias capias is granted William Wye in the suit brought by him agt George James Dunbar. (Pg 501)

Special imparlance is granted agt William Harper in the suit brought agt him by Phil Cavenaugh. (Pg 501)

Special imparlance is granted Philip Waters in the suit brought by him agt Joseph Read. (Pg 501)

The suit brought by Jeremiah Murdock agt Honour Woffendale is cont'd. (Pg 501)

An alias capias is granted Anthony Hainey in the suit brought by him agt Richard Green. (Pg 501)

An alias capias is granted Mary Harrison in the suit brought by her agt Richard Griffis. (Pg 501)

The suit brought by Saml Skinker agt Henry Jones is dismist. (Pg 502)

The suit brought by Charles Lewis agt William Owens is dismist. (Pg 502)

The suit brought by Daniel French agt Evan Price executor of the will of John Pratt decd is cont'd for the auditors to make their report. (Pg 502)

In the action upon the case between Thomas Smith & Ann Fowke his wife plts & Jeremiah Bronaugh & Rose his wife adminrs with the will annext of John Dinwiddie decd defs by consent of all parties it is ordered that William Strother gent, Benja Berryman, Robert Jones & Richard Bryant or any three of them audit, state & settle all accounts between the plts & the estate of the sd John decd & make their report to the next court. (Pg 502)

In the action upon the case between Thomas Monteith plt & Jeremiah Bronaugh & Rose his wife adminrs with the will annext of John Dinwiddie decd defs the sd suit is ordered to be cont'd till next court to argue the errors & it is ordered that no executions issue for evidences attendance in the sd suit till the sd suit is determined in this court & it is further ordered that the sd suit shall not abate by the death of either of the parties which the sd defs refuse to consent to. (Pg 502)

Ordered that William Thornton gent remove the barr & make such alteration therein as he shall think more convenient & that he remove the stocks & pillory provide hair cloth for the court house floor & build a house of office for the use of the court. (Pg 502)

In the action upon the case between John Washington gent plt & Alexander Turnbald def the def being called & not appearing judgment is granted the plt agt the def & Stephen Bowsing his security for what of the sum sued for in the declaration shall appear to be justly due unless the def appear at the next court & answer the sd action. (Pg 502)

In the action upon the case between John Toward plt & Jonas Williams adminr of George McDaniel decd def the def being called & not appearing judgment is granted the plt agt the def & Thomas Vivion gent sheriff of this co for what of the sum sued for in the declaration shall appear to be justly due unless the def appear at the next court & answer the sd action. (Pg 502)

In the action upon the case between John Williams plt & Saml Hensilly def the def being called & not appearing judgment is granted the plt agt the def & Henry Berry his security for what of the sum sued for in the declaration shall appearing to be justly due unless the def appear at the next court & answer the sd action. (Pg 503)

The petition of William Thatcher to chouse his guardian is cont'd till next court for the depositions John Gilbert & his (*sic*) Mary Tutt & Elizabeth Underwood. (Pg 503)

Then the court adjourned to court in course.

Court held for further examination of Mary Marshall & Hugh Straghan 3 Apr 1730. Present: William Robinson, Nich Smith, Wm Thornton, Joseph Strother, Saml Skinker, Rowld Thornton, gent justices. (Pg 503)

Mary Marshall & Hugh Strahan being committed unto the goal of this co for receiving sundry stolen goods belonging to James Nichols merchant upon hearing the evidence the court is of opinion that they be discharge. (Pg 503)

John Toward & Hugh Strahan came into court & ackn themselves to stand justly indebted to our Sovereign Lord the King in the sum of £40 each of them to be levied on their goods & chattels, lands & tenements if they perform not the condition hereafter required. The condition of this recognizance is such that if the sd Hugh Strahan appear at Wmsburgh at the trial of James Scott & James Dickinson to give his evidence for & on the behalf of our King agt the sd Scott & Dickinson then this obligation to be void. (Pg 503)

Mary Marshall came into court & ackn herself to stand justly indebted to our Sovereign Lord the King in the sum of £40 to be levied on her goods & chattels, lands & tenements if she performs not the condition hereafter required. The condition of this recognizance is such that if the sd Mary Marshall appear at Wmsburgh at the trial of James Scott & James Dickinson to give her evidence for & on the behalf of our King agt the sd Scott & Dickinson then this obligation to be void. (Pg 503)

Court held 1 May 1730. Present: William Robinson, William Thornton, Nicholas Smith, Joseph Strother, Rowld Thornton, William Strother, gent justices. (Pg 504)

Archdell Combes ackn his deed of lease to Mary Tutt which on the motion of William Tutt is admitted to record. (Pg 504)

William Strother gent by virtue of a power of atty from Thomas Riphley & Grace his wife ackn a deed & bond to Wm McBee which on the motion of the sd McBee is admitted to record. (Pg 504)

William Robinson gent ackn his lese & release to Maximilian Robinson gent which on the motion of the sd Maximilian is admitted to record. (Pg 504)

The suit brought by Henry Fitzhugh esqr agt Jeremiah Bronaugh adminr with the will annext of John Dinwiddie decd is cont'd till next court. (Pg 504)

The suit brought by Thomas Davis agt Edward Merret is cont'd. (Pg 504)

Thomas Thatcher & Katherine his wife ackn their lease, release & bond to William Wheeler the sd Katherine being solely & secretly examined confessed her free consent thereto which on the motion of the sd Wheeler is admitted to record. (Pg 504)

Lunsford Lomax gent presented into court a deed from Elizabeth Lomax widow which was proved by the oaths of John Champ, Charles Seale, Richard Jarvis & James Vaughan which on the motion of the sd Lunsford is admitted to record. (Pg 504)

In the action upon the case between John Finlason plt & Adam Christie def upon arguing the demurer the court is of opinion the demurer is not good & judgment per nihil dicit is granted the plt agt the def for what of the sum sued for in the declaration shall appear to be justly due upon a writ of enquiry to be had at the next court. (Pg 504)

The suit brought by Alexr Parker agt Robert Wilson is cont'd. (Pg 504)

The suit brought by Richard Bryant agt Mark Jones is cont'd. (Pg 504)

The suit brought by John Wilson agt Robert Raddish is dismist. (Pg 505)

The suit in chancery between Richard Barns complt & William Skrine respt is cont'd. (Pg 505)

In the attachmt obtained by Thomas Phillips agt Richard Cornelious it is ordered that the sheriff take Rowld Cornelious & him in his safe custody keep till he enter into bond with good & sufficient security that he render an account of the crop belonging to the sd Richard in his hands. (Pg 505)

Robert Engles of Stafford Co being sumoned an evidence by Robert Raddish agt John Wilson it is order'd that the sd Raddish pay the sd Engles for one days attendance for 6 miles coming & going according to law. (Pg 505)

The suit brought by John Savage agt Thomas Riphley is dismist. (Pg 505)

The scire facias brought by our Sovereign Lord the King agt Thomas Harper is cont'd till next court. (Pg 505)

The scire facias brought by our Sovereign Lord the King agt Thomas Monteith is cont'd till next court. (Pg 505)

The action upon the case between Edward Barradall plt & Charles Seale def is cont'd till next court at the plts cost. (Pg 505)

The suit brought by Samuel Skinker agt Esdras Theodor Edzard clk is cont'd till next court. (Pg 505)

On the motion of William Thatcher, Thomas Thatcher is appointed his guardian the sd Thomas together with Thomas Harper ackn their bond for £50 to save the court harmless. (Pg 505)

In the information brought by our Sovereign Lord the King agt John Popham the def being called & not appearing judgment per nihil dicit is granted our King agt the def for what shall appear to be justly due unless the def appear at the next court & answer the sd information. (Pg 505)

In the suit brought by Josiah Farguson agt John Diskin the def pleads in writing the plt has time to consider the sd plea & the same is cont'd till next court. (Pg 505)

The gectione firma between Thomas Thrustout plt & Ann Marsh def is cont'd. (Pg 505)

In the suit brought by Thomas Stribling agt William Loney the def being called & not appearing judgment per nihil dicit is granted the plt agt the def for what of the sum sued for in the declaration shall appear to be justly due unless the def appear at the next court & answer the sd action. (Pg 505)

In the suit brought by Marmaduke Beckwith agt Richard Gill & Joseph Seamons is cont'd till next court. (Pg 505)

In the suit brought by William Wye Junr agt George James Dunbar the def being called & not appearing judgment is granted the plt agt the def & Nicholas Smith gent his security for what of the sum sued for in the declaration shall appear to be justly due unless the def appear at the next court & answer the sd action. (Pg 506)

The suit brought by Phil Cavenaugh agt William Harper is cont'd till next court. (Pg 506)

In the suit brought by Phil Waters agt Joseph Read is cont'd till next court at the defs cost. (Pg 506)

In the suit brought by John Washington agt Alexr Turnbull the def being called & not appearing judgmt per nihil dicit is granted the plt agt the def for what of the sum sued for in the declaration shall appear to be justly due unless the def appear at the next court & answer the sd action. (Pg 506)

The suit brought by Jeremiah Murdock agt Honour Woffendale is cont'd till next court. (Pg 506)

In the suit brought by John Toward agt Jonas Williams adminr of [*blank*] McDonald decd the def being called & not appearing judgment per nihil dicit is granted the plt agt the def for what of the sum sued in the declaration shall appear to be justly due unless the def appear at the next court & answer the sd action. (Pg 506)

The suit brought by John Williams agt Saml Hensilly is con't till next court. (Pg 506)

In the suit brought by Anthony Hainey agt Richard Green the def being called & not appearing judgment is granted the plt agt the def & Thomas Vivion gent sheriff of this co for what of the sum sued for in the declaration shall appear to be justly due unless the def appear at the next court & answer the sd action. (Pg 506)

A plures capias is granted Mary Harrison in the suit brought by her agt Richard Griffis. (Pg 506)

Alias Capias is granted Alexr Carson in the suit brought by him agt Edward Henselly. (Pg 506)

The suit brought by William Sarjant agt Henry Goddard is dismist. (Pg 506)

Special imparlance is granted Richard Ellkins in the information brought agt him by our Sovereign Lord the King. (Pg 506)

Special imparlance is granted William Flowers in the suit brought agt him by our Sovereign Lord the King. (Pg 506)

In the suit in chancery between Ann Bronaugh complt & Jereh Bronaugh respt the respt has time till next (court) to consider the bill. (Pg 507)

The suit brought by Thomas Smith & Ann Fowke his wife agt Jeremiah Bronaugh & Rose his wife adminrs with the will annext of John Dinwiddie decd is cont'd. (Pg 507)

John Edy ackn his lease & release to Thomas Osbourne & Tobias Russell which on the motion of the sd Osbourne is admitted to record. (Pg 507)

In the petition brought by Thomas Vivion gent agt Robert Washington gent it is ordered that Danl White, Joseph Minton & John Gilbert view the road the sd Vivion proposes to turn & make their report to the next court. (Pg 507)

Joseph Berry, John Bradford, Charles Morgan, Garret Smith, John Smith, William Flowers, Saml Hoyle, Robert Strother, Francis Suttle, William Marshall, Joshua Farguson, Samuel Wharton, John Owens, George White, Charles Dean, John Payne & Richard Butler was sworne a grand jury for the body of this co who having received their charge withdrew & sometime after returned several presentments whereupon it is ordered that the several persons (viz) Thomas Williams Junr, Richard Green & Hannah Letich of Hanover Parish, Katherine Taylor, Margaret Carter & Ann Hinson of Sittenbourn Parish be sumoned by the sheriff of this co to answer the presentmts of the grand jury. (Pg 507)

Nicholas Smith & William Thornton gent trustees & directors of the Town of Falmouth ackn a deed for a lott in the sd town numbered 4 to Hancock Lee gent which on the motion of Thomas Turner gent in behalf of the sd Hancock is admitted to record. (Pg 507)

Adam Christie produced an account of £11:10:11 agt the estate of William Pattishall decd & made oath thereto whereupon it is ordered that the sd Christie be paid the sd sum out of the sd estate in the hands of William Strother gent. (Pg 507)

The attachment obtained by Thomas Goosehee agt Patrick Rian the sheriff having returned that he had attached 1 feather bed, 1 pair of blankets, 1 rug, 1 chest, 1 box iron & 1 pail, it is ordered that the sd goods be sold by the sheriff of this co to satisfie the plt the sum of 300 lbs of tobacco & cost. (Pg 507)

In the suit by petition between Daniel French & Margaret his wife agt Evan Price exr of the will of John Pratt decd the auditors having reported (viz) pursuant to an order of King George Co Court dated 7 Nov 1729 & continued from court to court we the subscribers have stated & settled the accounts in difference between the estate of John Pratt decd & Evan Price exr of the will of the sd decd also the accounts in difference between Daniel French & Margaret his wife & find the sd Evan stands indebted to the sd estate the quantity of 38,476 lbs of tobacco, we also find the sd estate indebted to the sd Evan £144:11:3 also £50:0:8, we also find the sd Daniel French & Margaret his wife indebted to the sd estate 2,771 lbs of tobacco & £212:18:8 out of which sd last sums the widows part is to be deducted given under our hands this 1st day of May 1730, Wil Robinson, Nicho Smith, T. Turner. (Pg 507)

Then the court adjourned to court in course.

Court held for proof of publick claims & certifying propositions & grievances 1 May 1730. Present: William Robinson, Nicholas Smith, William Thornton, Joseph Strother, Rowld Thornton, gent justices. (Pg 508)

John Kenyan produced a cert under the hand of William Strother gent for taken up a slave named Aaron belonging to Robert Carter esqr & made oath the sd service was real & bona fide made, done & performed & that no satisfaction had been received for the same which was ordered to be certifyed to the next General Assembly for allowance. (Pg 508)

John Lunsford produced a cert under the hand of Joseph Strother gent for taken up a slave named Tom belonging to the Bristol Iron Works & made oath the sd service was real & bona fide made, done & performed & that no satisfaction had been received for the same which was ordered to be certifyed to the next General Assembly for allowance. (Pg 508)

William Yicklin produced a cert under the hand of William Robinson gent for taken up a servt named Edward Rowell belonging to Thomas Turner gent & made oath the sd service was real & bona fide made, done & performed & that no satisfaction had been received for the same which was ordered to be certified to the next General Assembly for allowance. (Pg 508)

John Gilbert produced a cert under the hand of Thomas Vivion gent for taken up a runaway servant woman named Frances Jaques belonging to Henry Ward & made oath the sd service was real & bona fide made, done & performed & that no satisfaction had been received for the same which was ordered to be certified to the next General Assembly for allowance. (Pg 509)

John Bell produced a cert under the hand of William Strother gent for taken up a runaway slave named Bristol belonging to Bristol Iron Mines & made oath the sd service was real & bona fide made, done & performed & that no satisfaction had been received for the same which was ord'd to be certified to the next General Assembly for allowance. (Pg 509)

Francis Suttle produced a cert under the hand of Joseph Strother gent for taken up a slave named Prince belonging to William Quile & made oath the sd service was real & bona fide made, done & performed & that no satisfaction had been received for the same which was ordered to be certified to the next General Assembly for allowance. (Pg 509)

Robert Finch produced a cert under the hand of Nicholas Smith gent for taken up a runaway servt belonging to William Grant & made oath the sd service was real & bona fide made, done & performed & that no satisfaction had been received for the same which was ordered to be certified to the next General Assembly for allowance. (Pg 509)

Walter Anderson produced a cert under the hand of Samuel Skinker gent for taken up a runaway Negro slave belonging to George Eskridge gent & made oath the sd service was real & bona fide made, done & performed & that no satisfaction had been received for the same which was ordered to be certified to the next General Assembly for allowance. (Pg 509)

Benja Rush produced an account of 2,040 lbs of tobacco agt the co which is ordered to be certified to the next General Assembly for allowance. (Pg 509)

Thomas Turner presented an account of 1,000 lbs of tobacco agt the co which is ordered to be certified to the next General Assembly for allowance. (Pg 509)

Court held 5 Jun 1730. Present: Wm Thornton, Jos Strother, Saml Skinker, Jere Murdock, gent justices. (Pg 510)

William Robinson gent is appointed to take the list of tithables from the lower end of the co up to the mines. (Pg 510)

Samuel Skinker gent is appointed to take the list of tithables from the mines to Kays Swamp. (Pg 510)

William Thornton gent is appointed to take the list of tithables from Kays Swamp to the upper end of the co. (Pg 510)

On the motion of Edward Barradall atty for John Willis infant under the age of 21 agt John Jennings, it is ord'd that the sd Jennings commit no farther wast on the land untill the action depending is determined. (Pg 510)

Administration of the estate of John Ellkin decd is granted unto Elizabeth Ellkin his widdow the sd Elizabeth with John Owens & Henry Berry ackn their bond for £100 for the sd Elizabeth's faithfull administering the sd estate & to save the court harmless. (Pg 510)

James Kay, John Price, Francis Pain & Charles Jones or any three of them being first sworn & appointed to appraise in money the estate of John Ellkins decd that shall be brought to their view & make report to the next court. (Pg 510)

Daniel Frazier a servant boy to Thomas Thatcher is adjudged by the court to be 13 years of age & ord'd to be recorded. (Pg 510)

Duncan McDonald a servt boy to Thomas Thatcher is adjudged by the court to be 12 years of age & ord'd to be recorded. (Pg 510)

David Monroe a servt boy to Rebecca Quidley is adjudged by the court to be 14 years of age & ord'd to be recorded. (Pg 510)

William Stone & Richard Tout two servt boys belonging to Anthony Hainey was brought before the court & the sd Stone was adjudged to be 18 years & the sd Tout to 15 years of age which was ord'd to be recorded. (Pg 510)

Rice Hooe & Katherine his wife ackn their lease & release unto Thomas Turner the sd Katherine being solely examined ackn her free & voluntary consent thereto which on the motion of the sd Turner is admitted to record. (Pg 511)

William Lampton ackn his lease & release unto James Jones which on the motion of the sd Jones is admitted to record. (Pg 511)

Richard Griffis ackn deed of feoffment & bond unto Mary Harrison & Ann Griffis relinquished her right of dower thereto which on the motion of Edward Barradall atty for the sd Mary is admitted to record. (Pg 511)

Thomas Stribling is appointed surveyor of the highways in the room of Robert Benson & it is ord'd that he forthwith keep the same in repair according to law. (Pg 511)

The suit brought by Thomas Monteith agt Jeremiah Bronaugh & Rose his wife adminrs with the will annexed of John Dinwiddie decd is cont'd till next court for a fuller court. (Pg 511)

The accon upon the case between John Finlayson plt & Adam Christie def the plt not prosecuting is ord'd to be dismist. (Pg 511)

The suit brought by Alexander Parker agt Robert Wilson is cont'd for Nicholas Smith gent to return his report & the sd report to be final. (Pg 511)

The suit brought by Henry Fitzhugh esqr agt Jeremiah Bronaugh & Rose his wife the court being divided is cont'd till next court. (Pg 511)

The suit brought by Richard Bryant agt Mark Jones the court being divided is cont'd till next court. (Pg 511)

The motion of Daniel French & Margaret his wife for the sd Margt's dower to be assigned her of the estate of John Pratt decd the court being divided is cont'd till next court. (Pg 511)

Then the court adjourned to court in course.

Court held 3 Jul 1730. Present: Wm Robinson, Nicho Smith, Wm Thornton, Joseph Strother, Rowld Thornton, gent justices. (Pg 511)

William Munro a servant to Joseph Armstrong was adjudged by the court to be 16 years of age which is ord'd to be recorded. (Pg 511)

Alexander Mckenny a servant to Edward Pearle is adjudged by the court to be 16 years of age which is ord'd to be recorded. (Pg 511)

The suit brought by Thomas Davis agt Edward Merret is cont'd till next court. (Pg 512)

In the attachment obtained by Thomas Phillips agt Richard Cornelious the sheriff having returned that he had attached the crop of the sd Richard in the hands of Rowland Cornelious & the sd Rowland being sumoned to this court produced an acct agt the sd Richard & made oath thereto by which sd acct appeared there was nothing due to the sd Richard whereupon the sd attachment is ord'd to be dismist. (Pg 512)

The suit in chancery between Richard Barnes complt & William Skrine respt is cont'd till next court at the complts cost. (Pg 512)

The scire facias brought by our Sovereign Lord the King agt Thomas Harper is cont'd till next court. (Pg 512)

The suit brought by Samuel Skinker gent agt Esdras Theodor Edzard clerk is ord'd to be dismist. (Pg 512)

The information brought by our Sovereign Lord the King agt John Popham is ord'd to be cont'd. (Pg 512)

The suit brought by Josiah Farguson agt John Diskins is ord'd to be cont'd. (Pg 512)

The ejectione firma between Thomas Thrustout plt & Ann Marsh def is cont'd till next court. (Pg 512)

The suit brought by Thomas Stribling agt William Loney is dismist. (Pg 512)

The action upon the case between Thomas Smith & Ann Fowlk his wife plts & Jeremiah Bronaugh & Rose his wife adminrs with the will annexed of John Dinwiddie decd defs is cont'd. (Pg 512)

In the action upon the case between Edward Barradall plt & Charles Seale def, Samuel Wharton, Abraham Kenyan, Jonas Williams, Rush Hudson, Bryant OBannon, John Jennings, Christopher Man, Joseph Armstrong, Richard Gill, Thomas Dickinson, Rowland Cornelious & Alexander Clement were sworne a jury to try the issue who having heard the evidence & arguments of both parties withdrew & sometime after returned the following verdt (viz) we find for the plt £2:1:11, Samuel Wharton foreman, which verdt on the plts motion is admitted to record & judgmt is granted the plt agt the def for the sd sum which is ord'd to be paid with cost & one atty fee. (Pg 512)

In the suit brought by William Wye Junr agt George James Dunbar, Nicholas Smith gent entered himself special bail & pleaded that the def owes nothing the plt joines the issue & the sd suit lies till next court for trial. (Pg 512)

In the action upon the case between Philemon Cavenaugh plt & William Harper def the def has oyer of the acct. (Pg 513)

In the action upon the case between Phillip Waters plt & Joseph Reid def the def pleads in writing & the plt has time till next court to consider the sd plea. (Pg 513)

The suit brought by John Washington agt Alexander Turnbull is cont'd. (Pg 513)

The suit brought by Jeremiah Murdock gent agt Honour Woffendale is dismist. (Pg 513)

The suit brought by John Williams agt Samuel Hensilly is ord'd to be dismist the def agreeing to pay cost & one atty fee. (Pg 513)

In the action of assault between Anthony Hainey plt & Richard Green def the def pleads that it was of his own assault to which the plt replies & says it was of his own proper injury &c & prays it may be enquired of by the country & the def in like manner. (Pg 513)

The suit brought by Mary Harrison agt Richard Griffis is ord'd to be dismist. (Pg 513)

In the information brought by our Sovereign Lord the King agt Richard Ellkins the def pleads not guilty & Edward Barradall atty for our sd King joins the issue & the same lies till next court for trial. (Pg 513)

In the action of trespass between Marmaduke Beckwith plt & Richard Gill & Joseph Seamons defs for damages as is set forth in the declaration to which the defs pleaded severally not guilty, it is therefore ordered by the court that the sheriff of this co do sumon an able jury of the vicinage that is no ways concerned by affinity or consanguinity to any of the parties or in interest to the land in question nor liable to any other just exception to meet on the land in difference on the first Monday in Sep next if fair if not the next fair day who being first sworne by a justice of the peace do together with the surveyor proceed & survey the land of the plt according to the most known ancient & reputed bounds thereof having regard to all lawfull evidences & elder patents that shall be produced & if they find the defs or either of them trespassers that they value the damage & report their proceedings to the next court. (Pg 513)

In the suit in chancery between Ann Bronaugh complt & Jeremiah Bronaugh respt the respt having put in his answer & made oath thereto the complt has time till next court to consider the sd answer. (Pg 513)

In the suit brought by John Clark agt William Flower the plt has leave to mend his declaration & the def has time till next court to consider the same. (Pg 513)

A plures capias is granted unto Alexr Carson in the suit brought by him agt Edward Hensilly. (Pg 513)

Imparlance is granted unto William Peck in the suit brought agt him by William Quoil. (Pg 514)

In the suit brought by John Micou agt Robert Smith the def being called & not appearing judgment is granted the plt agt the def for what of the sum sued for in the declaration shall appear to be justly due unless the def appear at the next court & answer the sd action. (Pg 514)

In the suit brought by John Toward agt Adam Christie the def being called & not appearing judgment is granted the plt agt the def & Hugh French his security for what of the sum sued for in the declaration shall appear to be justly due unless the def appear at the next court & answer the sd action. (Pg 514)

In the suit brought by William Fling agt George Parsons the def being called & not appearing judgment is granted the plt agt the def for what of the sum sued

108

for in the declaration shall appear to be justly due unless the def appear at the next court & answer the sd action. (Pg 514)

The suit brought by James Nicoll agt Angus Mackay the plt not prosecuting is ord'd to be dismist. (Pg 514)

The suit brought agt Isaac Johnson by Robert Thomas is dismist. (Pg 514)

The suit brought by Samuel Hearn agt Jeremiah Brown is dismist. (Pg 514)

The suit brought by William Marshall agt William Knighton is dismist. (Pg 514)

In the suit brought by John Toward agt Thomas Reynolds the def being called & not appearing judgment is granted the plt agt the def & Thomas Vivion gent sheriff of this co for what of the sum sued for shall appear to be justly due unless the def appear at the next court & answer the sd action. (Pg 514)

In the suit brought by Joseph Crouch agt Elizabeth Ellkins adminr of John Ellkins decd the def being called & not appearing judgment is granted the plt agt the def & Thomas Vivion gent sheriff of this co for what of the sum sued for shall appear to be justly due unless the def appear at the next court & answer the sd action. (Pg 514)

Samuel Kendall ackn his lease, release & bond to Jeremiah Murdock gent which on his motion is admitted to record. (Pg 514)

Special imparlance is granted unto Thomas Smith in the suit brought agt him by William Brown. (Pg 514)

In the suit brought by John Brown agt Jeffery Johnson the def being called & not appearing judgment is granted the plt agt the def & Thomas Vivion gent sheriff of this co for what of the sum sued for in the declaration shall appear to be justly due unless the def appear at the next court & answer the sd action. (Pg 515)

In the suit brought by Robert Peck agt John Popham the def being called & not appearing judgment is granted the plt agt the def & Thomas Vivion gent sheriff of this co for what of the sum sued for in the declaration shall appear to be justly due unless the def appear at the next court & answer the sd action. (Pg 515)

The suit brought by William Brown agt Ralph Ellson is dismist. (Pg 515)

An alias capias is granted unto Edward Barradall in the suit brought by him agt Thomas Riphley. (Pg 515)

Joseph Cash & Howard Cash came into court & confessed judgment unto Edward Barradall for 30 shillings which is ord'd to be paid with cost. (Pg 515)

The suit brought by Angus Mackay agt James Nicoll the plt not prosecuting is ord'd to be dismist. (Pg 515)

An alias capias is granted unto Lazarus Tiller in the suit brought by him agt Isaac Johnson. (Pg 515)

The suit brought by Giles Carter agt John Fleming is dismist. (Pg 515)

The suit brought by James Markham agt George Burd is dismist. (Pg 515)

In the suit brought by Joseph Minton agt Samuel Tuson, Thomas Arnold entered himself special bail & imparlance is granted the def in the sd suit. (Pg 515)

Special imparlance is granted unto Thomas Waring in the suit brought agt him by Jeremiah Murdock gent. (Pg 515)

On the motion of Edward Barradall atty for John Willis agt John Jennings the former order prohibiting the sd Jennings from committing wast is cont'd. (Pg 515)

In the suit brought by John Willis Junr agt John Jennings the plt not prosecuting the sd action is nonsuit which is ord'd to be paid with cost & one atty fee. (Pg 515)

Thomas Williams being presented by the grand jury for coming drunk to church the 25th day of Dec last & now being called & not appearing judgment is granted the church wardens of Hanover Parish agt the sd Thomas for 5 shillings which is ordered to be paid with cost. (Pg 516)

Richard Green being presented by the grand jury for coming drunk to church the 25th day of Dec last & now being called & not appearing judgment is granted the church wardens of Hanover Parish agt the sd Richard for 5 shillings which is ordered to be paid with cost. (Pg 516)

The presentment of the grand jury agt Hannah Leitch is dismist. (Pg 516)

Katherine Taylor being presented by the grand jury for bringing a bastard child & now being called & not appearing judgment is granted the church wardens of Sittenbourne Parish agt the sd Katherine for 500 lbs of tobacco & cask which is ordered to be paid. (Pg 516)

Margt Carter being presented by the grand jury for bringing a bastard child & now being called & not appearing judgment is granted the church wardens of Sittenbourne Parish agt the sd Margaret for 500 lbs of tobacco & cask which is ordered to be paid. (Pg 516)

Ann Hinson being presented by the grand jury for bringing a bastard child & now being called & not appearing judgment is granted the church wardens of Sittenbourne Parish agt the sd Ann for 500 lbs of tobacco & cask which is ordered to be paid. (Pg 516)

In the scire facias brought by our Sovereign Lord the King agt Thomas Monteith judgment is renewed for £5 which is ordered to be paid with cost & one atty fee. (Pg 516)

On the motion of William Duff it is ordered that Mary May an infant serve the sd William & Elizabeth his wife the full sum of an indenture whereby she was bound to join John Dinwiddie & Rose his wife. (Pg 516)

Present Samuel Skinker & Jereh Murdock gent.

In the action upon the case between Thomas Monteith plt & Jeremiah Bronaugh & Rose his wife adminrs with the will annexed of John Dinwiddie decd defs, Edward Barradall atty for the defs moved that Thomas Stribling & Anthony Hainey two of the jurys that was sworne to try the issue in the sd suit should be sworne evidences in arguing the errors filed in arrest of judgment which motion of Zachary Lewis atty for the plt objected agt but the courts judgment is that they shall be admitted evidences. (Pg 517)

In the action upon the case between Thomas Monteith plt & Jeremiah Bronaugh & Rose his wife adminrs with the will annext of John Dinwiddie decd defs the jury having returned their verdt the defs filed errors in arrest of judgment the court on arguing the sd errors is of opinion that the fifth exception is error & that no judgment can be founded upon the sd verdt from which judgmt the plt prays an appeal to the 9th day of the next General Court which is granted him he having with Robert Richards entered into bond according to law to prosecute the sd appeal. (Pg 517)

On the motion of Rowland Thornton, Alexander Munro came into court & signed an indenture to serve the sd Rowland 7 years from the 30th day of Apr last. (Pg 517)

Then the court adjourn'd till tomorrow morning 8 o'clock.

Court held 4 Jul 1730. Present: William Robinson, Samuel Skinker, Rowland Thornton, Jeremiah Murdock, Joseph Strother, gent justices. (Pg 517)

The suit brought by Alexander Parker agt Robert Wilson is cont'd. (Pg 517)

In the suit brought by Richard Bryant agt Mark Jones the jury having returned a special verdt the court on arguing the sd verdt is of opinion that the def is not guilty whereupon it is ordered that the sd suit is dismist with cost & one atty fee. (Pg 517)

The suit brought by Henry Fitzhugh esqr agt Jeremiah Bronaugh & Rose his wife adminrs with the will annext of John Dinwiddie decd is cont'd. (Pg 517)

Then the court adjourned to court in course.

Court held 4 Jul 1730 for the examination of Robt Taylor. Present: William Robinson, Joseph Strother, Samuel Skinker, Rowland Thornton, Jeremiah Murdock, gent justices. (Pg 518)

Robert Taylor being committed by Nicholas Smith gent for advising, aiding & abetting Scott Dickenson in the felonious breaking open the store house belonging to Capt William Strother & stealing from thence divers European goods belonging to James Nicolls factor for William Mackay & Company merchants in Inverness, James Scott & James Dickinson being the only evidences produced the court is of opinion that they are not lawfull wits whereupon it is ordered that the sd Taylor be discharged. (Pg 518)

Then the examining court concluded.

Court held 7 Aug 1730. Present: Nicholas Smith, Joseph Strother, Samuel Skinker, William Strother, gent justices. (Pg 518)

Elizabeth Ellkins returned the inventory of the estate of John Ellkins decd which is admitted to record. (Pg 518)

Samuel Green ackn his deed of feofment to Francis Suttle together with the livery & seizing thereon & is admitted to record. (Pg 518)

Martin Gollothan, John Jennings & Giles Carter ackn the bond for £50 for the sd Martin's faithfull administration of the estate of Xopher Pritchett decd. (Pg 518)

112

Robert Wilson, Giles Carter, Joseph Carpenter & John Quisenbury or any three
of them are appointed being first sworne to appraise in mony the estate of
Xopher Pritchett decd & make report thereof. (Pg 518)

John Pope ackn his lease, release & bond to Joshua Farguson & Thos Turner by
vertue of a power of atty from Elizabeth Pope w/o the sd John relinquished her
right of dower & thirds at the comon law in & to the same which on the motion
of the sd Farguson is admitted to record. (Pg 519)

On the petition of Ralph Falkner setting forth that the Main Road that leads by
the Iron Works is prejudiciall to the sd works & praying the same may be turned,
it is ordered that Rowland Thornton gent, Isaac Arnold & Rush Hudson or any
two of them view the road where the sd Falkner proposes to turn it & make their
report to the next court. (Pg 519)

Alexander Mackentosh a servt to John Ambrose is adjudged by the court to be
14 years of age & ordered to be recorded. (Pg 519)

On the motion of Thomas Phillips & he having entered into bond with Richard
Gill his security to our Sovereign Lord the King for 10,000 lbs of tobacco the sd
Thomas Phillips is licenced to keep ordinary on his now dwelling plantation the
year ensuing. (Pg 519)

George Keesee brought Thomas Frankline a servant man before the court to be
adjudged for running away time & expences for taking him up & making oath
that he had paid 350 lbs of tobacco, it is ordered that he serve his sd master for
the same & for 68 days absence according to law. (Pg 519)

The suit brought by Alexander Parker agt Robert Wilson is cont'd. (Pg 519)

The suit brought by Henry Fitzhugh esqr agt Jeremiah Bronaugh & Rose his
wife is cont'd at the plts costs. (Pg 519)

In the scire facias brought by our Sovereign Lord the King agt Thomas Harper
judgment is renewed for £5 which is ordered to be paid. (Pg 519)

In the information brought by our Sovereign Lord the King agt John Popham def
pleads not guilty the plt joins the issue & the same lyes till next court for tryal.
(Pg 519)

The suit brought by Marmaduke Beckwith agt Richard Gill & Joseph Seamons
is cont'd. (Pg 519)

In the suit brought by Thomas Smith & Ann Fowke his wife agt Jeremiah Bronaugh & Rose his wife adminrs with the will annext of John Dinwiddie decd, it is ord'd that Benja Berryman, Robert Jones, Abraham Kenyan & Richard Bryant or any three of them audit, state & settle all accounts & difference between the sd plt & def on the estate of the sd John decd & make report to the next court. (Pg 519)

The suit brought by William Wye agt George James Dunbar is dismist. (Pg 520)

The suit brought by Phillamon Cavenaugh agt Wm Harper is cont'd. (Pg 520)

The suit brought by Phil Waters agt Joseph Read is cont'd. (Pg 520)

The suit brought by John Washington agt Alexr Turnbull is cont'd. (Pg 520)

Special imparlance is granted John Ambrose in the suit brought agt him by Angus Mackay. (Pg 520)

The suit brought by Angus Mackay agt Lunsford Lomax is cont'd. (Pg 520)

Special imparlance is granted Benjamin Rush in the suit brought agt him by Angus Mackay. (Pg 520)

Special imparlance is granted John Branham in the suit brought agt him by Angus Mackay. (Pg 520)

In the suit brought by Thomas Davis agt Edward Merret the plt having obtained a judgment for 30 shillings & cost the def by leave of the court having filed a bill of injunction to stay execution untill the matter be heard in equity the plt has time till next court to consider the sd bill. (Pg 520)

George Parsons & Thomas Dickenson came into court & confessed judgment unto William Fling for 500 lbs of tobacco which is ordered to be paid with cost & one atty fee. (Pg 520)

In the accon upon the case between Josiah Farguson plt & John Diskin def the def having pleaded in writing the plt joins the plea & the suit is referred till next court for tryall. (Pg 520)

In the suit in chancery [?] between Richard Barns complt & Nicholas Smith gent adminr of the goods & chattels of William Skrine decd respdt upon hearing the bill & answer the court are of opinion that the matters in the sd bill contained are not sufficient to set aside the verdt obtained by the sd Wm Skrine agt the sd

Richard Barns at comon law, it is therefore considered by the court & decreed that the sd bill of injunction be dissolved & that the sd Nicholas Smith have the effect of the verdt afsd agt the sd Richard Barns together with the cost in this suit expended. (Pg 520)

In the accon upon the case between Angus Mackay plt & Richard Tutt def the def being called & not appearing the plt on his motion had liberty to mend his declaration & judgment is granted the plt agt the def & Thomas Vivion gent sheriff of this co for what of the sum sued for in the declaration shall appear to be justly due unless the def appear at the next court & answer the sd accon. (Pg 521)

In the accon of trespass & assault between Robert Taylor plt & Angus Mackay def the plt not appearing to give security for his cost nonsuit is granted the def agt the sd Robt which is ordered to be paid with cost & one atty fee. (Pg 521)

The suit brought by John Branham agt John Davis is dismist. (Pg 521)

The suit brought by George Paine agt James Hinson is dismist. (Pg 521)

Special imparlance is granted Howard Cash in the suit brought agt him by Robert Richards. (Pg 521)

The suit brought by Rowland Thornton agt Joseph Bates is dismist. (Pg 521)

The suit brought by Richard Green agt Frans Woffendale is dismist. (Pg 521)

Alias capias is granted William Strother agt Mary Marshall. (Pg 521)

The suit brought by Jeremiah Murdock agt Thomas Waring is cont'd. (Pg 521)

In the accon of debt between Joseph Minton plt & Samuel Tuson def the def being called & not appearing judgmt per nihil dicit is granted the plt agt the def for 750 lbs of tobacco due by bill which is ordered to be paid with cost & one atty fee. (Pg 521)

Special imparlance is granted Isaac Johnson in the suit brought agt him by Lazs Tilly. (Pg 521)

Plures capias is granted Edward Barradall agt Thomas Riphley. (Pg 521)

In the accon of trespass & assault between Robert Peck plt & John Popham def the def being called & not appearing judgmt per nihil dicit is granted the plt agt the def unless the def appear at the next court & answer the sd accon. (Pg 521)

In the accon upon the case between William Brown plt & Thomas Smith def the def pleads in writing & the plt joins it & the sd suit is referred till next court for trial. (Pg 521)

The accon of debt brought by John Micou agt Robert Smith is dismist by consent the def paying cost & one atty fee. (Pg 521)

In the accon upon the case between Joseph Crouch plt & Elizabeth Ellkins def judgmt is granted the plt agt the def for 300 lbs of tobacco which is ord'd to be paid with cost. (Pg 522)

In the accon upon the case between John Toward plt & Thomas Reynolds def judgmt is granted the plt agt the def for what of the sum sued for in the declaration shall appear to be justly due upon a writ of inquiry to be executed at the next court. (Pg 522)

Upon the motion of Evan Price exec of the will of John Pratt decd it is ordered that William Robinson & Nicholas Smith gent & Thomas Turner reinspect the accounts between Danl French & Margaret his wife & the estate of the sd John Pratt decd & make their report to the next court. (Pg 522)

In the accon upon the case between John Toward plt agt Adam Christie def judgment is granted the plt agt the def for what of the sum sued for in the declaration shall appear to be justly due upon a writ of inquiry to be executed at the next court. (Pg 522)

In the accon upon the case between William Quoil plt & Robert Peck def the def pleads not guilty the plt joins it & the same lyes till next court for tryall. (Pg 522)

A plures capias is granted Alexander Carson agt Edward Hensilly. (Pg 522)

In the accon upon the case between John Clark plt & Willm Flowers def the def being called & not appearing judgment per nihil dicit is granted the plt agt the def unless the def appear at the next court & answer the sd accon. (Pg 522)

In the petition between Thomas Vivion gent plt & Robert Washington gent def the viewers having returned their report upon arguing the same the sd petition is ordered to be dismist & that the sd Thomas pay the sd Robert his cost in this suit expended from which judgment the plt prays an appeal to the 9th day of the next General Court which is granted him he having with Thomas Turner entered into bond to prosecute the sd appeal according to law. (Pg 522)

In the accon upon the case between John Ambrose plt & Angus Mackay def the def being called & not appearing the sd suit is ordered to be cont'd till next court for the def to give special bail. (Pg 522)

In the accon of wast between John Willis by Rush Hudson his next friend plt & John Jennings def the sd Rush Hudson is appointed to prosecute the sd suit in behalf of he sd Willis & on the defs motion special imparlance is granted the def till next court. (Pg 523)

In the accon upon the case between Angus Mackay plt & Joseph Read def the def being called & not appearing the plt on his motion has leave to mend his declaration & judgment is granted the plt agt the def for what of the sum sued for in the declaration shall appear to be justly due unless the def appear at the next court & answer the sd accon. (Pg 523)

In the accon of detinue between John Brown plt & Jeffery Johnson def the def pleads that he does not detain the plt joins the issue & it is ordered that a deddimus issue to take the deposition of Ann Marsh. (Pg 523)

In the suit in chancery between Ann Bronaugh complt & Jeremiah Bronaugh respdt the respdt having given in his answer the complt puts in her exceptions to the sd answer & the respdt has time till next court to consider them. (Pg 523)

John Carder of Spotsilvania Co being sumoned an evidence by Richard Barns agt William Skrine & making oath that he had come four times & attended four days on the sd suit & it appearing that he lived 50 miles from the sd court it is ordered that the sd Barns pay the sd Carder for the same according to law. (Pg 523)

Aaron Pinson of Spotsilvania Co being sumoned an evidence by Nicholas Smith gent adminr of the goods & chattels of William Skrine decd agt Richard Barns & making oath that he had come four times & attended four days on the sd suit & it appearing that he lived 45 miles from the sd court it is ordered that the sd Smith pay the sd Pinson for the same according to law together with his ferriages at Seales. (Pg 523)

Then the court adjourned to court in course.

Court held 4 Sep 1730. Present: Nicholas Smith, Joseph Strother, Samuel Skinker, William Strother, gent justices. (Pg 524)

The inventory of the estate of Christopher Pritchett decd is returned & admitted to record. (Pg 524)

Administration on the estate of John Bowling decd is granted unto Judeth his widow the sd Judeth with John Wise ackn their bond of £10 for the sd Judeth's faithfull administration on the sd estate. (Pg 524)

John Kenyan, Rowland Thornton, John Higdon & Humphery Sawyer or any three of them being first sworne are appointed to appraise in mony the estate of John Bowling decd that shall be presented to their view & make report to the next court. (Pg 524)

A deed from under the hand & seale of Samuel Green to Francis Suttle was proved by the oath of Stafford Lightbourn, John Hudson & Francis Woffendale evidences thereto together with the livery & seizing thereon which on the motion of the sd Francis is admitted to record. (Pg 524)

Upon hearing the petition of John Pritchett it appearing to the court that the sd John was by indenture bound to Christopher Pritchett decd & not to his assigns it is therefore ordered that the sd John Pritchett be discharged from the service of the executor of the sd Christopher decd. (Pg 524)

Upon hearing the petition of Henry Williams it appearing to the court that the sd Henry was by indenture bound to Christopher Pritchett decd & not his assigns it is therefore ordered that the sd Henry Williams be discharged from the service of the executor of the sd Christopher decd. (Pg 524)

On the petition of Simon Miller, Thomas Turner is appointed guardian to the sd Simon & it is ordered that John Miller be summoned to the next court held for this co to answer the other pt/o the sd petition. (Pg 524)

On the petition of Ralph Falkner it was last court ordered that Rowland Thornton gent, Isaac Arnold & Rush Hudson or any two of them should view the road proposed to be turned by the sd Ralph & now having returned their report it is ordered that the sd Ralph have liberty to turn the Main Road in the sd petition menconed provided the sd Ralph clear's it according to law. (Pg 525)

In the action upon the case brought by Alexander Parker agt Robert Wilson it being by consent of both partys referred to Nicholas Smith gent who having reported that he found 30 shillings due to the sd Alexander, it is ordered that the sd Robert pay the sd Alexander the sd 30 shillings together with the costs of this suit. (Pg 525)

The suit brought by Henry Fitzhugh agt Jeremiah Bronaugh & Rose his wife adminrs with the will annext of John Dinwiddie decd is cont'd. (Pg 525)

The suit brought by Thomas Davis agt Edward Merret is cont'd. (Pg 525)

The suit brought by Josiah Farguson agt John Diskins is cont'd plts costs. (Pg 525)

The ejectione firma brought by Thomas Thrustout agt Ann Marsh is cont'd. (Pg 525)

In the action of trespass between Marmaduke Beckwith plt & Richard Gill & Joseph Seamons defs for damages as is set forth in the declaration the former order made in this cause not being complied with it is ordered that the sheriff sumon an able jury pursuant to the sd former order to meet on the land in difference on the 2nd Monday in Oct next if fair if not the next fair day who being first sworne by a justice of the peace for the sd co do together with the surveyor of the sd co proceed & survey the land of the plt according to the most known ancient & reputed bounds thereof having regard to all lawfull evidence & elder patents that shall be produced & if they find the defs or either of them trespassers that they value the damage & report their proceedings to the next court. (Pg 525)

In the action upon the case between Thomas Smith & Ann Fowke his wife agt Jeremiah Bronaugh & Rose his wife adminrs with the will annext of John Dinwiddie decd the former in this cause not being complied with is ordered to be cont'd to the next court & that the sd auditors return their report thereto. (Pg 525)

In the action upon the case between Philemon Cavenaugh plt & William Harper def the def pleads in writing & the plt has time till next court to consider the sd plea. (Pg 525)

In the action upon the case between Phillip Waters plt & Joseph Read def the plt replies & the def has time till next court to consider the sd replication. (Pg 525)

In the action upon the case between John Washington plt agt Alexander Turnbull def, Isaac Arnold, Richard Tutt, Thomas Dickenson, Richard Butler, William Peck, William Sommerton, John Jennings, Alexander Clement, Francis Suttle, Francis Woffendale, Thomas Thatcher & Charles Baker were sworne a jury to enquire into the damages who having heard the arguments of both partys withdrew & sometime after returned the following verdt (viz) we find for the def, Isaac Arnold foreman, which verdt is admitted to record & the sd suit is ordered to be dismist with cost. (Pg 526)

In the suit for chancery between Ann Bronaugh complt & Jeremiah Bronaugh respdt the complt having excepted the answer upon arguing the exceptions the court is of opinion that the answer is insufficient & it is ordered that the respondt make a more perfect answer to the next court & that he pay the complt half a crown cost. (Pg 526)

On the motion of Margaret Simmonds a free mulatto woman it is ordered that Rachel Simmond serve William Strother gent till she come to the age of 21 years the sd Rachel being 12 years of age last Oct. (Pg 526)

Judgment is granted unto Nicholas Smith gent agt the estate of Christopher Pritchett decd for the quantity of 2,189 lbs of tobacco which is ordered to be paid with cost in the hands of Martin Gollathan executor of the will of the sd Christopher. (Pg 526)

Present William Thornton gent.

Alexander Turnbull def in an action brought agt him by John Washington made oath in court that the sd Washington refused to trust the sd Alexander but that he did look to Robert Bolling for his pay which on the motion of Edward Barradall atty for the sd John is ordered to be recorded. (Pg 526)

In the information between our Sovereign Lord the King plt & John Popham def, Isaac Arnold, Richard Tutt, Thomas Dickenson, Richard Butler, William Peck, William Summerton, John Jennings, Alexander Clement, Francis Suttle, Francis Woffendale, Thomas Thatcher & Charles Baker were sworne a jury to try the issue joined who having heard the evidence & arguments of both partys withdrew & sometime after returned the following verdt, viz, we find the def not guilty, Isaac Arnold foreman, which verdt is admitted to record & the sd suit is ordered to be dismist. (Pg 526)

George Rust & Sarah his wife ackn their deed of lease & release to Enoch Innis the sd Sarah being solely examined ackn her free consent thereto which on the motion of the sd Enoch is admitted to record. (Pg 527)

In the suit brought by John Clark agt William Flowers the def pleads he owes nothing the plt joins the issue & the same lyes till next court for tryal. (Pg 527)

A plures capias is granted Alexander Carson agt Edward Hensilly. (Pg 527)

The suit brought by William Quoil agt Robert Peck is cont'd. (Pg 527)

The suit brought by John Brown agt Jeffery Johnson is cont'd. (Pg 527)

In the action of trespass & assault between Robert Peck plt & John Popham def the def pleads not guilty the plt joins the issue & the same is referred till next court for tryal. (Pg 527)

The suit brought by Edward Barradall agt Thomas Riphley is dismist. (Pg 527)

In the suit brought by Lazarus Tilly agt Isaac Johnson the def pleads in writing & the plt has time till next court to consider the sd plea. (Pg 527)

On the motion of Charles Seale & he having entered into bond with Benjamin Rush his security to our Sovereign Lord the King for 10,000 lbs of tobacco the sd Charles Seale is licenced to keep ordinary in his now dwelling plantation the year ensuing. (Pg 527)

In the suit brought by Jeremiah Murdock agt Thomas Waring the def pleads he owes nothing the plt joines the issue & the same lyes till next court for tryal. (Pg 527)

William Brown came into court & confessed judgment unto Mosely Battaley for £1:15:6 which is ordered to be paid with costs. (Pg 527)

John Diskin ackn his deed of lease & release to Samuel Skinker gent which on the motion of the sd Samuel is admitted to record. (Pg 527)

In the action upon the case between John Toward plt & Jonas Williams def adminr of George McDaniel decd def, Isaac Arnold, Richard Tutt, Thomas Dickenson, Richard Buttler, William Peck, William Summerton, John Jennings, Alexander Clement, Francis Suttle, Francis Woffendale, Thomas Thatcher & Charles Baker were sworn a jury to enquire into the damages who having heard the argument of both parties withdrew & sometime after returned the following verdt (viz) we find for the plt £1:10, Isaac Arnold foreman, which verdict on the plts motion is admitted to record & judgment is granted the plt agt the estate of the sd George in the hands of the sd Jonas which is ordered to be paid with cost & on the motion of Edward Barradall atty for the def time is granted him till next court to assign errors in arrest of judgment. (Pg 527)

On the motion of Thomas Vivion gent sheriff of this co Charles Seale is admitted under sheriff he having taken the oaths by law appointed & signed the test. (Pg 528)

The suit brought by William Brown agt Thomas Smith is cont'd. (Pg 528)

In the suit by petition between Hugh French plt & Daniel Harper def the def pleaded he owed nothing plt joins the issue upon hearing the arguments of both parties judgment is granted the plt agt the def for 595 lbs of tobacco which is ordered to be paid with cost & one atty fee. (Pg 528)

Jonas Williams adminr of George McDaniel decd produced an account of 1,447 lbs of tobacco agt the estate of the sd McDaniel & made oath thereto which is ordered to be allowed agt the sd estate. (Pg 528)

Whereas it was ordered last Apr Court that the clerk of this co should issue no executions for evidences attendance till the cause depending between Thomas Monteith plt & Jeremiah Bronaugh & Rose his wife adminrs with the will annext of John Dinwiddie decd defs should be determined in this court & whereas the sd suit is now determined in this court by an appeal had last Jul court, on the motion of the clerk of this court it is ordered that he issue executions for such of the respective evidences that shall demand the same. (Pg 528)

Then the court adjourned to court in course.

Court held 2 Sep 1730 for the examination of Peter Robinson. Present: William Robinson, Joseph Strother, Samuel Skinker, Rowland Thornton, William Strother, gent justices. (Pg 528)

Peter Robinson servant to William Thornton gent being committed under the hands & seals of Joseph Strother & Samuel Skinker gent justices for the sd co & charged with buggering of a mare, on hearing the evidence the court is of opinion that the proof is not sufficient to touch his life but there appearing to the court prenant circumstances of his guilty, it is considered by the court & ordered that the sheriff take the sd Peter to the common whiping post & give him 39 lashes on the bare back well laid on & that the sd sheriff commit him again into the goal till next Friday at 2 o'clock & that he then give him 39 lashes more on the bare back & that he be then delivered to his sd master. (Pg 528)

Court held 2 Oct 1730. Present: William Robinson, Joseph Strother, Rowland Thornton, William Strother, gent justices. (Pg 529)

Ordered that the sheriff sumon a sufficient number of men to serve for a grand jury for the body of this co.

Bloomfield Long & Elizabeth his wife ackn their lease, release & bond to Thomas Turner gent the sd Eliza being solely examined confessed her free consent thereto which on the motion of the sd Turner is admitted to record. (Pg 529)

On the petition of Simon Miller son of William Miller decd, John Miller produced an account settled by Thomas Turner gent on behalf of the sd Simon which is ordered to be recorded & it is ordered that the sd John pay the sd Turner the ballance in the sd account for the use of the sd Simon. (Pg 529)

John Miller presented an account agt the whole estate of William Miller decd which is admitted to record. (Pg 529)

Linsfield Sharp ackn his lease, release & bond to Muttoone (Mulloone?) Lewis which on the motion of the sd Lewis is admitted to record. (Pg 529)

Judeth Bowling returned the inventory of the estate of John Bowling decd which is admitted to record. (Pg 529)

In the accon upon the case between John Peyton plt & William Harper def the def being called & not appearing judgment is granted the plt agt the def & Thomas Vivion gent sheriff of this co for what of the sum sued for in the declaration shall appear to be justly due unless the def appear at the next court & answer the sd accon. (Pg 529)

The suit brought by James Markham agt Thomas Blassingham is cont'd. (Pg 529)

The suit brought by Edward Barradall agt William Hensilly is dismist. (Pg 529)

The suit brought by Thomas Vivion agt Jona Williams is dismist. (Pg 529)

The suit brought by Thomas Davis agt Edward Merret is cont'd defs cost. (Pg 529)

The action of trespass between Marmaduke Beckwith plt & Richard Gill & Joseph Simmons defs is cont'd. (Pg 529)

In the attachment between Farguhar Matheson plt & John Watford def the sheriff having attached all the estate of the sd John Watford in the hands of John hall it is ordered that the sd John Hall be sumoned to the next court to answer the same. (Pg 529)

The suit brought by Thomas Smith & uxor agt Jeremiah Bronaugh & uxor is dismist. (Pg 529)

The suit brought by Philemon Cavenaugh agt William Harper the def having pleaded the plt has further time to consider the sd plea. (2nd Pg 529)

In the accon upon the case between Phillip Waters plt & Joseph Read def the def having pleaded in writing the plt demurs to the first pt/o the sd plea & takes issue on the latter part & the def joines his demurer & the suit lyes till next court. (2nd Pg 529)

In the action upon the case between John Toward plt & Jonas Williams adminr of George McDaniel decd def the def having filed errors in arrest of judgment the sd suit is cont'd till next court to argue the sd errors. (2nd Pg 529)

In the suit in chancery between Ann Bronaugh complt & Jeremiah Bronaugh respdt & the respdt having giving in his answer the court is of opinion the sd answer is insufficient & it is ordered that the respdt pay to the complt half a crown & the sd respdt has time till next court to put in a fuller answer. (2nd Pg 529)

The suit brought by Henry Fitzhugh agt Jeremiah Bronaugh is cont'd def costs. (2nd Pg 529)

The suit brought by Josiah Farguson agt John Diskin is cont'd plts costs. (2nd Pg 529)

The ejectione firma brought by Thomas Thrustout agt Ann Marsh is cont'd defs costs. (2nd Pg 529)

The suit brought by John Clark agt William Flowers is cont'd defs cost. (2nd Pg 529)

The suit brought by Anthony Hainey agt Richard Green is cont'd defs costs. (2nd Pg 529)

In the action of trespass & assault between Alexander Carson plt & Edward Hansilly def the def being called & not appearing on the plts motion an attachment is granted him agt the estate of the sd def returnable to the next court. (2nd Pg 529)

124

The suit brought by John Toward agt Adam Christie is cont'd plts costs. (2nd Pg 529)

The suit brought by John Toward agt Thomas Reynolds is cont'd plts costs. (2nd Pg 529)

The suit brought by Robert Peck agt John Popham is cont'd defs costs. (2nd Pg 529)

Thomas Turner gent by vertue of a power of atty under the hand & seale of Jane Ingram proved by the oath of Thomas Grymes relinquished her right of dower & thirds at the comon law to a certain tr of land sold by her husband Tobias Ingram to Samuel Skinker gent which is admitted to record. (2nd Pg 529)

Thomas Turner gent presented into court a power of atty from under the hand & seale of Jeremiah Murdock gent which was proved by the oath of Edward Barradall & admitted to record. (Pg 530)

The suit brought by John Brown agt Jeffery Johnson is cont'd defs cost. (Pg 530)

The suit brought by William Brown agt Thomas Smith is cont'd plts cost. (Pg 530)

The suit brought by Lazarus Tilly agt Isaac Johnson the def having pleaded the plt has further time to consider the sd plea. (Pg 530)

The suit brought by Jeremiah Murdock gent agt Thomas Waring is cont'd. (Pg 530)

The suit brought by Angus Mackay agt Richard Tutt is dismist. (Pg 530)

The suit brought by Angus Mackay agt John Ambrose is dismist. (Pg 530)

The suit brought by Angus Mackay agt Lunsford Lomax is cont'd. (Pg 530)

The suit brought by John Ambrose agt Angus Mackay ... [blank] ... . (Pg 530)

The suit brought by John Willis agt John Jennings is cont'd defs cost. (Pg 530)

The suit brought by Angus Mackay agt Joseph Read is dismist. (Pg 530)

The suit brought by Charles Seale agt Samuel Skinker is cont'd defs cost. (Pg 530)

The suit brought by Robert Richards agt Howard Cash is cont'd defs cost. (Pg 530)

The suit brought by Robert Strother agt Mary Marshall is dismist. (Pg 530)

The suit brought by Richard Bullock agt John Jones is dismist. (Pg 530)

The accon of trespass & assault between Robert Johnson plt & Francis Woffendale def is cont'd. (Pg 530)

In the accon of trespass & assault between John Branham plt & Joseph Wing def the def being called & not appearing judgment is granted the plt agt the def & Mary Brock his security for what of the sum sued for in the declaracon shall appear to be justly due unless the def appear at the next court & answer the sd action. (Pg 530)

The suit brought by Thomas Thatcher agt John Gilbert is dismist. (Pg 530)

In the action of trespass between Maxfield Rose plt & Robert Hughs def the def being called & not appearing judgment is granted the plt agt the def & Simon Hughs his security for what of the sum sued for in the declaration shall appear to be justly due unless the def appear at the next court & answer the sd action. (Pg 530)

The suit brought by William Grant agt John Newbank is dismist. (Pg 530)

The suit brought by Ebenr Ram agt James Lewis is dismist. (Pg 530)

A power of atty under the hand & seale of Elizabeth Diskin to Thomas Turner gent being proved in court by the oath of John Farguson the sd Turner relinquished her right of dower & thirds at the comon law of a certain tr of land sold by her husband John Diskin to Samuel Skinker gent which is admitted to record. (Pg 531)

Richard Bryant being sumoned by the sheriff to tend the court this day for a juryman & being called & not appearing it is ordered that he be fined 5 shillings to our Sovereign Lord the King for the sd contempt which is ordered to be paid with cost. (Pg 531)

Anthony Hainy being sumoned by the sheriff to tend the court this day for a juryman & being called & not appearing it is ordered that he be fined 5 shillings to our Sovereign Lord the King for the sd contempt which is ordered to be paid with cost. (Pg 531)

John Grant being sumoned by the sheriff to tend the court this day for a juryman & being called & not appearing it is ordered that he be fined 5 shillings to our Sovereign Lord the King for the sd contempt which is ordered to be paid with cost. (Pg 531)

John Fox being sumoned by the sheriff to tend the court this day for a juryman & being called & not appearing it is ordered that he be fined 5 shillings to our Sovereign Lord the King for the sd contempt which is ordered to be paid with cost. (Pg 531)

In the suit by petition between Daniel French & Margaret his wife agt Evan Price executor of the will of John Pratt decd the auditors having reinspected the accounts in difference & made their report as followeth (viz) pursuant to an order of King George Co Court dated 7 Aug last we the subscribers have reinspected the accounts in difference between the estate of John Pratt decd & Evan Price executor of the will of the sd decd also the accounts in difference between Daniel French & Margaret his wife & the sd estate & find the sd Evan stands indebted to the sd estate the quantity of 34,485 lbs of tobacco, we also find the sd estate indebted to the sd Evan £144:11:3 & £52:5:8, we also find the sd Daniel French & Margaret his wife indebted to the sd estate 9,181 lbs of tobacco & the sum of £215:15:8 out of which sd sum of 9,181 lbs of tobacco & £215:15:8 the widows part is to be deducted for the sd Margaret, given our hands this 28 Sep 1730, William Robinson, Nicho Smith, T. Turner. (Pg 531)

In the action of trespass upon the case between William Quoill plt & Robert Peck def, Richard Tutt, Thomas Dickenson, John Jennings, John Sharp, Samuel Hoyle, Fras Woffendale, Fras Triplet, Thomas Thatcher, Robert Johnson, Alexander Clement, Darby Calliham & Richard Butler were sworne a jury to try the issue joined who having heard the evidence & arguments of both partys withdrew & sometime after returned the following verdict (viz) we find for the def, Richard Tutt foreman, which verdt on the defs motion is admitted to record & the sd suit is ordered to be dismist with cost & one atty fee. (Pg 532)

Then the court adjourned to court in course.

Court held 6 Nov 1730. Present: Nicholas Smith, William Thornton, Joseph Strother, Samuel Skinker, William Strother, gent justices. (Pg 532)

Elizabeth Kitchen ackn her deed to Margaret Tutt which on the motion of the sd Tutt is admitted to record. (Pg 532)

Samuel Wharton ackn his deed of lease & release to Robt Johnson & Ann w/o the sd Samuel relinquished her right of dower & thirds at the comon law in & to the same which on the motion of the sd Robert is admitted to record. (Pg 532)

Thomas Conway ackn his deed to Bryant Bredin which on the motion of the sd Bryant is admitted to record. (Pg 532)

William Morton ackn his deed together with the livery & seizing to John Piper & Samuel Reeds by virtue of a power duely proved in court from Ann Morton w/o the sd William relinquished her right of dower & thirds at the comon law in & to the same which on the motion of the sd John is admitted to record. (Pg 532)

William McBee ackn his deeds of lease & release to Emanuel Cumbee & James McDonnel by virtue of a power of atty duely proved in court from Susanah w/o the sd William relinquished her right of dower & thirds at the comon law in & to the same which on the motion of the sd Cumbee is admitted to record. (Pg 532)

Thomas Welch ackn his deeds of lease & release to Samuel & Jeremiah Bronaugh & William Strother gent & John Wright by virtue of a power of atty duely proved in court from Doras Welch w/o the sd Thomas relinquished her right of dower & thirds at the common law in & to the same which at their motion is admitted to record. (Pg 532)

Benjamin Rush by virtue of a power of atty under the hand & seale of Rosemond Steward relinquished her right of dower & thirds at the common law to a certain parcel of land sold by her husband John Steward to Joseph Steward which is admitted to record. (Pg 533)

James Kay ackn his deeds of lease & release to Saml Skinker gent & Mary w/o the sd James relinquished her right of dower & thirds at the common law in & to the same which on the motion of the sd Skinker is admitted to record. (Pg 533)

An order of this court dated 5 Dec 1724 together with a report of Nicholas Smith gent was presented into court by William Jett (viz) pursuant to the within order I did within a few days after the date thereof state & settle all the accounts therein menconed & found yet remaining £11:11:6 of the estate of Francis Jett in the hands of his son William Jett, Nicholas Smith. (Pg 533)

William Strother gent presented into court a power of atty from under the hand & seale of Angus Mackay, the same being proved by the oath of Nicholas Smith & Edward Barradall gent which is admitted to record. (Pg 533)

In the suit in chancery between Ann Bronaugh complt & Jeremiah Bronaugh respdt the respdt gave in his answer & made oath thereto & the complt has time till next court to consider the sd answer. (Pg 533)

On the motion of Walter Anderson & he having entered in bond with William Harrison his security to our Sovereign Lord the King for 10,000 lbs of tobacco the sd Walter Anderson is licenced to keep ordinary in his now dwelling plantation the year ensuing. (Pg 533)

William Lampton, John Grigsby & Ann his wife ackn their deeds of lease & release to James Jones the sd Ann being solely examined confessed her free consent thereto which on the motion of the sd Jones is admitted to record. (Pg 533)

Jacob Hubard brought Alexander Mackenny a servant man before the court to be adjudged for runaway time & expences in taking him up & produced an account of £6 & made oath thereto, it is ordered that the sd Mckenny serve the sd Hubard or his assigns for the sd term after the rate of 100 lbs of tobacco for every 10 shillings after his time by indenture custom or hire expired together with the cost according to law. (Pg 533)

Francis Triplet brought John Nun a servant man before the court & produced an account of 375 lbs of tobacco & 10 shillings & made oath thereto, it is ordered that the sd Nun serve the sd Triplet for the same & for 17 days absence according to law after his time by indenture, custom or hire is expired together with his cost. (Pg 534)

Thomas Smith & Ann Fowke his wife ackn their deed to Henry Willis gent the sd Ann being solely examined confessed her free consent thereto which on the motion of the sd Willis is admitted to record. (Pg 534)

King George Co. To Edward Abbot for 5 wolves heads, Daniel Marr for 5 ditto, Lunsfield Sharp & John Sharp for counting tobacco plants, Samuel Skinker gent for 3 inquests, John Bourne his acct, Edward Barradall a Westmoreland clks note, ditto for Kings atty, Thomas Turner his acct, ditto clerk of co, Walter Anderson his acct, William Stringfellow his acct, Benja Rush his acct, Thomas Jefferies his acct, William Longmire & Henry Taylor for watching the prison, James Jones his acct. 13,130 lbs tobacco. Credits by William Strother gent for credit to this co by the country & ordered in King William Co, by increase of tithables. It is ordered that every tithable person in this co pay to the sheriff 1 lb of tobacco to discharge the co levy & that the sheriff pay the same to the respective creditors according to law. (Pg 534)

It is ordered that Isaac Arnold be surveyor of the Forest Road from Moons Quarter to Fagans Pine & that he forthwith keep the same in repair according to law. (Pg 534)

Ordered that Rowland Thornton gent be surveyor of the Forest Road from Fagans Pine to William Duff's & that he forthwith keep the same in repair according to law. (Pg 534)

Ordered that Samuel Skinker gent be surveyor of the Forest Road from William Duff's to Robert Strother's. (Pg 534)

Ordered that John Champe be surveyor of the Forest Road from Robert Strother's to the Widow Steward's. (Pg 535)

Ordered that John Farguson be surveyor of the Forest Road from Widow Steward's (the best way) into the Main Road by James Jones & that he forthwith keep the same in repair according to law. (Pg 535)

It is ordered that William Strother gent receive from the sheriff of Accomack Co what tobacco is levied in the sd co for this co & that he dispose of the same as he shall think convenient. (Pg 535)

John Farguson, Jeremiah Strother, Max Brown, Thomas Dickeson, Samuel Reeds, John Triplet, John Pain, George Franklin, Giles Carter, John Steward, John Owens, John Smith, Richard Rosser, Jonas Williams, Richard Butler, William Grant, Samuel Hoyle, Rowland Thornton & John Sharp being swore a grand jury for the body of this co & having received their charge withdrew & sometime after returned the following presentments. (Pg 535)

We present Katherine Store (or Hore?) alias Nash of Hanover Parish for having a bastard child sometime in the month of Jun last past. (Pg 535)

Wee present Elizabeth Hickman of Hanover Parish for having a bastard child sometime in the month of Jul last past by the informacon of Robert Peck. (Pg 535)

Wee present Richard Griffis of Hanover Parish for retailing liquour contrary to law at the Race Ground in Mr. Tarjants old field sometime in the month of Sep last. (Pg 535)

We present Joseph Reed of Sittenbourn Parish for being drunk this present day. (Pg 535)

130

We present William Welsh of Hanover Parish for being drunk & swearing one oath sometime in the month of Oct last past. (Pg 535)

We present John McDaniel of Hanover Parish for retailing liquor contrary to law in his own house sometime in Sep last past. (Pg 535)

We present Daniel McKenny of Hanover Parish for retailing liquor contrary to law in his own house sometime in the month of Oct last past. (Pg 535)

Ordered that Katherine Nore (*sic*) alias Nash, Eliza Hickam, Richard Griffis, Joseph Read (*sic*), William Welch, John McDaniel, Daniel McKenny be sumoned to the next court to answer the sd presentments. (Pg 535)

Then the court adjourned to court in course.

Court held 4 Dec 1730. Present: William Robinson, William Thornton, Rowland Thornton, William Strother, gent justices. (Pg 536)

An additional inventory of the estate of Jonathan Gibson gent decd was presented into court & admitted to record. (Pg 536)

George Tankersley presented into court a deed of gift from Henry Long Senr which on his motion is admitted to record. (Pg 536)

Ordered that John Turner an orphan boy being 13 years old the 15th of Feb serve Robert Richards & his assigns till he come to the age of 21 years the sd Robert Richards promising in open court that the sd John shall be learned to read & write & at the expiration of the sd term to pay him such freedom dues as the law directs to servants imported. (Pg 536)

The suit in chancery between Edward Merret complt & Thomas Davis respdt is cont'd at the complt costs. (Pg 536)

Present Joseph Strother gent.

In the action upon the case between Henry Fitzhugh esqr plt & Jeremiah Bronaugh & Rose his wife adminrs with the will annext of John Dinwiddie decd defs the defs having pleaded fully administred, Richard Bryant, John Gilbert, Thomas Dickenson, William Peck, Robert Johnson, William Strother, Neal McCormack, John Farguson, John Price, Henry Berry, Rush Hudson & Robert Strother were sworn a jury to try the issue joined who having heard the evidence & arguments of both parties withdrew & sometime after returned the following verdt (viz) we find assetts in the defs hand 4,980 lbs of tobacco,

Richard Bryant foreman, which verdt on the plts motion is admitted to record & judgment is granted the plt agt the estate of the sd John in the hands of the sd defs for the sum of 1305 lbs of tobacco or so much to be found if not out of the estate of the sd Jeremiah which is ordered to be paid with cost. (Pg 536)

In the action upon the case between Josiah Farguson plt & John Diskin def, Richard Bryant, John Gilbert, Thomas Dickenson, William Peck, Robert Johnson, William Strother, Neal McCormack, John Farguson, John Price, Henry Berry, Rush Hudson & Robert Strother were sworne a jury to try the issue joined who having heard the evidence & arguments of both parties withdrew & sometime after returned the following verdt (viz) we find for the plt £4:10, Richard Bryant foreman, which verdt on the plts motion is admitted to record & judgment is granted the plt agt the def which is ordered to be paid with cost & one atty fee. (Pg 536)

The suit brought by John Branham agt Angus Mackay the def pleads in writing & the plt has time till next court to consider the sd plea. (Pg 537)

John Farguson being sumoned as an evidence by Josiah Farguson agt John Diskin & making oath that (he) attended three days, it is ordered that the sd Josiah pay the sd John for the same with cost according to law. (Pg 537)

Baldwin Matthews ackn his lease, release & bond to John Champ gent which on the motion of the sd Champ is admitted to record. (Pg 537)

Sambo a Negro man belonging to Mark Jones now in the possession of Richard Bryant being committed under the hand & seale of William Thornton gent & charged with stealing a hog from Thomas Smith upon examination the sd Sambo confessed the fact, it is ordered that the sheriff take the sd Sambo & carry him to the common whipping post & give him 39 lashes on the bare back well laid on & that he be delivered to his sd master. (Pg 537)

The suit brought by Philemon Cavenaugh plt & William Harper def the plt has leave to mend his declaracon & account the def pleads he did not assume & the plt has time till next court to consider the sd plea. (Pg 537)

Timothy Reading ackn his lease & release to John Tayloe & Company & Thomas Turner by virtue of a power of atty duely proved in court from Sarah w/o the sd Timothy relinquished her right of dower in & to the same which on the motion of John Champ gent on behalf of the sd Tayloe & Company is admitted to record. (Pg 537)

The suit in chancery between Ann Bronaugh complt & Jeremiah Bronaugh respdt the respdt having put in his answer the complt has further time to consider the sd answer. (Pg 537)

The suit brought by Lazs Tilly plt agt Isaac Johnson def the plt demurs def has time till next court to consider the demurer. (Pg 537)

Special imparlance is granted Lunsford Lomax in the suit brought agt him by Angus Mackay. (Pg 537)

The suit brought by Angus Mackay agt Benja Rush the def pleads in writing plt has time till next court to consider the sd plea. (Pg 537)

John Cannon being sumoned an evidence for Josiah Farguson agt John Diskin & making oath he attended three days on the sd suit it is ordered that the sd Farguson pay the sd Cannon for the same with cost according to law. (Pg 537)

In the accon of trespass & assault between Alexander Carson plt & Edward Hemsilly def the def being called & not appearing judgmt is granted the plt agt the def for what of the sum sued for in the declaracon shall appear to be justly due upon a writ of inquiry to be executed next court. (Pg 537)

In the ejectione firma between Thomas Thrustout plt & Ann Marsh def, Richard Bryant, John Gilbert, Thomas Dickenson, William Peck, Robert Johnson, William Strother, Neal McCormack, John Farguson, John Price, Henry Berry, Rush Hudson & Robert Strother were sworn a jury to try the issue who having heard the evidence & arguments of both parties withdrew & sometime after returned the following verdt (viz) we find a proprietors deed for 541 a. of land in King George Co granted to John Brown 8 Apr 1723, we find a plat of the sd land under the hand of John Copedge dated 22 Jan 1722/3, we find a lease in writing under the hand of John Brown the lessor of the plt dated 25 Jan 1724 for 100 a. of the sd land made to George Mash & Ann his wife the now def for the term of 21 years, we find a counterpart of the sd lease under the hands & seals of George Mash & Ann Mash dated the same day & year, we find John Brown procured 100 apple trees for the sd George & Ann Marsh to plant on the plantation, we find the sd George & Ann Mash have planted out seventy odd apple trees & have as many in a nursery as will make up 100, we find the sd Ann Mash has barked five while oaks for tanning her own leather, we find the sd plantation of the def is on the n side of Browns Run & within 200 & odd strides of commons line, if upon the whole the court shall adjudge the law be with the plt we find for him 1 shilling damage otherwise we find for the def, Richard Bryant foreman, which verdt is admitted to record & the plt has time till next court to consider the sd verdict. (Pg 538)

Darby Callihan being sumoned an evidence by Ann Mash agt Thomas Thrustout making oath that he attended seven days on the sd suit it is ordered that the sd Mash pay the sd Callihan for the same with cost according to law. (Pg 538)

James McDaniel being sumoned an evidence by Thomas Thrustout agt Ann Mash & making oath that he attended seven days on the sd suit it is ordered that the sd Thrustout pay the sd McDaniel at the rate of 30 lbs of tobacco per day with cost according to law. (Pg 538)

Christopher Man being sumoned an evidence by Thomas Thrustout agt Ann Mash & making oath that he attended seven day son the sd suit it is ordered that the sd Thrustout pay the sd Man at the rate of 30 lbs of tobo per day with cost according to law. (Pg 538)

Alexander Clement being sumoned an evidence by Thomas Thrustout agt Ann Mash & making oath that he attended seven days on the sd suit it is ordered that the sd Thrustout pay the sd Clement at the rate of 30 lbs of tobacco per day with cost according to law. (Pg 538)

John Hammons being sumoned an evidence by Ann Mash agt Thomas Thrustout & making oath that he attended three days on the sd suit it is ordered that the sd Mash pay the sd Hammons for the same at the rate of 30 lbs of tobacco per day with cost according to law. (Pg 538)

Court held 5 Dec 1730. Present: William Robinson, Joseph Strother, Rowland Thornton, William Thornton, gent justices. (Pg 539)

The suit brought by Marmaduke Beckwith agt Richard Gill & Joseph Seamons is cont'd. (Pg 539)

The suit brought by Philip Waters agt Joseph Read, John Champ, William Duling, Robert Johnson, John Price, Thomas Dickenson, Rush Hudson, Robert Peck, Richard Gill, Charles Baker, Robert Wilson, John Jennings & Anthony Hainey were sworn a jury to try the issue joined who having heard the evidence & arguments of both partys withdrew & sometime (after) returned the following verdt (viz) we find for the plt £1:13:9 & 1,200 lbs of tobacco, John Champ foreman, which verdt on the plts motion is admitted to record & judgment is granted the plt agt the def which is ordered to be paid with cost & one atty fee. (Pg 539)

The suit brought by John Clark agt William Flowers is dismist. (Pg 539)

The suit brought by John Toward agt Jonas Williams is dismist. (Pg 539)

The suit brought by John Toward agt Adam Christie is cont'd. (Pg 539)

In the accon of trespass & assault between Anthony Hainy plt & Richard Green def, John Champe, Richard Elkins, William Duling, Jeffery Johnson, Thomas Dickison, John Jennings, Rush Hudson, Robert Peck, Evan Price, Richard Gill, Charles Baker & Robert Willson were sworne a jury to try the issue joined who having heard the evidence & arguments withdrew & sometime after returned the following verdt (viz) we find for the plt 25 shillings, John Champ foreman, which verdict on the plts motion is ordered to be recorded & judgment is granted the plt agt the def which is ordered to be paid with cost & one atty fee. (Pg 539)

Ordered that Richard Green give bond & security in the sum of £40 for his being of the good behaviour for a year & a day next coming & that he remain in custody till bond given. (Pg 539)

In the informacon brought by our Sovereign Lord the King agt Richard Ellkins, John Champ, William Duling, Robert Peck, Richard Gill, Charles Baker, Robert Wilson, John Jennings, John Price, Robert Johnson, Thomas Dickeson, Rush Hudson & Anthony Hainy were sworne a jury to try the issue joined who having heard the evidence & arguments of both partys withdrew & sometime after returned the following verdt, we find the def guilty of retailing liquors contrary to the within mentioned Acts of Assembly, John Champe foreman, the def having liberty to file errors in arrest of judgmt on arguing the sd errors the court is of opinion the informacon is uncertain & that no judgment can be founded thereon whereupon the sd informacon is ordered to be dismist. (Pg 539)

The suit brought by William Quoil agt Robert Peck is dismist. (Pg 539)

Judgment is granted unto John Toward agt Thomas Reynolds for 500 lbs of tobacco which is ordered to be paid with cost & one atty fee. (Pg 539)

Richard Bryant being summoned an evidence by Anthony Hainy agt Richard Green & making oath that he attended five days on the sd suit it is ordered that the sd Hainy pay the sd Bryant for the same at 30 lbs of tobacco per day with cost. (Pg 540)

Robert Johnson being sumoned an evidence by Richard Green agt Anthony Hainy & making oath he attended six days on the sd suit it is ordered that the sd Green pay the sd Johnson for the same at 30 lbs of tobacco per day with cost. (Pg 540)

In the accon of detinue between John Brown plt & Jeffery Johnson def, John Champe, William Duling, Robert Peck, Richard Gill, Charles Baker, Robert

Wilson, John Jennings, Jno Price, Robert Johnson, Thomas Dickeson, Rush
Hudson & Anthony Hainy were sworne a jury to try the issue joined who having
heard the evidence & arguments of both partys withdrew & sometime after
returned the following verdt (viz) we find for the def, John Champ foreman,
which verdict on the defs motion is admitted to record & the sd suit is ordered to
be dismist with cost. (Pg 540)

Charles Baker being summoned an evidence by Jeffery Johnson agt John Brown
& making oath he attended five days on the sd suit it is ordered that the sd
Johnson pay the sd Baker for the same at 30 lbs of tobacco per day with cost.
(Pg 540)

Thomas Hampton being sumoned an evidence by Jeffery Johnson agt John
Brown & making oath he attended five days on the sd suit it is ordered that the
sd Johnson pay the sd Hampton for the same at 30 lbs of tobacco per day with
cost. (Pg 540)

Jacob Jacobs being sumoned an evidence by John Brown agt Jeffery Johnson &
making oath he attended two days on the sd suit it is ordered that the sd Brown
pay the sd Jacobs for the same at 30 lbs of tobacco per day with cost. (Pg 540)

In the accon of trespass & assault between Robert Peck plt & John Popham def,
John Champ, William Duling, Richard Ellkins, Richard Gill, Charles Baker,
Robert Wilson, John Jennings, John Price, Robert Johnson, Thomas Dickeson,
Rush Hudson & Anthony Hainy were sworne a jury to try the issue joined who
having heard the evidence & arguments of both partys withdrew & sometime
after returned the following verdt (viz) we find for the def, John Champ
foreman, which verdt on the defs motion is admitted to record & the sd suit is
ordered to be dismist with cost. (Pg 540)

Benjamin Strother being sumoned an evidence by John Popham agt Robt Peck
& making oath he attended three days on the sd suit it is ordered that the sd
Popham pay the sd Strother for the same at 30 lbs of tobacco per day with cost.
(Pg 540)

Francis Woffendale being sumoned an evidence by John Popham agt Robert
Peck & making oath he attended three days on the sd suit it is ordered that the sd
Popham pay the sd Woffendale for the same at 30 lbs of tobacco per day with
cost. (Pg 540)

Henry Reins of Spotsilvania Co being sumoned an evidence by Philip Waters
agt Joseph Read & having attended two days on the sd suit & it appearing he

lived 15 miles from the sd court it is ordered that the sd Waters pay the sd Reins for the same with his ferriage at Seals according to law. (Pg 540)

John Lee being sumoned an evidence by John Brown agt Jeffery Johnson & being called & failing to appear it is ordered that the sd Lee be fined according to law unless he appear at the next court to shew cause why he failed this. (Pg 540)

Robert Wilson being sumoned an evidence by Philip Waters agt Joseph Read & having attended two days on the sd suit it is ordered that the sd Waters pay the sd Read for the same at 30 lbs of tobacco per day with cost. (Pg 540)

In the suit by petition between Daniel French & Margaret his wife plts & Evan Price executor of the will of John Pratt decd def the auditors having returned their report it is ordered that the tobacco menconed in the sd report be valued at 10 shillings per cent & it is also ordered that 1/3 pt/o the estate of the sd John decd be set apart for the sd Margaret from which judgmt the sd Evan prays an appeal to the 9th day of the next General Court which is granted him he having with John Popham entered into bond to prosecute the sd appeal according to law. (Pg 541)

Then the court adjourned to court in course.

Court held 5 Feb 1730. Present: William Thornton, Joseph Strother, Samuel Skinker, William Strother, gent justices. (Pg 541)

Ordered that Richard Griffis be sumoned to answer the informacon of our Sovereign Lord the King. (Pg 541)

Ordered that John McDaniel be sumoned to answer the informacon of our Sovereign Lord the King. (Pg 541)

Ordered that Daniel McKenny be sumoned to answer the informacon of our Sovereign Lord the King. (Pg 541)

Ordered that Robert Rankins be surveyor of the Forest Road from William Duff's to Robert Strother's & that he forthwith keep the same in repair according to law. (Pg 541)

Ordered that John Champe be surveyor of the Forest Road from Robert Strother's to the Rolling Road by Benjamin Rush's & that he forthwith keep the same in repair according to law. (Pg 541)

Administration of the estate of Barbare Kersey decd is granted unto Daniel McKensay & Dorothy his wife the sd Daniel with Edward Pearle & James Williams ackn their bond of £50 for the sd Daniel & Dorothy's faithfull administracon of the sd estate. (Pg 541)

William Welch, Richard Butler, John Glendening & James Grant being first sworn are ordered to appraise in mony the estate of Barbare Kersey decd that shall be presented to their view & make their report to the next court. (Pg 541)

In the suit in chancery between Edward Merret complt & Thomas Davis respdt the respdt having filed his answer the complt has time till next court to consider the sd answer. (Pg 541)

Ordered that Lazs Dameron be surveyor of the highway from the lower side of Deep Run to the upper end of the Red Oak Quarter & that he forthwith keep the same in repair according to law. (Pg 541)

Ordered that Richard Gill be surveyor of the highway from the lower side of Deep Run to the lower side of the Horsepen Run & that he forthwith keep the same in repair according to law. (Pg 541)

Ordered that Robert Doniphan be sumoned to the next court to answer the petition of William Cave & Joseph Waugh. (Pg 542)

In the ejectione firma between Thomas Thrustout plt & Ann Mash def the plt not prosecuting the sd suit is ordered to be dismist with cost & one atty fee. (Pg 542)

The suit brought by Marmaduke Beckwith plt & Richard Gill & Joseph Seamons defs the court being divided is ordered to be cont'd till next court. (Pg 542)

In the suit between Philemon Cavenaugh plt agt William Harper def the def pleads he did not assume the plt joins the issue & the same lyes till next court for tryall. (Pg 542)

In the accon of trespass & assault between Alexander Carson plt & Edward Hensilly def, Richard Bryant, Samuel Hoyle, Thomas Steward, Jonas Williams, Joseph Berry, Robert Strother, John Price, Richard Elkins, John Steward, Robert Richards, Giles Carter & John Triplet were sworne a jury to try the issue who having heard the evidence & arguments of both parties withdrew & some time after returned the following verdt (viz) we find for the plt £5, Richard Bryant foreman, which verdict on the plts motion is admitted to record & judgment is granted the plt agt the def for the sd sum of £5 which is ordered to be paid with cost & one atty fee & it appearing by the return of the sheriff that he has attached all the estate of the sd Edward in the hands of Samuel Hensilly it is ordered that the sd Samuel has time till next court to finish the defs crop. (Pg 542)

The suit brought by John Toward agt Adam Christie is cont'd. (Pg 542)

The suit brought by William Brown agt Thomas Smith is cont'd plts cost. (Pg 542)

The suit brought by Lazs Tilly agt Isaac Johnson the plt having demur'd to the defs plea the def joins it & the same lyes till next court to be argued. (Pg 542)

In the accon of debt between Jeremiah Murdock gent plt & Thomas Waring gent def, Richard Bryant, Samuel Hoyle, Thomas Steward, Jonas Williams, Joseph Berry, Robert Strother, John Price, Richard Ellkins, John Steward, Robert Richard, Giles Carter & John Triplet were sworne a jury to try the issue joined who having heard the evidence & arguments of both parties withdrew & sometime after returned the following verdt (viz) we find for the def, Richard Bryant foreman, which verdt on the defs motion is admitted to record & the sd suit is ordered to be dismist with cost & one atty fee. (Pg 542)

The suit brought by Angus Mackay agt Lunsford Lomax is cont'd. (Pg 542)

The suit brought by Angus Mackay agt Benjamin Rush is cont'd. (Pg 542)

The accon of wast brought by John Willis agt John Jennings the def having pleaded in writing the plt has time till next court to consider the sd plea. (Pg 542)

The suit brought by Robert Richards agt Howard Cash the plt not prosecuting is dismist. (Pg 542)

The suit brought by John Branham agt Joseph Wing the plt not prosecuting is dismist. (Pg 542)

The suit brought by Robert Johnson agt Francis Woffendale the plt not prosecuting is dismist. (Pg 542)

In the accon of trespass upon the case between Daniel McDonald plt & George Mackay def the def being called & not appearing judgment is granted the plt agt the def & Thomas Vivion gent sheriff of this co for what of the sum sued for in the declaracon shall appear to be justly due unless the def appear at the next court & answer the sd accon. (Pg 542)

Special imparlance is granted Robert Hughs in the suit brought agt him by Max(field) Rose. (Pg 542)

The suit brought by John Peyton agt William Harper the plt not prosecuting is dismist. (Pg 542)

The suit brought by Farqhar Matheson agt John Watford the plt not prosecuting is dismist. (Pg 543)

The suit brought by John Grant agt Thomas Magee the plt not prosecuting is dismist. (Pg 543)

The suit brought by John Fox agt Isaac Johnson the plt not prosecuting is dismist. (Pg 543)

The suit brought by Robert Wilson agt John Jones the plt not prosecuting is dismist. (Pg 543)

The suit brought by Elizabeth Lomax agt Charles Seale is cont'd. (Pg 543)

In the accon upon the case between William Anderson plt & Elizabeth Ellkins adminr of John Ellkins decd def the def being called & not appearing judgment is granted the plt agt the def & Thomas Vivion gent sheriff of this co for what of the sum sued for in the declaracon shall appear to be justly due unless the sd def appear at the next court & answer the sd accon. (Pg 543)

In the accon upon the case between John Price plt & James Kay def the def being called & not appearing judgment is granted the plt agt the def & Samuel Hoyle his security for what of the sum sued for in the declaracon shall appear to be justly due unless the def appear at the next court & answer the sd accon. (Pg 543)

Special imparlance is granted William Fickling in the suit brought agt (him) by Wm Pannell. (Pg 543)

The suit brought by Thomas Humpston agt Alexander Turnbull the plt not prosecuting is dismist. (Pg 543)

In the accon upon the case between John Champe plt & Elizabeth Ellkins adminr of John Ellkins decd def the def being called & not appearing judgment is granted the plt agt the def & Thomas Vivion gent sheriff for what of the sum sued for in the declaracon shall appear to be justly due unless the def appear at the next court & answer the sd accon. (Pg 543)

An alias capias is granted William Kennan agt William Brown. (Pg 543)

The suit brought by Elizabeth Berryman agt Jeffery Johnson the plt not prosecuting is dismist. (Pg 543)

The suit brought by Nicholas Smith gent agt Angus Mackay is cont'd. (Pg 543)

Special imparlance is granted John McCarty in the suit brought agt him by Wm Serjant. (Pg 543)

An alias capias is granted John Mercer agt John Snow. (Pg 543)

In the accon of debt between Jeremiah Murdock gent plt & William Harper def the def being called & not appearing judgment is granted the plt agt the def & Thomas Harper Junr his security for what of the sum sued for in the declaracon shall appear to be justly due unless the def appear at the next court & answer the sd accon. (Pg 543)

In the accon of trespass upon the case between Samuel Earl plt & James Moor def the def being called & not appearing judgment is granted the plt agt the def & Thomas Harper his security for what of the sum sued for in the declaracon shall appear to be justly due unless the def appear at the next court & answer the sd accon. (Pg 543)

The suit brought by William Harper agt James Moor the plt not prosecuting is dismist. (Pg 543)

An alias capias is granted George James Dunbar agt Robert Finch. (Pg 544)

In the petition brought by John Marks agt Simon Hughs the sd Simon being called & not appearing judgmt is granted the plt agt the def for 550 lbs of tobacco which is ordered to be paid with cost & one atty fee. (Pg 544)

Three suits brought by Israel Illingsworth agt John Davis, the plt not prosecuting are dismist. (Pg 544)

The suit brought by Howson Hooe agt Charles Lewis the plt not prosecuting is dismist. (Pg 544)

The suit brought by James Baxter agt William Whiting the plt not prosecuting is dismist. (Pg 544)

The suit brought by William Stevenson agt Willm Whiting the plt not prosecuting is dismist. (Pg 544)

The suit brought by Thomas Wood agt Henry Query the plt not prosecuting is dismist. (Pg 544)

The suit brought by Charles Seale agt Jonathan Williams the plt not prosecuting is dismist. (Pg 544)

James Jones presented into court the depositions of Ann Mcpherson & Mary Reynolds they making oath thereto which on the motion of the sd Jones is admitted to record. (Pg 544)

Elizabeth Ellkins adminr of John Ellkins decd came into court & confessed judgmt to Thos Vivion gent for 510 lbs of tobacco which is ordered to be paid with cost. (Pg 544)

In the attachment obtain'd by John Mercer agt Robert Taylor the sheriff having returned that he had attacht 216 lbs of tobacco in his own hands it being pt/o the sd Robert's claim from the country its ordered that the sheriff pay the sd 216 lbs of tobacco to the sd John & that the sd Robert pay the sd John 84 lbs of tobacco together with the cost of this suit. (Pg 544)

In the suit brought by Mary Morton adminr of the goods, chattels & credits of John Morton decd plt agt Katherine Hay executrix of John Hay decd the def pleads she is not executrix the plt joines the issue & the same lyes till next court for tryall. (Pg 544)

In the bill in chancery brought by Francis Stone agt John Plaile & uxor the respdts has time till next court to answer the sd bill. (Pg 544)

John Lee being sumoned an evidence by John Brown agt Jeffery Johnson & being called & not appearing to give his evidence it was ordered in Dec Court last that unless the sd John appear at this court to shew cause whey he then failed to give his evidence the sd John should be fined according to law the sd John being now called & failing to appear it is ordered that he pay the sd Brown 350 lbs of tobacco with cost. (Pg 544)

The suit in chancery between Ann Bronaugh complt & Jeremiah Bronaugh respdt is cont'd till next court for hearing the bill, answer & replicacon. (Pg 544)

Then the court adjourn'd to court in course.

142

Court held 13 Mar 1730 for the examination of William Cooke. Present: Wm Thornton, Jos Strother, Saml Skinker, Row Thornton, gent justices. (Pg 545)

William Cooke being comitted by mittimus under the hand & seale of William Robinson gent for stealing eight pair of shoes from Ralph Falkner of this co, upon hearing the evidence the court is of opinion that the proof is not sufficient to touch his life but the sd Cooke appearing to be a man of very ill behaviour it is ordered that the sheriff take him to the whipping post & give him 39 lashes on the bare back well laid on & that he be then discharged. (Pg 545)

Court held 2 Apr 1731. Present: Wm Thornton, Jos Strother, Row Thornton, Wm Strother, gent justices. (Pg 545)

The will of Timothy Stamps decd was presented into court by Margaret his widdow & extrix who made oath thereto & the same was proved by the oath of Linsfield Sharp & John Sharp two of the evidences thereto & admitted to record. (Pg 545)

The inventory of the estate of Barbara Kersey decd is returned into court & admitted to record. (Pg 545)

It is ordered that George White & Francis James be sum'd to the next court to answer the petition of James Quisenbury. (Pg 545)

It is ord'd that Joseph Suttle be sumoned to the next court to answer the petition of Enoch Berry. (Pg 545)

Peter Coffee being bound for his appearance to this court for abusing his servant woman named Jane Lewis & appearing to the court to be a person of ill behaviour, it is ordered that he remain in custody of the sheriff till he give bound & security for his good behaviour. (Pg 545)

Peter Coffee & John Triplett came into court & entered into recognizance & assumed to pay to our Sovereign Lord the King the sum of £20 to be levied on their goods & chattels, lands & tenements on condition hereafter mentioned. The condition of this recognizance is such that if the sd Peter Coffee be of the good behaviour for a year & a day next ensuing to all his Majesties subjects that then the sd recognizance to be void otherwise to remain in full force & virtue. (Pg 545)

The will of John Dinwiddie gent decd was presented into court by Rose Bronaugh, Thomas Monteith & Jeremiah Bronaugh Senr executors therein named who made oath thereto & the same was ordered to be certified. (Pg 546)

Jeremiah Bronaugh Junr & Rose his wife, Thomas Monteith & Jeremiah
Bronaugh Senr executors of the will of John Dinwiddie gent decd ackn their
lease, release & bond unto William Stevenson which on his motion are admitted
to record. (Pg 546)

Then the court adjourned to court in course.

*Court held 7 May 1731. Present: Wm Robinson, Jos Strother, Saml Skinker,
Wm Strother, gent justices.* (Pg 546)

John Seamons ackn his lease, release & bond unto Edward Burges & Elizabeth
w/o the sd John relinquished her right of dower & thirds thereto which on the
motion of the sd Edward are adm'd to record. (Pg 546)

It is ord'd that the clerk of the co return a particular account of what orphans are
in the co together with a list of their securities to the next court.

Administration of the estate of James Quidley decd is granted unto Rebecca his
widdow the sd Rebecca having with John Ambrose & Rowland Thornton ackn
their bond of £100 for her faithfull administration of the sd estate. (Pg 546)

John Kenyan, Abraham Kenyan, Jonas Williams & William Taylor or any three
of them being first sworn are appointed to appraise in money the estate of James
Quidley decd that shall be brought to their view & make report to the next court.
(Pg 546)

William Stringfellow presented into court a lease & release under the hand &
seale of William Sarjant to the sd Stringfellow which were proved by the oath of
Thomas Waring, Richard Bryant & Moseley Battaley & Thomas Waring gent by
virtue of a power of atty under the hand & seale of Jane w/o the sd William
duely proved in court relinquished the right of dower & thirds of the sd Jane in
& to the sd land which on the motion of the sd Stringfellow are admitted to
record. (Pg 546)

Administration on the estate of William Pitman decd is granted unto Margaret
his widdow the sd Margaret & Jeremiah Bronaugh ackn their bond of £100 for
her faithfull administration of the sd estate. (Pg 547)

John Farguson, Robert Richards, Benjamin Stribling & John Burne or any three
of them are appointed to appraise in money the estate of William Pitman decd
that shall be brought to their view & report to the next court. (Pg 547)

Robert Doniphan ackn his lease & release unto William Thornton gent & Edward Barradall by virtue of a power of atty from Mary w/o the sd Robert proved in court by the oath of Rowland Thornton & Edward Pearle relinquished the right of the sd Maries dower & thirds at the comon law in & to the sd land which on the motion of the sd Thornton is admitted to record. (Pg 547)

Richard Bryant, William Remey, Giles Carter, George White, John Plaile, John Triplett, Thomas Dickeson, William Pitman, William Harrison, Jeremiah Strother, Robert Rankins, Joseph Berry, Enoch Berry, Samuel Hoyle, Richard Gill, Rowland Thornton, Edward Burges, Richard Owens, John Price & William Flower were sworne a grand jury for the body of this co who having rec'd their charge withdrew & sometime after returned the following presentments. (Pg 547)

We present George Harper of Hanover Parish for being drunk at church the 25th day of Dec last past. (Pg 547)

We present Martha Taylor of Sittenbourne Parish for having a base born child within six months last past. Richard Bryan foreman. (Pg 547)

It is ord'd that George Harper of Hanover Parish & Martha Taylor of Sittenbourne Parish be sumoned to appear at the next court to answer the presentments of the grand jury. (Pg 547)

In the suit in chancery depending between Edward Merret complt & Thomas Davis respdt the complt having replied to the respts answer the respdt has time till next court to consider the replication. (Pg 547)

In the action of trespass between Marmaduke Beckwith plt & Richard Gill & Joseph Seamons defs the defs came into court & confessed judgment unto the plt for 1 shilling which is ord'd to be paid with cost & one atty fee. (Pg 547)

John Grayson ackn his lease, release & bond unto Joseph Strother gent & Benjamin Rush by virtue of a power of atty from Susannah w/o the sd John proved in court by the oath of James Strother & John Standley relinquished her right of dower & thirds thereto which on the motion of the sd Strother are admitted to record. (Pg 548)

In the suit in chancery between Ann Bronaugh complt & Jeremiah Bronaugh respt by consent of both parties it is ordered that the report of Joseph Strother, William Strother gent & John Farguson or any two of them be made the decree of this court. (Pg 548)

Edward Barradall presented a lease & release into court under the hand & seale of Robert Carter esqr unto Nicholas Smith gent which were proved by the oath of Thomas Turner, William Stevenson & Edward Barradall which on the motion of the sd Edward Barradall were admitted to record. (Pg 548)

William Duff came into court & ackn his lease unto William Hambleton which on the motion of the sd Hamilton is admitted to record. (Pg 548)

In the action upon the case between Philemon Cavenaugh plt & William Harper def, Anthony Hainey, Thomas Stribling, John Jennings, Francis Martin, William Remey, John Price, Henry Head, Robert Doniphan, Richard Rosser, Jeremiah Strother & George White were sworne a jury to try the issue who having heard the evidence & arguments withdrew & sometime after returned their verdt (viz) we find for the plt £1:10, Anthony Hainey foreman, which verdt on the plts motion is admitted to record & judgmt is granted the plt agt the def for the sd sum which is ord'd to be paid with cost & one atty fee. (Pg 548)

Thomas Dickeson being sumoned an evidence by William Harper agt Philemon Cavenaugh & making oath he attended 11 days on the sd suit, it is ord'd that the sd Harper pay the sd Dickeson for the same at 30 lbs of tobacco per day & cost. (Pg 548)

In the action of trespass & assault between Alexander Carson plt & Edward Hensilly def, Samuel Hensilly garnishee being called & failing to appear, it is ord'd that unless the sd Samuel appear at the next court & produce an acct of the crop of the sd Edward that judgment shall be entered up agt the sd Samuel for £5 together with the cost of this suit. (Pg 548)

In the action of the case between Lazarus Tilly plt & Isaac Johnson def the plt having demurr'd to the defs plea the court on arguing the demurrer is of opinion that it is not good & the sd suit is ord'd to be dismist with cost & one atty fee. (Pg 548)

In the action on the case between John Toward plt & Adam Christie def, Anthony Hainey, Robert Richards, John Jennings, Francis Martin, William Remey, John Price, Henry Head, Robert Doniphan, Thomas Stribling, Richard Rosser, Jeremiah Strother & George White were sworne a jury to enquire into the damages who having heard the evidence & arguments withdrew & sometime after returned the following verdt (viz) we find for the plt £11:8:6, Anthony Hainey foreman, which verdt on the plts motion is admitted to record & judgmt is granted the plt agt the def for the sd sum which is ord'd to be paid with cost & one atty fee. (Pg 549)

146

Then the court adjourned till tomorrow morning 8 o'clock.

Court held 8 May 1731. Present: Wm Robinson, Jos Strother, Saml Skinker, Wm Strother, gent justices. (Pg 549)

In the action upon the case between William Brown plt & Thomas Smith def, Anthony Hainey, Robert Richards, John Jennings, Francis Martin, William Remey, John Price, Henry Head, Robert Doniphan, Thomas Stribling, Richard Rosser, Jeremiah Strother & George White were sworne a jury to try the issue who having heard the evidences & argumts withdrew & sometime after returned the following verdt (viz) we find for the plt 11 shillings 4 pence ½ penny, Anthony Hainey foreman, which verdt on the plts motion is admitted to record & judgmt is granted the plt agt the def for the sum which is ord'd to be paid with cost & on atty fee. (Pg 549)

In the action of debt between Mary Morton adminr of John Morton decd plt & Catherine Hays extrix of John Hays decd def, Anthony Hainey, Robert Richards, John Jennings, Francis Martin, William Remey, John Price, Henry Head, Robert Doniphan, Thomas Stribling, Richard Rosser, Jeremiah Strother & George White were sworn a jury to try the issue who having heard the evidence & argumts withdrew & sometime after returned their verdt (viz) we find in the hands of Catherine Hays extrix of John Hays decd 620 lbs of tobacco, we find the bill to be due to the plt, Anthony Hainey foreman, which verdt on the plts motion is admitted to record & judgmt is granted the plt agt the def for the sum of 620 lbs of tobacco which is ord'd to be paid with cost. (Pg 549)

The suit brought by Angus Mackay agt Benjamin Rush is cont'd till next court. (Pg 549)

In the action upon the case between Angus Mackay plt & Lunsford Lomax def the def pleads that he did not assume the def joins the issue & the sd suit lies till next court for trial. (Pg 550)

INDEX

ABBOT; Edward, 59, 128; Robert,
38; Rodger, 37; Roger, 35, 42,
43, 44, 47 , 51
ABBOTT; Roger, 12
ACCOMACK COUNTY, 129
ALEXANDER, Robert, 19
ALLEN, Joseph, 28, 42; Mary, 42
ALSUP, William, 65
AMBROSE, John, 11, 12, 16, 18, 19,
21, 37, 45, 51, 59, 65, 77, 85, 91,
112, 113, 116, 124, 143
ANDERSON, Walter, 2, 8, 15, 16,
19, 21, 26, 33, 35, 37, 44, 47, 56,
58, 59, 70, 103, 128 ; William,
139
ANGUS, Alexander, 46
APPERSON, Thomas, 45
ARCHARD, Mary, 3
ARLET, John, 48
ARMSTRONG, Joseph, 105, 106
ARNOLD, Isaac, 12, 13, 19, 36, 45,
51, 59, 68, 75, 112, 117, 118,
119, 120, 129; Thomas, 109
ATTWOOD, Francis, 11
AYRES, Thomas Akers, 70
BACK ROAD, 50, 51, 85
BAGGE, John, 19
BAKER, Charles, 118, 119, 120,
133, 134, 135
BARLETT, Thomas, 18
BARNES, Richard, 17, 20, 21 , 24,
43, 46, 50, 53, 57, 70 , 79, 105;
Thomas, 2, 6, 16, 17, 21 , 23;
William, 16
BARNS, Richard, 33, 38, 40, 84, 98,
113, 114, 116
BARRADALL, Edward, 2, 10, 15,
18, 22, 27, 28, 31, 36, 54, 59,
74, 77, 79, 86, 87, 88, 93, 94,
98, 103, 104, 106, 107, 108, 109,

110, 114, 119, 120, 122, 124,
127, 128, 144, 145
BARRET, Richard, 13
BARTLET, Henry, 40
BARTLETT, Henry, 25, 33, 41;
Jacob, 20, 24, 32
BASHAW, Peter, 19
BATES, Joseph, 114
BATTALEY, Moseley, 28, 79, 91,
143; Mosely, 3, 25, 28, 49, 51,
53, 55, 63, 68, 69, 72, 120
BATTALY, Mosely, 60
BAXTER, James, 140; William, 20
BEACH, Thomas, 66
BEBY, John, 19
BECKWITH, Marmaduke, 22, 95,
99, 107, 112, 118, 122, 133,
137, 144
BELL, John, 37, 102
BENDALL, Isaac, 57
BENNET, Isaac, 74
BENSON, Robert, 7, 42, 65, 104;
Thomas, 7, 8, 60, 64, 90
BERKLEY, John, 83
BERRY, Enoch, 18, 19, 91, 94, 142,
144; Henry, 68, 82, 96, 103,
130, 131, 132; Joseph, 51, 90, 91,
92, 94, 95, 101, 137, 138, 144
BERRYMAN, Benjamin, 4, 11, 12,
60, 65, 71, 74, 85, 95, 113;
Elizabeth, 140
BEVERLEY, William, 30, 66
BEVERLY, William, 31, 34
BEVERSHAM, Elizabeth, 20
BIDDEFORD MAN OF WAR, 45
BIRCHNEL, Charles, 15, 57, 68
BIRCHNELL, Charles, 43, 46, 50,
54, 62, 72
BIRK, Thomas, 67
BLASINGHAM, Thomas, 62

BLASSINGHAM, Thomas, 9, 61, 63, 66, 77, 84, 88, 122
BODDINGTON, James, 66
BOLDWIRE, William, 24
BOLLING, John, 62, 67, 84; Robert, 119
BOUORNE, John, 70
BOURNE, John, 69, 81, 94, 128; Robert, 42
BOWLING, John, 117, 122; Judeth, 117, 122
BOWLWARE, Richard, 32; William, 20
BOWSHOTT, Jane, 2, 3
BOWSING, Stephen, 96
BOYLE, Margaret, 69; Thomas, 69
BOYLES, Margaret, 65; Thomas, 14, 65
BRADFORD, John, 28, 101
BRANHAM, John, 4, 11, 12, 113, 114, 125, 131, 138
BREDIN, Bryant, 127
BRIANT, Richard, 54
BRIDGFORTH, Thomas, 48, 52, 54, 60, 69
BRISTOL, 46
BRISTOL IRON MINES, 9, 10, 57
BRISTOL IRON WORKS, 59, 102
BROCK, Mary, 4, 11, 12, 125
BROMADGE, Samuel, 6, 16, 21, 23
BRONAUG, Jeremiah, 50; Rose, 50
BRONAUGH, Ann, 100, 107, 116, 119, 123, 128, 132, 141, 144; Jeremiah, 1, 4, 6, 12, 13, 14, 15, 16, 17, 18, 21, 23, 24, 25, 26, 27, 31, 32, 33, 36, 37, 38, 39, 40, 41, 43, 45, 46, 50, 51, 53, 54, 55, 56, 57 , 59, 60, 61, 68, 69, 71, 72, 74, 75, 76, 78, 79, 80, 81, 82, 83, 84, 87, 91 , 95, 96, 97, 100, 104 , 106, 107, 110, 111, 112, 113, 116, 118, 121, 123,
127, 128, 130, 132, 141, 142, 143, 144; Jermiah, 119; Rose, 1, 4, 6, 13, 14, 15, 16, 23, 24, 25, 32, 36, 37, 41, 43, 46, 50, 51, 54, 55, 56, 57 , 59, 61, 68, 69, 71, 74, 75, 76, 79, 80, 81, 82, 83, 84, 87, 95, 96, 100, 104 , 106, 110, 111, 112, 113, 118, 121, 130, 142, 143
BROOKE, Richard, 59
BROOKES, Richard, 6
BROOKS, William, 34
BROWN, Jeremiah, 1, 7 , 108; John, 94 , 108, 116, 120, 124, 132, 134, 135, 136, 141; Mary, 20, 24, 33; Max, 129; William, 79, 108, 115, 120, 121, 124, 138, 140, 146
BROWNS RUN, 132
BRYAN, Richard, 144
BRYANT, Richard, 36, 38, 40, 41, 49, 56, 61, 62, 63, 68, 72, 94, 95, 98, 104, 111, 113, 125, 130, 131, 132, 134, 137, 138, 143, 144
BUCKNER, Elizabeth, 10; Richard, 10
BUCY, Joel, 35
BULLOCK, Richard, 125
BUMBERRY, Thomas, 20
BURBRIDGE, William, 44, 48, 52
BURCHNELL, Charles, 24, 32, 37
BURD, George, 109
BURGES, Edward, 143, 144; Joseph, 84
BURNE, John, 143
BURTON, John, 41
BUSHNEL, Charles, 6
BUTLER, Richard, 90, 101, 118, 119, 126, 129, 137
BUTTLER, Richard, 120
CALDWALLS, David, 31, 36
CALE, Alice, 70

CALFEE, Elinor, 42; Henry, 41, 42
CALLIHAM, Darby, 54, 55, 56, 60, 126
CALLIHAN, Darby, 81, 94, 133
CAMERON, John, 77, 78
CANNON, John, 132
CARDER, John, 40, 70, 116
CARNABY, Anthony, 23
CAROLINE COUNTY, 8, 9, 16, 26, 34, 53, 75, 79, 80, 81
CARPENTER, Joseph, 112
CARSON, Alexander, 66, 67, 100, 107, 115, 120, 123, 132, 137, 145
CART ROAD, 83
CARTER, Charles, 29; Giles, 109, 111, 112, 129, 137, 138, 144; John, 30; Margaret, 101, 110; Robert, 27, 30, 83, 102, 145; William, 35, 58
CASH, Howard, 109, 114, 125, 138; Joseph, 109
CASSEDY, Peter, 5, 16
CATLETT, Thomas, 26
CAVE, William, 137
CAVENAUGH, Philemon, 66, 106, 118, 123, 131, 137, 145; Philip, 84, 95, 99; Phillamon, 113
CAVES, Patrick, 47
CHADWELL, Bryant, 45, 57; John, 55, 61, 75
CHAMBERLAINE, William, 25, 34
CHAMBERLAYNE, William, 37
CHAMP, John, 37, 86, 98, 131, 133, 135
CHAMPE, John, 6, 7, 8, 12, 24, 36, 43, 48, 66, 68, 77, 78, 129, 134, 136, 139
CHEW, Larkin, 4, 5; Thomas, 4, 5
CHILTON, John, 2, 3
CHININGHANE, Adam, 27
CHRISTE, Adam, 31

CHRISTIE, Adam, 11, 16, 44, 47, 48, 49, 52, 53, 54, 55, 60, 64, 65, 67, 71, 72, 74, 79, 90, 91, 98, 101, 104, 107, 115, 124, 134, 138, 145; Mary, 11, 16, 53, 57, 65, 71, 74
CLARK, Alexander, 19; John, 29, 40, 107, 115, 119, 123, 133; William, 66
CLATOR, Thomas, 83
CLAYTER, Thomas, 85
CLEMENT, Alexander, 106, 118, 119, 120, 126, 133
COBURN, John, 4, 12, 13, 49, 82, 84, 94
COCKE, Catesby, 26, 29, 30, 75
COFFEE, Peter, 142
COMBES, Archdell, 97
CONNER, John, 64, 91
CONWAY, Thomas, 127
COOKE, John, 55, 62; William, 57, 142
COPEDGE, John, 132
CORBIN, John, 59; William, 38
CORNELIOUS, Richarad, 105; Richard, 93, 98; Rowland, 15, 16, 18, 21, 65, 93, 98, 105, 106
CORNELIUS, Richard, 88; Rowland, 38, 85, 88, 92
COX, John, 48, 52, 54, 60, 69
CRAWLEY, Samuel, 16
CRESSAP, Thomas, 15
CRISTIE, Adam, 50
CROUCH, Joseph, 64, 65, 108, 115
CROWS SWAMP, 10, 36
CUMBEE, Emanuel, 127
CUNINGHAM, George, 46
DAMERON, Lazarus, 18, 56, 59, 63, 137
DAVIS, Elizabeth, 41; George, 5, 14, 16, 21; John, 114, 140; Thomas, 7, 11, 15, 16, 19, 21, 24, 33, 34,

41, 63 , 68 , 78 , 92, 97, 105,
113, 118, 122, 130, 137, 144
DEAN, Charles, 3, 12, 26, 27, 31,
33, 35, 37, 101
DEANE, Charles, 33, 34
DEEP RUN, 2, 11, 39, 42, 137
DEFOE, James, 48
DELANY, Joseph, 16
DICKENSON, Scott, 111; Thomas,
39, 113, 118, 119, 120, 126, 130,
131, 132, 133
DICKESON, Thomas, 129, 134, 135,
144, 145
DICKINSON, James, 89, 90, 97, 111;
Thomas, 106
DICKISON, Thomas, 134
DIER, John, 45
DILLEN, Thomas, 8
DINWIDDIE, John, 1, 4, 6, 11, 13,
24, 26, 32, 36, 43, 50, 54, 55, 56,
57 , 59, 61, 71, 74, 75, 76, 79,
80, 81, 82, 83, 84, 87, 91, 95,
96, 97, 100, 104, 106, 110, 111,
113, 118, 121, 130, 142, 143;
Rose, 110
DISKIN, Elizabeth, 125; John, 43, 56,
59, 75, 83, 85, 91, 94 , 99, 113,
120, 123, 125, 131, 132
DISKINS, John, 8, 18, 31 , 33, 34,
42, 49, 105, 118
DODD, John, 56, 83
DOGUE BRIDGE, 7
DOGUE SWAMP, 36
DONIPHAN, Mary, 144; Mott, 80,
91; Robert, 18, 22, 61, 68, 91,
137, 144, 145, 146
DOOLING, William, 25, 34, 35
DOWNING, George, 6, 25, 33, 55,
61, 62, 67, 69, 84, 88
DOYLE, William, 17
DRAKE, Francis, 85

DUDLEY, Peter, 19; Robert, 5, 8, 9,
15, 16, 34
DUFF, Elizabeth, 110; William, 50,
64, 110, 129, 136, 145
DULING, William, 85, 133, 134,
135
DUNAHOE, Edmund, 87
DUNBAR, George James, 78, 95,
99, 106, 113, 140; Peter, 58, 75
DUNBARR, George James, 58;
Peter, 58
DUNCAN, John, 3; Robert, 56;
Thomas, 78
DUNCOM, Thomas, 78
DUNCOMB, Robert, 43, 63; Thomas,
41, 64, 68
DURHAM, Mary, 63, 68, 91, 92;
Samuel, 91
EARL, Samuel, 140
EASTER, Giles, 4
EDRINGTON, Christopher, 10, 18,
19, 59, 61, 66
EDWARDS, Elizabeth, 11; John, 25,
33
EDY, John, 100
EDZARD, Esdras Theodor, 17, 66,
86, 94, 98, 105; Esdras Theodore,
45
ELKIN, John, 66
ELKINS, Richard, 59, 134, 137
ELLIOT, Elizabeth, 7
ELLISTON, Elliner, 73, 74; Robert,
22, 35, 73
ELLKIN, Elizabeth, 103; John, 9,
103; Richard, 75
ELLKINS, Elizabeth, 108, 111, 115,
139, 141; John, 48, 77, 103, 108,
111, 139, 141; Richard, 31, 33,
34, 67, 79, 90, 100, 107, 134,
135, 138
ELLSON, Ralph, 108
ELMES, Edward, 11

ELSON, John, 26
ENGLES, Robert, 98
ENGLISH, Jane, 92; Robert, 5, 14,
  15, 79, 91
ESKRIDGE, George, 7, 18, 103
ESSEX COUNTY, 9, 17, 19
ESTER, Giles, 11, 12, 13
EVANS, Robert, 34, 58
FAGAN, Edward, 3
FAGANS PINE, 129
FALKNER, Elizabeth, 10; Ralph, 10,
  112, 117, 142
FALMOUTH, 101
FALMOUTH TOWN, 29, 30
FARGUSON, Isaac, 26; John, 18, 31
  , 33, 34, 35, 40, 41, 42, 43, 45,
  49, 51, 56, 59, 72, 78, 125, 129 ,
  130, 131 , 132, 143, 144; Joshua,
  27, 36, 38, 39, 40, 41, 48, 101,
  112; Josiah, 85, 94, 99, 105,
  113, 118, 123, 131, 132; Josua,
  29
FEWELL, William, 7, 8, 9
FICKLING, William, 1, 7, 139
FINCH, Elizabeth, 62; John, 18;
  Robert, 62, 102, 140
FINLASON, John, 53, 67, 72, 90, 98
FINLAYSON, John, 55, 60, 104
FISHPOOL, George, 27, 78
FITZHUGH, Henry, 47, 52, 56, 61,
  69, 84, 91, 97, 104, 111, 112,
  118, 123, 130
FLEMING, John, 78, 109
FLING, William, 107, 113
FLOWER, William, 107, 144
FLOWERS, William, 29, 40, 68, 78,
  100, 101, 115, 119, 123, 133
FOLICOPHER, Christopher, 2
FOREST ROAD, 129, 136
FOSTER, John, 41; William, 28
FOWKE, Ann, 113

FOX, John, 27, 36, 38, 40, 41, 61,
  72, 73, 75, 76, 80, 85, 87, 126,
  139
FRANKLIN, George, 23, 27, 31, 33,
  34, 51, 66, 129
FRANKLINE, Thomas, 112
FRAZIER, Daniel, 103
FRENCH, Daniel, 6, 15, 18, 23, 32,
  40, 43, 46, 50, 53, 58, 59, 62, 65,
  69, 72, 74, 84, 95, 101, 105, 115,
  126, 136; Daniell, 39, 41; Hugh,
  67, 107, 121; Margaret, 6, 15, 18,
  23, 43, 46, 53, 58, 59, 62, 65, 69,
  72, 74, 84, 101, 105, 115, 126,
  136; Margrett, 32, 39
FRY, Richard, 10
GAMON, Charles, 79
GARNER, John, 71
GIBSON, Elizabeth, 70; Jona, 56;
  Jonathan, 14, 20, 22, 28, 32, 58,
  60, 70, 130
GILBERT, John, 10, 12, 13 , 14, 18 ,
  19, 51, 68, 71, 73, 81, 84, 96,
  100, 102, 125, 130, 131, 132
GILL, Richard, 22, 23, 45, 47, 48,
  64, 78, 94, 95, 99, 106, 107, 112
  , 118, 122, 133 , 134, 135, 137 ,
  144
GILLISON, James, 8, 66
GINGOTEAGUE, 7, 10
GLENDENING, John, 19, 137
GOBLE, John, 51
GODDARD, Henry, 100
GOFF, Thomas, 28, 58
GOLF, Thomas, 84
GOLLATHAN, Martin, 83, 119;
  Mary, 83
GOLLOP, Henry, 59
GOLLOTHAN, Martin, 111
GOOCH, William, 2, 49
GOOSEHEE, Thomas, 101
GORDING, William, 72

GRADY, Edward, 45; Patrick, 59
GRANT, James, 137; John, 7, 8, 54,
    56, 61, 91, 126, 139; William, 1,
    6, 7, 8, 15, 24, 32, 36, 37, 38,
    39, 40, 41, 43, 46, 50, 54, 57, 62,
    64, 68, 70, 72, 78, 102, 125, 129
GRAY, Mary, 20
GRAYSON, Benjamin, 76; John, 73,
    144; Susanah, 73; Susannah, 144
GREAT FALLS, 2, 11, 39, 42
GREEN, Richard, 63, 84, 95, 100,
    101, 106, 109, 114, 123, 134 ;
    Robert, 40, 70; Samuel, 111, 117
GREENIAN, James, 21, 25
GREENING, Owen, 5
GRIFFIN, Richard, 22; Thomas, 26,
    33, 43, 46, 51, 54, 62
GRIFFIS, Ann, 5, 15, 17, 23, 31,
    104; Francis, 9; Richard, 44, 45,
    49, 62, 63, 66, 67, 71, 78, 84,
    85, 86, 95, 100, 104, 106, 129,
    130, 136
GRIFFITH, Richard, 14, 78
GRIGGSBY, Benjamin, 38; John, 38
GRIGSBY, Ann, 128; Benjamin, 79;
    John, 44, 128; Rose, 59; Thomas,
    55, 59
GRIMSLEY, Thomas, 15, 17, 19, 22
GRIMSLY, Thomas, 14
GRYMES, Thomas, 124
HACKLEY, James, 12, 31; William,
    31
HACKNEY, William, 19, 33, 34 ,
    38, 41, 42, 44, 45, 59, 64
HAINEY, Anthony, 51, 54, 56, 57,
    60, 73, 75, 95, 100, 104, 106,
    110, 123, 133, 145, 146
HAINY, Anthony, 26, 60, 72, 125,
    134 , 135
HALL, John, 123
HAMBLETON, William, 145
HAMILTON, Gilbert, 54, 59

HAMMONS, John, 133
HAMPTON, 76, Thomas, 135
HANDY, Anthony, 59
HANOVER PARISH, 12, 35, 39, 48,
    64, 76, 79, 88, 101, 109, 129,
    130, 144
HANSFORD, Stephen, 91
HANSILLY, Edward, 123
HANSLEY, William, 91
HARBUT, Thomas, 73
HARDIN, Mark, 31, 33, 34, 48, 54,
    56
HARDY, John, 3, 5, 7, 8, 14, 15
HARPER, Daniel, 121; George, 144;
    Thomas, 71, 77, 86 , 87, 93, 98,
    99, 105, 112, 140; William, 26,
    95, 99, 106, 113, 118, 122, 123,
    131, 137, 139, 140, 145
HARRISON, Margaret, 18; Margrett,
    32; Mary, 95, 100, 104, 106;
    Robert, 51; Thomas, 18, 32;
    William, 12, 18, 19, 25, 35, 36,
    37, 38, 44, 47, 128, 144
HARRISSON, Margaret, 23; Thomas,
    23
HARTSHORNE, Bersheba, 65; John,
    65
HARVIE, John, 11
HARWOOD, Thomas, 18, 23, 25,
    31, 34, 39, 41, 42, 65, 68, 71, 74
    , 77
HASELLS, Joseph, 21
HASETTS, Joseph, 21
HASTY, John, 75
HAWKINGS, Benjamin, 72
HAWKINS, Benjamin, 67
HAY, John, 141; Katherine, 141
HAYS, Catherine, 146; John, 146
HEAD, Alford, 49; Anthony, 49, 65,
    84; George, 14, 15, 25, 34, 35,
    37, 44, 47, 49; Henry, 36, 38,
    41, 85, 145, 146; James, 49

HEARN, Samuel, 64, 108
HEDGMAN, Nathaniel, 52; Peter, 12,
   29, 40, 52, 83
HELLIER, John, 10
HEMSILLY, Edward, 132
HENRICO COUNTY, 45
HENSELLY, Edward, 100
HENSILLY, Edward, 107, 115, 120,
   137, 145; Samuel, 96, 100, 106,
   138, 145; William, 122
HENSLEY, Benjamin, 14, 47, 48,
   77; Joseph, 26 , 33, 34, 37, 44 ,
   47; Samuel, 36, 91; Samuell, 38,
   40, 41; William, 11, 12, 13, 14,
   53, 55 , 69, 72, 77, 79, 88, 93
HENSLY, William, 4, 60
HEWES, Ralph, 54
HEWS, Ralph, 60, 69; Rose, 20
HICKAM, Elizabeth, 130
HICKMAN, Elizabeth, 129
HIGDON, John, 78, 86, 117
HILLIER, John, 45, 49
HILLING, John, 77; Nathaniel, 48
HINSON, Ann, 101, 110; James, 78,
   114
HOLDFAST, William, 88
HOLDSWORTH, Elizabeth, 6
HOLEBROOKE, Randolph, 5
HOLLAND, James, 66
HOOE, Howson, 140; Katherine,
   104; Rice, 104
HOPPER, John, 41, 59
HORE, Katherine, 129
HORNBY, Daniel, 6, 16, 20, 23, 31,
   37, 38; Daniell, 36
HORSEPEN RUN, 137
HORSNAIL, James, 93
HORTON, Snodel, 12, 19
HOYLE, Samuel, 4, 7, 8, 15, 18, 45,
   48, 65, 87, 101, 126, 129, 137,
   138, 139, 144
HOYLES, Samuel, 14

HUBARD, Jacob, 128
HUBBARD, Mathew, 48
HUBBERD, Mathew, 52
HUDNALL, John, 42 , 51, 52;
   Joseph, 18, 41, 42, 43, 51, 59
HUDSON, John, 117; Rush, 54, 56,
   72, 84 , 106, 112, 116, 117, 130,
   131, 132, 133, 134, 135; Sarah,
   84; William, 84, 85, 91
HUGHS, Ralph, 3, 59; Robert, 125,
   139; Simon, 20, 24, 32, 39, 43,
   46, 52, 53, 56, 125, 140
HULLOCK, John, 4, 5
HUME, George, 93
HUMPHREY, Jane, 69; John, 69;
   William, 69
HUMPSTON, Thomas, 139
HUNDLEY, Caleb, 2
HUNDLY, Caleb, 11
HUTCHINSON, William, 34
ILLINGSWORTH, Israel, 67, 140
INGRAM, Jane, 124; Tobias, 57, 124
INNIS, Enoch, 27, 119
INVERNESS, 111
IRISH, Richard, 26
IRON WORKS, 112
JACKSON, Robert, 28
JACOBS, Jacob, 135
JAMES, Francis, 13, 24, 142;
   Thomas, 19, 84, 94
JAQUES, Frances, 102
JARVIS, John, 31; Richard, 98
JEFFERIES, Thomas, 81, 128
JEFFERYS, Thomas, 49
JENKINS, John, 19; Jonas, 35
JENNINGS, John, 3, 14, 15, 18, 19,
   21, 23, 58, 68, 87, 91, 94, 103,
   106, 109, 111, 116, 118, 119,
   120, 124, 126, 133, 134, 135,
   138, 145, 146
JETT, Elizabeth, 12, 74; Francis, 63,
   68, 71, 74, 127; John, 23, 34, 38,

44, 63, 68 , 71, 74; Mary, 74;
Thomas, 74; William, 56, 58, 59,
68, 127
JOHNSON, Benjamin, 11; Elizabeth,
45; Isaac, 34, 85, 108, 109, 114,
120, 124, 132, 138, 139, 145;
Jeffery, 108, 116, 120, 124, 134
, 135, 136, 140, 141; Margaret,
11; Robert, 36, 38, 40, 41, 59,
125, 126, 127, 130, 131, 132,
133, 134 , 135, 138; Thomas, 55,
60, 69, 72, 78
JONES, Charles, 5, 14, 15, 37, 78,
103; George, 42; Henry, 95;
Howell, 78, 86; James, 15, 16,
19, 20, 31, 32, 36 , 38, 40, 41,
49, 53, 56, 59, 104, 128 , 129,
141; John, 4, 5, 26, 125, 139;
Katherine, 42; Mark, 63, 68, 94,
98, 104, 111, 131; Robert, 2, 29,
30 , 31, 59, 65, 66, 71, 78, 95,
113
KAY, James, 55, 61, 68, 77, 103,
127, 139; Mary, 127; Walter, 46
KAYS LANDING, 53
KAYS SWAMP, 46, 103
KEESEE, George, 112
KEIRN, Robert, 39
KENDALL, Samuel, 34, 108
KENNAN, Robert, 55, 61 , 62, 67,
72, 73; William, 37, 44, 45, 47,
48, 52, 54, 63, 67, 68, 140
KENNEY, James, 29
KENYAN, Abraham, 18, 31, 33, 34,
35, 45, 85, 106, 113, 143; John,
19, 59, 85, 102, 117, 143
KERSEY, Barbara, 142; Barbare, 137
KINDALL, Samuell, 23
KING, Higgason, 5; John, 11, 76
KING WILLIAM COUNTY, 128
KIRTLEY, Francis, 20
KIRTLY, Francis, 24

KITCHEN, Elizabeth, 126
KNIGHTON, Moses, 39; Mosses, 27;
William, 45, 108
LACOM, Francis, 18
LAMPTON, William, 104, 128
LANCASTER COUNTY, 52
LEE, Elizabeth, 35; Hancock, 101;
Isaac, 35; John, 35, 136, 141;
Thomas, 93
LEITCH, Andrew, 7; Ann, 45;
Hannah, 109
LETICH, Hannah, 101
LEWIS, Charles, 6, 21, 25, 33, 95,
140; Henry, 38, 44; James, 125;
Jane, 142; Martha, 38, 44;
Mulloone, 122; Muttoone, 122;
Z., 87, 88; Zachary, 110
LIGHTBOURN, Stafford, 117
LITTLE, Thomas, 59
LOMAX, Elizabeth, 98, 139; John, 2,
3, 46; Lunsford, 46, 98, 113,
124, 132, 138, 146
LONEY, William, 94, 99, 106
LONG, Bloomfield, 54, 56, 66, 122;
Elizabeth, 122; Henry, 36, 85,
130; John, 5, 8, 16, 25, 33, 40,
41; Richard, 79
LONGMAN, Richard, 4, 16, 20, 24,
32, 38, 44, 47, 52, 54, 63, 67, 72,
79, 83
LONGMIRE, William, 128
LUNSFORD, John, 102
MCBEE, Susanah, 127
MCBEE, Susannah, 2; William, 2
MCBEE, William, 66, 97, 127
MCCARTY, John, 140
MCCORMACK, Neal, 28
MCCORMACK, Neal, 54
MCCORMACK, Neal, 56, 72, 130,
131, 132

MCDANIEL, George, 85, 90, 96, 120, 121, 123; James, 133; John, 130, 136

MCDONALD, Daniel, 138; Duncan, 104; George, 66, 74

MCDONNEL, James, 127

MCFARLANE, Alexander, 63

MCGUFFY, John, 48, 59

MCGUIRE, John, 12, 18

MACKAY, Angus, 1, 7, 108, 109, 113, 114, 116 , 124, 127, 131, 132, 138, 140, 146; George, 138; William, 111

MCKENNY, Alexander, 105

MACKENNY, Alexander, 128

MCKENNY, Daniel, 130, 136

MCKENSAY, Daniel, 137; Dorothy, 137

MACKENTOSH, Alexander, 112

MCKIE, Henry, 82; Jeas, 82

MCMAHONE, Mathew, 76

MCMAHONE, Mathew, 77, 86, 87; Matthew, 84

MCMCMAM, John, 25

MCNEMARA, John, 7, 13, 21, 45, 59

MCPHERSON, Ann, 141; Archbell, 10

MAGEE, Thomas, 139

MAGGEE, Patrick, 3

MAIN ROAD, 2, 7, 51, 112, 117, 129

MAN, Christopher, 106, 133

MARKHAM, James, 5, 8, 9, 15, 16, 48, 59, 79, 109, 122

MARKHAMS RUN, 7

MARKS, John, 140

MARR, Daniel, 12, 18, 19, 59, 128; John, 7, 64

MARSH, Ann, 88, 99, 105, 116, 118, 123, 132; George, 132

MARSHALL, Mary, 89, 96, 97, 114, 125; William, 18, 68, 101, 108

MARTIN, Francis, 145, 146; Jacob, 55, 61; John, 55, 61; Sarah, 55, 61

MASH, Ann, 132, 133, 137; George, 132

MASON, French, 55, 60, 69, 72; George, 9, 59

MATHESON, Farguhar, 122; Farqhar, 139

MATHEWS, John, 49, 51, 63, 68

MATTHEWS, Baldwin, 28, 39, 131; John, 28, 39

MAVER, Alexander, 12

MAXFIELD, Abraham, 71

MAY, Mary, 110

MERCER, John, 9, 76, 85, 140, 141

MERRET, Edward, 63, 68, 92, 97, 105, 113, 118, 122, 130, 137, 144

MICOU, John, 107, 115

MILLER, David, 48; John, 4, 17, 20, 21 , 24, 48, 117, 122; Simon, 117, 122; William, 122

MINES SWAMP, 36

MINTO, Joseph, 13

MINTON, John, 23; Joseph, 77, 100, 109, 114

MITCHELL, John, 5

MONROE, David, 104; Thomas, 18

MONTEITH, Thomas, 1, 6, 11, 15, 16, 26, 32, 33, 36, 37, 41, 43 , 45, 46, 50 , 51, 54, 57, 59, 68, 69, 71, 74, 75, 76, 77, 79, 80, 81, 82, 83, 86, 87, 88, 93, 96, 98, 104, 110, 121, 142, 143

MONTIETH, Thomas, 24, 25

MOON, Samuel, 10, 68, 72, 75

MOONEY, John, 5

MOONS QUARTER, 129

MOONY, John, 16

MOOR, James, 140
MOREHEAD, John, 28, 41, 42
MORGAN, Charles, 19, 43, 101;
    Dennis, 55, 60; James, 19
MORRIS, Hannah, 48; Lewis, 28, 49
MORRISON, Mary, 8; William, 4, 8,
    14, 17, 23, 31, 39, 43, 50, 51,
    53, 57
MORRISS, Hannah, 45
MORTON, Ann, 127; John, 141, 146;
    Mary, 141, 146; William, 127
MUMFORD, Katherine, 2; William,
    5, 65, 66
MUNRO, Alexander, 110; William,
    105
MURDOCK, Jeremiah, 2, 3, 5, 6, 9,
    10, 11, 12, 14, 17, 19, 20, 22, 26,
    27, 33, 35, 36, 38, 41, 45, 51, 58,
    59, 64, 67, 68, 69, 71, 73, 74,
    75, 76, 78, 83, 85, 94, 95, 99,
    103, 106, 108, 109, 110, 111,
    114, 120, 124, 138, 140
NASH, Katherine, 129, 130
NEGRO, Aaron, 102; Abraham, 11;
    Bassett, 11; Bristol, 11, 102;
    Councellor, 29; Dick, 9, 10, 71,
    74; Dingey, 71, 74; George, 11;
    Judy, 29; Mingo, 71, 74; Prince,
    102; Sambo, 131; Scipio, 71, 74;
    Tom, 102
NEW ENGLAND, 40
NEWBALD, Samuel, 64
NEWBANK, John, 125
NEWGEN, Dominic, 23; Edward, 23
NEWGENT, Domine, 31; Edward,
    31, 36, 47; Frances, 31, 44;
    Francis, 36, 37, 47; Peter, 37, 40
NICHOLLS, James, 55, 61, 89, 90;
    Mary, 70, 73; Samuel, 70, 73
NICHOLS, James, 97
NICOLL, James, 108, 109
NICOLLS, James, 111

NORE, Katherine, 130
NORMAN, Isaac, 20, 24, 33
NUBALD, Samuel, 95
NUGENT, Peter, 49
NUN, John, 128
OBANNON, Briant, 11, 21; Bryant,
    12, 16, 45, 68, 69, 106
OBANON, Ann, 29; Bryant, 29
OBRIAN, Jeremiah, 47, 53
OBRIANT, Jeremiah, 34
OSBOURNE, Thomas, 45, 100
OSWALD, Alexander, 46; Betty, 46;
    David, 46; Isabell, 46
OWEN, John, 31
OWENS, John, 18, 68, 101, 103,
    129; Richard, 144; William, 15,
    95
OXSHAW, Samuel, 79
PAGE, Mann, 30
PAIN, Francis, 103; George, 53;
    John, 129
PAINE, George, 114
PANNELL, William, 139
PARKER, Alexander, 61, 67, 79, 91,
    98, 104, 111, 112, 117;
    Elizabeth, 75
PARSONS, George, 5, 8, 14, 58, 64,
    107, 113
PATTISHALL, William, 53, 65, 71,
    74, 101
PAYNE, John, 23, 101
PAYTON, John, 19
PEARLE, Edward, 105, 137, 144
PEATROSS, John, 64
PECK, Robert, 22, 108, 115, 120,
    124, 126, 129, 133, 134, 135;
    William, 22, 107, 118, 119, 120,
    130, 131, 132
PERCIVALL, Peter, 57
PEYTON, John, 64, 122, 139
PHILIPS, Thomas, 23, 88

PHILLIPS, Thomas, 78, 86, 93, 95, 98, 105, 112
PHILSHER, Edward, 4
PICKFORD, Samuel, 45
PINSON, Aaron, 40, 70, 116
PIPER, John, 11, 50, 85, 127
PITMAN, Margaret, 143; William, 143, 144
PLAILE, John, 141, 144
PLANT, John, 16
PLUNKETT, John, 27, 36, 38, 39, 40, 41
POPE, Elizabeth, 112; John, 112
POPES CREEK, 31
POPETER BRIDGE, 31
POPHAM, John, 11, 73, 86, 94, 99, 105, 108, 112, 115, 119, 120, 124, 135, 136
POPLAR SWAMP, 50
POTTER, Miles, 65, 66, 78, 84
PRATT, John, 6, 15, 18, 23, 32, 46, 53, 58, 59, 65, 69, 72, 74, 84, 95, 101, 105, 115, 126, 136; Margaret, 6, 18
PRICE, Evam, 101; Evan, 6, 7, 8, 14, 15, 18, 23, 32, 39, 43, 46, 50, 53, 58, 59, 62, 65, 69, 72, 74, 84, 95, 115, 126, 134, 136; John, 103, 130, 131, 132, 133, 135, 137, 138, 139, 144, 145, 146
PRITCHET, Christopher, 17; John, 17; Thomas, 17
PRITCHETT, Christopher, 111, 112, 117, 119; John, 117
PROCTER, William, 31
PROCTOR, George, 80; William, 51, 61, 68
PROSSER, Roger, 9, 10, 16
PULLEIN, William, 19
PULLEINS SWAMP, 7
PULLEN, William, 39
QUERY, Henry, 141

QUIDLEY, James, 143; Rebecca, 90, 104, 143
QUILE, William, 102
QUISENBURY, Elizabeth, 27, 83; Humphrey, 13; James, 142; John, 27, 68, 83, 112; Thomas, 18; William, 27
QUOIL, William, 107, 115, 120, 134
QUOILL, William, 126
RACE GROUND, 129
RADDISH, Elinor, 92; Robert, 63, 85, 92, 98
RADING, Timothy, 34
RAINES, Patrick, 21
RAM, Ebenezer, 125
RAMSAY, Thomas, 46
RANKINS, Robert, 136, 144
RAREDON, Henry, 57
RASINS, Richard, 93
READ, Joseph, 95, 99, 113, 116, 118, 123, 124, 130, 133, 135, 136
READE, Joseph, 3
READING, Sarah, 131; Timothy, 131
RED OAK QUARTER, 137
REDMAN, Bartholomew, 44, 59, 62, 66, 67, 84
REED, Elizabeth, 71; Joseph, 129; Samuel, 68; Thomas, 71
REEDS, Elizabeth, 68, 71, 74; Mary, 68, 71, 74; Samuel, 63, 68, 71, 74, 127, 129; Thomas, 68, 71, 74; William, 71, 74
REEMY, William, 68
REID, Joseph, 106
REINS, Henry, 135; Patrick, 25
REMEY, William, 41, 83, 144, 145, 146
RETTERFORD, John, 20
REYNOLDS, Mary, 141; Thomas, 108, 115, 124, 134
RIAN, Patrick, 101

RICHARD, Robert, 138
RICHARDS, Robert, 14, 15, 18, 110,
    114, 125, 130, 137, 138, 143,
    145, 146
RICHMOND COUNTY, 19, 21, 26,
    33, 43, 45, 54, 59, 62
RIGBY, Alexander, 13
RIPHLEY, Grace, 74, 97; Thomas, 6,
    62, 63, 66, 67, 74, 78, 84, 86,
    87, 93, 94, 97, 98, 108, 114, 120
RITTERFORD, John, 24
ROBERTS, Hugh, 6
ROBERTSON, Ann, 35, 36; Daniel,
    1; James, 18, 22, 35, 36, 65
ROBINSON, Ignatius, 55;
    Maximilian, 6, 59, 97; Peter, 121;
    William, 1, 3, 10, 17, 26, 32, 46,
    50, 53, 65, 68, 73, 75, 76, 78,
    83, 85, 89, 90, 92, 96, 97, 101,
    102, 103, 105, 111, 115, 121,
    126, 130, 133, 142, 143, 146
ROBIRTSON, James, 25
ROBISSON, Ignatious, 64
RODGERS, Christopher, 36, 38, 78;
    Margrett, 38
ROGERS, Chrisopher, 41;
    Christopher, 38, 40
ROLLING ROAD, 74, 136
ROOF, William, 22
ROSE, Maxfield, 3, 125, 139
ROSS, John, 45, 57; Walter, 6
ROSSER, Richard, 68, 81, 129, 145,
    146
ROWELL, Edward, 102
ROWLEY, William, 18, 61, 71
ROY, John, 7, 8
ROYSTON, Thomas, 64
RUSH, B., 7; Benjamin, 7, 30, 31,
    49, 58, 64, 73, 103, 113, 120,
    127, 128, 132, 136, 138, 144,
    146; William, 18
RUSSEL, William, 19

RUSSELL, Andrew, 55, 62; Grace,
    28; Tobias, 100; William, 28, 71
RUST, George, 119; Sarah, 119
RYMER, Catherine, 18, 23;
    Katherine, 32
SAISE, Martha, 45; Ralph, 45
SALTASH, Ester, 10; William, 10
SARJANT, Cornelious, 46; William,
    100, 143
SAVAGE, John, 5, 16, 78, 86, 87,
    93, 98
SAWYER, Frances, 82; Humphery,
    117; Humphrey, 51
SCOTT, James, 89, 90, 97, 111
SEAL, Charles, 53, 62
SEALE, Anthony, 19, 59, 61, 68;
    Charles, 5, 6, 7, 14, 16, 18, 20,
    21, 25, 31, 36, 37, 38, 44, 47,
    48, 51, 52, 54, 55, 61, 62, 63,
    66, 68, 69, 77, 82, 85, 86, 94, 98,
    106, 120, 121, 124, 139, 141;
    David, 59, 85, 94
SEAMONS, Elizabeth, 143; John,
    143; Joseph, 95, 99, 107, 112,
    118, 133, 137, 144
SEATON, James, 80
SEBASTIAN, William, 5
SENLVON, Charles, 23
SERJANT, William, 140
SETTLE, Francis, 61; John, 59
SHARP, Frances, 69; John, 12, 18,
    29, 31, 33, 34, 69, 126, 128,
    129, 142; Judith, 69; Linefield,
    31; Linsfield, 18, 19, 69, 122,
    142; Lunsfield, 128
SHARPE, John, 45
SHEILDS, Hannah, 8
SHELTON, Robert, 78
SIMMOND, Margaret, 4, 17, 21
SIMMONDS, Margaret, 119; Rachel,
    119
SIMMONS, Joseph, 122

SIMPSON, Ann, 18, 35, 39; John, 55, 60, 67
SINCLAIR, Thomas, 79, 80
SISE, Martha, 42, 48; Ralph, 42
SITTENBOURN PARISH, 101, 129
SITTENBOURNE PARISH, 109, 110, 144
SKAGGS, Charles, 49
SKINKER, Samuel, 1, 3, 4, 6, 7, 9, 10, 12, 14, 15, 18, 19, 20, 21, 24, 26, 27, 28, 32, 34, 36, 37, 38, 41, 43, 44, 45, 46, 47, 48, 49, 50, 53, 55, 56, 57, 59, 60, 64, 67, 70, 73, 75, 76, 77, 78, 83, 86, 89, 90, 92, 94, 95, 96, 98, 103, 105, 110, 111, 117, 120, 121, 124, 125, 126, 127, 128, 129, 136, 142, 143, 146; Samuell, 37
SKINNER, Samuel, 25; Samuell, 22
SKRINE, Margaret, 27, 56; William, 5, 15, 17, 20, 23, 24, 27, 31, 33, 38, 39, 40, 43, 46, 50, 53, 56, 57, 70, 79, 84, 93, 98, 105, 113, 116
SKRINE MILL, 36
SMITH, Ann Fowke, 95, 100, 118, 128; Ann Fowlk, 106; Augustin, 75; Elizabeth, 9; Garret, 101; John, 90, 101, 129; Nicholas, 1, 9, 10, 19, 20, 27, 28, 29, 35, 36, 39, 50, 56, 59, 65, 68, 69, 70, 73, 76, 83, 90, 91, 96, 97, 99, 101, 102, 104, 105, 106, 111, 113, 114, 115, 116, 117, 119, 126, 127, 140, 145; Robert, 7, 9, 107, 115; Thomas, 4, 15, 25, 28, 31, 33, 34, 37, 54, 56, 60, 65, 71, 74, 86, 88, 91, 94, 95, 100, 106, 108, 113, 115, 118, 121, 123, 124, 128, 131, 138, 146; William, 45, 61
SNELL, John, 44, 47, 50, 54, 60, 67, 71, 79, 91
SNOW, John, 140
SOMMERTON, William, 118
SPARKS, James, 4, 15
SPICER, Mary, 26, 35, 37; Rosser, 78
SPOTSILVANIA COUNTY, 70, 73, 75, 80, 93, 116, 135
SPOTSWOOD, Robert, 37, 44, 47, 48, 55, 60, 67
SPOTSYLVANIA COUNTY, 40
STAFFORD COUNTY, 13, 19, 20, 54, 59, 75, 76, 79, 80, 81, 91, 92, 98
STAMPS, Margaret, 142; Timothy, 142
STANDLEY, John, 34, 144
STANDLY, John, 28
STANNING, Abraham, 38
STANNINGS, Abraham, 44
STERN, David, 16, 24, 33, 34; Davis, 21
STEVENSON, William, 55, 64, 141, 143, 145
STEWARD, John, 14, 49, 72, 127, 129, 137, 138; Joseph, 14, 15, 127; Rosemond, 127; Thomas, 137, 138; Widow, 129
STONE, Francis, 56, 141; William, 104
STORE, Katherine, 129
STRAGHAN, Hugh, 96
STRAHAN, Hugh, 89, 97
STRANGHAN, Thomas, 9
STRIBING, John, 7
STRIBLING, Benjamin, 42, 143; John, 1, 4, 14, 20; Thomas, 21, 58, 59, 61, 68, 75, 78, 94, 99, 104, 106, 110, 145, 146
STRINGER, Mary, 11
STRINGFELLOW, Jane, 143; William, 64, 128, 143
STROTHER, Anthony, 70; Benjamin, 36, 58, 75, 135; James, 144;

160

Jeremiah, 68, 72, 83, 129, 144, 145, 146; Joseph, 1, 5, 18, 20, 21, 33, 34, 37, 38, 39, 46 , 47, 49, 51, 53, 56, 58, 59, 64, 67, 69, 70, 73, 75, 76, 78, 83, 89, 90, 92, 96, 97, 102, 103, 105, 111 , 117, 121, 126, 130, 133, 136, 142, 143, 144 , 146; Margaret, 43; Margrett, 28; Robert, 22, 42, 54, 56, 68, 91, 94, 101, 125, 129, 130, 131, 132, 136, 137, 138; William, 2, 5, 6, 10, 11, 12, 16 , 18, 19 , 20, 21, 22, 25, 26 , 27, 28, 32, 33, 38, 41, 43, 45, 47, 48, 49, 50, 51, 52, 53 , 56, 57, 58, 59, 64, 65, 67, 70, 71, 73, 74, 76, 78, 83, 86, 87, 89, 95 , 97 , 101, 102, 111, 114, 117, 119, 121, 126, 127 , 128, 129, 130 , 131, 132, 136, 142, 143, 144, 146

STUARD, Robert, 64

SULLEVAN, Owen, 8

SULLIVAN, Owen, 8, 51

SULLIVANT, Darby, 51; Elizabeth, 51; Owen, 51

SUMMERTON, William, 119, 120

SUTTLE, Francis, 45, 101, 102, 111, 117, 118, 119, 120; John, 41; Joseph, 142

SWEETING, Edward, 62

TALIAFERRO, John, 25, 26; Robert, 21, 81

TANKERSLEY, George, 130; Richard, 22, 35, 85

TANKERSLY, Richard, 45

TARJANT, Mr., 129

TAYLOE, John, 44, 70, 131

TAYLOR, Edward, 50; Henry, 128; James, 35, 37, 38, 44, 47, 51; John, 2, 50; Katerine, 101; Katherine, 109; Martha, 144;

Richard, 47, 53; Robert, 90, 111, 114, 141; William, 143

THARP, William, 26, 33, 43, 46, 51, 54

THARPE, William, 62

THATCHER, Katherine, 62, 97; Thomas, 12, 67, 68, 70, 72, 87, 94, 97, 99, 103, 104, 118, 119, 120, 125, 126; William, 13, 14, 76, 84, 96, 99

THATCHERS DAM, 7, 10, 51

THOMAS, Robert, 108

THOMPSON, Dorothy, 64

THORNLEY, Aaron, 2

THORNLY, Aaron, 27; Aron, 22; Mary, 22

THORNTON, Anthony, 79; Francis, 10, 65, 85, 86, 88, 92, 93, 94; Rowland, 1, 10 , 12, 17, 20, 22, 35, 36, 41, 45, 50, 51, 53, 58, 60, 68, 69, 71, 72, 73, 74, 75, 76, 78, 90, 91, 92, 96, 97, 102, 105, 110, 111 , 112, 114, 117, 121, 129 , 130, 133, 142, 143, 144; William, 1, 3, 9, 10, 12, 14, 17, 18, 19 , 20, 22, 24, 26, 28, 29 , 30, 32 , 38, 40, 41, 43, 45, 46, 50 , 51, 56, 58, 60, 61, 64, 67, 69, 70, 73, 75, 76, 78, 83, 89, 90, 92, 96 , 97, 101, 102, 103, 105, 119, 121, 126, 130, 131, 133, 136, 142 , 144

THORTON, Rowland, 56

THRUSTOUT, Thomas, 88, 94, 99, 105, 118, 123, 132, 133, 137

TILLER, John, 23; Lazarus, 109

TILLY, Lazarus, 71, 85, 114, 120, 124, 132, 138, 145

TIMMONS, Samuel, 52, 54, 60, 69

TIPPET, Elizabeth, 29; William, 3, 39

TODD, Richard, 6

TOMLINSON, William, 16 , 20, 24, 32
TOUT, Richard, 104
TOWARD, John, 89, 96, 97, 100, 107, 108, 115, 120, 123, 124, 133, 134 , 138, 145
TRAVIS, John, 19, 64, 65, 75, 79; Margaret, 75
TRAVISE, John, 54
TRICE, John, 6, 15, 24, 32
TRIPLET, Francis, 5, 126, 128; John, 3, 45, 129, 137, 138
TRIPLETT, Francis, 8 ; John, 25, 33, 51, 61, 72, 142, 144
TURNBALD, Alexander, 96
TURNBULL, Alexander, 99, 106, 113, 118, 119, 139
TURNER, James, 34; John, 130; Nathan, 20; Sarah, 58; T., 101, 126; Thomas, 4, 6, 7, 10 , 11, 18, 24, 27 , 28, 29, 30, 31, 38, 39, 43, 50, 58, 59, 65, 70, 73, 74, 76, 84, 93, 101, 102, 103, 104, 112, 115, 116, 117, 122, 124, 125, 128, 131, 145
TUSON, Mary, 1, 7, 13; Samuel, 1, 7, 13, 109, 114; Samuell, 24
TUTT, Margaret, 126; Mary, 27, 87, 96, 97; Richard, 10, 13 , 14, 27, 42, 114, 118, 119, 120, 124, 126; William, 97
TYPETT, William, 48
UNDERWOOD, Elizabeth, 96
VAUGHAN, James, 98
VIVION, Thomas, 3, 4, 6, 9, 10, 12, 14, 17, 19, 20, 22, 26, 36, 45, 46, 49, 50, 55, 58, 59, 66, 73, 85, 91, 96, 100 , 102, 108 , 114, 115, 121, 122, 138, 139, 141
WARD, Henry, 102
WARING, Thomas, 109, 114, 120, 124, 138, 143

WARNER, John, 12, 29, 30
WARREN, James, 48, 64
WASHINGTON, Augustine, 22; John, 96, 99, 106, 113, 118, 119; Robert, 91, 100, 115
WATERS, Edward, 48; Katherine, 65; Philip, 95, 99, 113, 133, 135, 136; Phillip, 106, 118, 123
WATFORD, John, 122, 139
WATS, Richard, 2
WATTS, Edward, 47, 48, 52, 56; Richard, 3
WAUGH, Joseph, 137
WELCH, Doras, 127; Thomas, 55, 60, 74, 87, 94, 127; William, 45, 130, 137
WELLS, Thomas, 23, 27
WELSH, William, 130
WESTMORELAND COUNTY, 13, 18, 20, 22
WESTMORELAND COURT, 31
WHARTON, Ann, 58, 127; Samuel, 22, 33, 34, 35, 42, 45, 58, 61, 85, 101, 106, 127; Samuell, 31
WHEELER, John, 80; William, 97
WHITE, Daniel, 18 , 19, 45, 58, 100; George, 7, 8, 12, 13, 18, 24, 35, 45, 58, 101, 142, 144, 145, 146
WHITEING, William, 13
WHITING, William, 140, 141
WILIAMS, James, 137
WILLIAMS, Henry, 17, 117; John, 10 , 14, 15, 29, 43, 51, 57, 66, 70, 96, 100, 106; Jonas, 74, 75, 85, 90, 96, 100, 106, 120, 121, 123, 129, 133, 137, 138, 143; Jonathan, 77, 88, 93, 122, 141; Thomas, 35, 95, 101, 109
WILLIAMSBURGH, 89, 90, 97
WILLIS, Henry, 128; John, 28, 84 , 103, 109, 116, 124, 138
WILLSON, Robert, 134

WILSON, James, 19; John, 22, 28,
    55, 63, 64, 68, 85, 91, 92, 98;
    Margaret, 91, 92; Mary, 63, 68;
    Robert, 3, 61, 67, 79, 91, 98,
    104, 111, 112 , 117, 133, 134,
    135, 136, 139
WING, Joseph, 3, 7, 8, 125, 138
WINTER, Richard, 19
WISE, John, 117

WOFFENDALE, Frances, 37, 40, 41;
    Francis, 18, 25, 26, 31, 33, 34,
    35, 43, 44 , 47 , 51, 52, 54, 56,
    62, 63, 67, 68, 72, 75, 79, 83,
    114, 117, 118, 119, 120, 125,
    126, 135, 138; Honour, 95, 99,
    106
WOFFENDALL, Francis, 72
WOOD, Thomas, 141; William, 90
WRIGHT, John, 18, 59, 127
WYE, William, 95, 99, 106, 113
YATES, Elias, 20, 24, 32, 39, 43, 46,
    52, 53; Thomas, 15
YERBY, John, 52
YEWBANK, John, 64, 78
YICKLIN, William, 102

Heritage Books by Mary Marshall Brewer:

Abstracts of Administrations of Montgomery County, Pennsylvania, 1822–1850

Abstracts of Land Records of King George County, Virginia, 1752–1783

Abstracts of Land Records of Richmond County, Virginia, 1692–1704

Abstracts of the Wills of Montgomery County, Pennsylvania, 1824–1850

Early Union County, New Jersey Church Records, 1750–1800

Essex County, Virginia Land Records, 1752–1761

Essex County, Virginia Land Records, 1761–1772

Essex County, Virginia Land Records, 1772–1786

Kent County, Delaware Guardian Accounts: Aaron to Carty, 1752–1849

Kent County, Delaware Guardian Accounts: Caton to Edinfield, 1753–1849

Kent County, Delaware Guardian Accounts: Edmondson to Hopkins, 1744–1855

Kent County, Delaware Guardian Accounts: Houston to McBride, 1739–1856

Kent County, Delaware Guardian Accounts: McBride to Savin, 1739–1851

Kent County, Delaware Guardian Accounts: Savin to Truax, 1754–1852

Kent County, Delaware Guardian Accounts: Truitt to Young, 1755–1849

Kent County, Delaware Land Records, Volume 2: 1702–1722

Kent County, Delaware Land Records, Volume 3: 1723–1734

Kent County, Delaware Land Records, Volume 4: 1735–1743

Kent County, Delaware Land Records, Volume 5: 1742–1749

Kent County, Delaware Land Records, Volume 6: 1749–1756

Kent County, Delaware Land Records, Volume 7: 1756–1764

PDF: Kent County, Delaware Land Records, Volume 7: 1756–1764

Kent County, Delaware Land Records, Volume 8: 1764–1768

Kent County, Delaware Land Records, 1776–1783

Kent County, Delaware Land Records, 1782–1785

Kent County, Delaware Land Records, 1785–1789

Kent County, Delaware Land Records, 1788–1792

King George County, Virginia Court Orders, 1721–1724

King George County, Virginia Court Orders, 1724–1728

King George County, Virginia Court Orders, 1728–1731

King George County, Virginia Court Orders, 1731–1736

King George County, Virginia Court Orders, 1736–1740

King George County, Virginia Court Orders, 1740–1746

King George County, Virginia Court Orders, 1746–1751

King George County, Virginia Court Orders, 1751–1754

King George County, Virginia Court Orders, 1754–1756

Land Records of Sussex County, Delaware, 1681–1725

PDF: Land Records of Sussex County, Delaware, 1681–1725

Land Records of Sussex County, Delaware, 1753–1763

Land Records of Sussex County, Delaware, 1763–1769

Land Records of Sussex County, Delaware: Various Dates:
1693–1698, 1715–1717, 1782–1792, 1802–1805

Land Records of York County, Pennsylvania, Libers A and B, 1746–1764

Land Records of York County, Pennsylvania, Libers C and D, 1764–1771

Land Records of York County, Pennsylvania, Libers E and F, 1771–1775

Land Records of York County, Pennsylvania, Libers G and H, 1775–1793

New Castle County, Delaware Wills, 1800–1813

Northumberland County, Virginia: Deeds, Wills, Inventories, etc., 1737–1743

Northumberland County, Virginia: Deeds, Wills, Inventories, etc., 1743–1749

Probate Records of Kent County, Delaware, Volume 1: 1801–1812

Probate Records of Kent County, Delaware, Volume 2: 1812–1822

Probate Records of Kent County, Delaware, Volume 3: 1822–1833

Quaker Records of Cedar Creek Monthly Meeting: Virginia, 1739–1793

Spotsylvania County, Virginia Deed Books, 1722–1734

Spotsylvania County, Virginia Deed Books, 1734–1751

York County, Virginia Deeds, Orders, Wills, Etc., 1698–1700

York County, Virginia Deeds, Orders, Wills, Etc., 1700–1702

York County, Virginia Deeds, Orders, Wills, Etc., 1705–1706

York County, Virginia Deeds, Orders, Wills, Etc., 1714–1716

York County, Virginia Deeds, Orders, Wills, Etc., 1716–1718

York County, Virginia Deeds, Orders, Wills, Etc., 1718–1720

York County, Virginia Deeds, Orders, Wills, Etc., 1728–1732

York County, Virginia Land Records: 1694–1713

York County, Virginia Land Records: 1713–1729

York County, Virginia Land Records: 1729–1763

York County, Virginia Land Records: 1763–1777

York County, Virginia Wills, Inventories and Court Orders, 1702–1704

York County, Virginia Wills, Inventories and Court Orders, 1732–1737

York County, Virginia Wills, Inventories and Court Orders, 1737–1740

York County, Virginia Wills, Inventories and Court Orders, 1740–1743

York County, Virginia Wills, Inventories and Court Orders, 1743–1746

York County, Virginia Wills, Inventories and Court Orders, 1745–1759

www.ingramcontent.com/pod-product-compliance
Lightning Source LLC
Chambersburg PA
CBHW070840300326
41935CB00038B/1157